UNSUNG EAGLES

UNSUNG EAGLES

*True Stories of America's
Citizen Airmen in the Skies
of World War II*

JAY A. STOUT

CASEMATE
Philadelphia & Oxford

Published in the United States of America and Great Britain in 2013 by
CASEMATE PUBLISHERS
908 Darby Road, Havertown, PA 19083
and
10 Hythe Bridge Street, Oxford, OX1 2EW

ISBN 978-1-61200-209-5
Digital Edition: ISBN 978-1-61200-210-1

Cataloging-in-publication data is available from the Library of Congress and
the British Library.

10 9 8 7 6 5 4 3 2 1

Printed and bound in the United States of America.

For a complete list of Casemate titles please contact:

CASEMATE PUBLISHERS (US)
Telephone (610) 853-9131, Fax (610) 853-9146
E-mail: casemate@casematepublishing.com

CASEMATE PUBLISHERS (UK)
Telephone (01865) 241249, Fax (01865) 794449
E-mail: casemate-uk@casematepublishing.co.uk

CONTENTS

PREFACE

THIS WORK FOCUSES ON THE EXPERIENCES AND REALITIES OF those Americans who fought World War II in the air. These are not the already-told-and-retold stories of the celebrated icons of the air war. Rather, they are accounts from the masses of largely unrecognized airmen who—in the aggregate—actually won it. They are the recollections of your Uncle Frank who shared them only after having enjoyed a beer or seven at the family reunion, and of your old girlfriend's grandfather who passed away about the same time she dumped you. And of the craggy guy who ran the salvage yard on the south side of town; a dusty, fly-specked B-24 model hung over the front counter. In other words these are the everyman—but important—narratives that are fast disappearing as the last of the generation passes away.

No other work describes how Ensign Ray Crandall was shot down by friendly fire a couple of days prior to the Battle of Leyte Gulf. Or how, miserably hung over, he climbed into his torpedo bomber aboard the escort carrier *Manila Bay* and flew through multi-colored, phosphorescing explosions of antiaircraft fire to attack the marauding Japanese fleet. "They fired their main batteries—their big guns—at us, which kicked up huge sprays of water that we had to fly through." Or how, absolutely terrified, Crandall almost refused to fly a second mission that day: "I told them that when everyone else in the Navy had done it once, then I would go a second time . . ." Or how, after having somewhat recovered his composure, he flew a third mission that same afternoon: "For some dumbass reason the Japanese had turned around and were running north. We were really ready to hurt them this time."

The *New World Encyclopedia* and other authoritative sources describe the clash in which Crandall fought thusly: "The Battle of Leyte Gulf, also known as the Second Battle of the Philippine Sea, was the largest naval battle in modern history. It was fought in the Pacific Theater of World War II, in the seas surrounding the Philippine island of Leyte, from October 23 to October 26, 1944, between the Allies and the Empire of Japan." It's a fine overview but it doesn't describe the humanness of the battle—it doesn't help the reader relive it. It doesn't describe how it really was for Ray Crandall and tens of thousands of men like him.

Likewise, other overarching descriptions fail to include the personal accounts of the men who fought the other great air battles of World War II. It is a gap that this work helps to fill.

However, this is no Greatest Generation love fest. Although the men who fought the war were indelibly imprinted by the Great Depression and the war that ended it, their innate core was no different than that of the generations that preceded and succeeded them. Great men and bad men were part of this group but the vast majority represented themselves as typical. And this was my experience as I interviewed them. I found one or two that might be counted as extraordinary but the majority of the men— except for their experiences—were unremarkable. I also encountered a couple of first-rate jackasses. In fact, in a couple of instances, the little, mean man in me overpowered the objective historian and decided not to pursue otherwise promising stories simply because the men who lived them were boorish—even contemptible.

Although I have—in order to provide some context—included some amount of background together with brief discussions of strategy and tactics, the stories in this work concentrate on the individuals. It is important for the reader to get a sense of who they were and where they came from. Too, it is important to understand what motivated them. And although their accounts were lightly edited for clarity and accuracy, a primary goal was to ensure that their voices were preserved as unique and individual.

As I worked with these men I was struck by a number of different aspects. Firstly, it was remarkable that so much was done so quickly. From a flat-footed start during the late 1930s until the end of the war in 1945, a very short span, the United States produced nearly 300,000 aircraft and trained more than two million airmen. And it was done without computers. From today's perspective, when it can take a decade or more to design, fund and build a relatively simple highway project, this achievement is almost incredible.

Nevertheless, it was hardly smooth and not always efficient. This was the conflict that gave us Catch-22 and SNAFU. Leadership was occasionally poor and equipment was sometimes shoddily designed and manufactured. Petty rivalries got in the way of greater things and men often were lost, injured or killed in the great crush of creating a military that could win the war.

Additionally, as already noted, was the fact that these men were not innately special. Rather they lived, adapted and survived during a special time. Their personalities and inherent qualities were no different than those of my peers. And although we tend to see or remember them as old and grandfatherly, they very often drank and caroused and chased skirts with a vigor and enthusiasm that would land them in jail today.

They were human. If it is popular to declare that today's generations are wanting, it should be considered that they are the products of the World War II generation. From those men came McCarthyism and the mistakes of Vietnam. Their children were the baby boomers, the caricatures of the 1960s; they were the flower children, the druggies, the hippies and the draft dodgers. That fact notwithstanding, the World War II generation also raised brilliant, less flashy progeny while winning the Cold War and making our nation—with its manifold positive attributes—into the world leader it is today.

The fact is that these men were individuals who came together to win a great cause. And much of that cause was won in dangerous skies. The stories here describe that winning.

PROLOGUE

ALL AT ONCE THE OLD MAN STOPPED TALKING AND TILTED HIS face to the ceiling so that the wet in his eyes wouldn't turn into tears and run down his cheeks. He remembered something and it was suddenly difficult for him to talk about friends long gone—friends lost to an enemy who has become one of our nation's closest allies. "It doesn't seem fair," he said, "for the rest of us to have gone on and lived so long—married and children. And those poor guys . . . we didn't even bring most of them home. They were just gone. I still remember their faces."

The man remembered the war and his friends as he knew them nearly seventy years ago. He remembered them as young, strong-willed, strong-bodied men who answered their nation's call to war. They were like young men of any generation. But unlike most young men, their lives were tempered in horrific ways by the skies of war.

For so many of us though, what comes to mind when we think of the men who fought World War II, is a cartoon image of an old man with an odd-looking, pin-festooned hat at the Veterans Day parade. Or the stooped-over gentleman who ushers us to our pew at church. Or perhaps the diminutive docent at the museum—shrunken with age, but always neatly dressed in a jacket and slacks and in unfailing good spirits.

But they know—and have known for a long time—that war is a complicated and brutal thing. They know that it isn't someone else who kills and dies; the killers and the dead are friends, and brothers, and sons, and husbands.

After coming of age during the Great Depression, and winning World War II, they put away the hurt, came home, married, and built lives for themselves. In so doing they raised this nation to a position of eminence that no other has known. And in the process, they created a better world.

But in the becoming, and in the creating and in the being, they were burdened with memories and feelings that are impossible to fathom. "You can't understand," one man said. "No one who wasn't there can understand."

He was right. I can't know the horrors and heartaches that these unsung eagles experienced. And I can't ever really understand the men themselves.

But I can honor them with a record of who they were and what they did. And that is this book.

CHAPTER 1
AMERICANS UNDER OTHER FLAGS

During the first years of World War II—before the United States became a belligerent—many young American men were anxious to travel overseas to fly and fight against the Axis powers. Although the cause was noble it was often secondary. These barely-men, some still in their teens, were as much fascinated by the glory they imagined was aerial combat as they were in the struggle for right and justice. Beleaguered Britain was quite often their destination as the English, isolated and alone, were desperately short of the skilled pilots they needed to hold the line against Nazi Germany.

John A. Campbell

JOHN A. CAMPBELL WAS BORN AT HOME ON NOVEMBER 2, 1921. He grew up south of San Diego in Chula Vista during the Great Depression and fell in love with military aviation at an early age. "I grew up reading the pulp magazines that were popular back then. *G-8 and his Battle Aces* was one that everyone liked," he said. "I started hanging around the local airport when I was fourteen. If I wasn't supposed to be in school, or if I wasn't home in bed, then I was at the airport. I did anything the guys wanted in trade for flying time. I fueled or washed airplanes—whatever. My first half-hour of flight instruction was in an American Eagle biplane. I got that in exchange for helping a guy put a brick floor in a hangar."

By the time he graduated from high school in 1940, Campbell had logged 220 flight hours and earned a Limited Commercial License. "I tried to get on with the airlines," he remembered, "but they weren't very interested in me. I was only eighteen and didn't have much multi-engine time.

During that period they could afford to pick and choose who they wanted. I had the same problem with the Army Air Corps. They wanted two years of college, or at least the equivalent, and I didn't have that. Essentially, I was too young and too stupid for both the airlines and the Army Air Corps."

Nevertheless, there was another way into military flying. During the summer and fall of 1940 the Royal Air Force was bitterly contesting the skies over England against Hitler's Luftwaffe in the Battle of Britain. The United Kingdom was desperately short of pilots and recruited young fliers from throughout the Commonwealth as well as from the United States. One of the areas that recruiters targeted was southern California where there was a high concentration of young men with flying experience.

Campbell was inspired to investigate the notion of flying for Great Britain's Royal Air Force, the RAF, when three brothers stopped to visit him where he was working at the local airport. They were on their way to Los Angeles to visit with the recruiter and they urged him to follow suit. He did so a few days later. "The guy's name was Wadell," Campbell recalled. "His office, so to speak, was in a garage. He was a building contractor. When I walked in he was talking to a woman about a building or something. He saw the logbook in my hand and right away told me to go wait in his office. He went through my logbook and my qualifications, and noted that I was kind of young and asked if I had permission from my parents. I told him no, but that I didn't think it would be a problem."

A couple of weeks later, having just celebrated his nineteenth birthday, and with a note from his parents, Campbell went back to Los Angeles and was accepted for service in the RAF. He started training with the Polaris Flight Academy on December 8, 1940, at Grand Central Airport in Glendale, California. "There were two big reasons they had us there," he remembered. "The first was so that they could run a security check on us. The second was to check us out and make sure we could actually fly. We were trained in formation flying, aerobatics and instrument flight. From December 1940 to March 1941 we received about a hundred hours of flight instruction."

After Campbell and his comrades completed their training they were supposed to travel to England in one large group of about ten pilots. "But there were four guys there who had the draft breathing down their necks.

One of them, who had already gotten his draft notice, was sent straight to New York and the other three were sent to Canada where one of them joined the Royal Canadian Air Force. The other two, along with some others, were shipped out to England."

A couple of weeks later, Campbell and the other remaining pilots were sent to England via Canada. "In Ottawa the Royal Canadian Air Force tried to recruit us," Campbell recalled. "In fact, they offered us commissions as flying officers. They wanted us to fly as instructors. But I still wanted to fly fighters and I found out that if I accepted a commission with the Canadians I'd get stuck instructing and would never get sent overseas."

Campbell refused the Canadian offer and on March 31, 1941, boarded the *Jean Jadot*, a Belgian ship which was part of a convoy bound for England. "The British met us [on April 18] when we made port and put us on a train where we spent the first night. The blackout was in effect and there was bombing and all sorts of excitement. We arrived in London the next day, which was a Saturday, and were taken down to the Air Ministry. There, they fed us and informed us that we were going to fly fighters, and additionally told us what we should expect, and so on."

The following day Campbell and his companions were taken to Moss Brothers, an outfitter for gentlemen, to have their uniforms made. "The tailor was measuring my inseam and he asked me whether I dressed right or left." Campbell didn't understand the question until it was explained to him that the tailor was asking which way he "hung." It was common to provide a gentleman a certain extra measure of room in the favored trouser leg. "About that time," Campbell recalled, "there was an air raid siren and I was practically up and running. The tailor looked up at me and said, 'we carry on quite as usual sir.' Well, I stuck around. I figured if he could stand it, then I could, too."

That same afternoon they picked up their new uniforms and were put on a train to No. 56 Operational Training Unit at Sutton Bridge. It was during his second day at Sutton Bridge when Campbell first flew with an RAF instructor pilot in the British advanced trainer—the Miles Master. "It was similar to the American advanced trainers, but had some nasty stall characteristics," Campbell remembered. "The instructor did a landing first and then I did two. He stopped and got out and called to Bill Geiger who was from the group I had come over with. The Master was easier to land three-point with two people in it, so poor Bill had to ride in the rear seat on my solo!"

Later that day Campbell was sent to do a cockpit check on a Hurricane that was up on jacks in one of the hangars. The RAF's first modern monoplane fighter and its first aircraft to exceed 300 miles per hour, the Hurricane was also by this time the grizzled veteran of the Battle of Britain. Easy to maintain, rugged, and readily built—if not for the Hurricane, the Luftwaffe might have dominated the skies of England during the critical summer months of 1940. The design was produced until 1944 and more than 14,000 were manufactured. It flew in every theater of war in which the RAF served. Campbell was excited at the prospect of flying it someday.

Someday came quickly. The following morning, the nineteen-year-old Campbell was told to grab his parachute and get ready to fly. He started for the Miles Master with his parachute slung over his shoulder. He was stopped and admonished, "No, no, not that! Get in the Hurricane. You've already flown the Master."

"That was the attitude of the English the whole way through. It was a great confidence builder. Looking back, I can't imagine what I must have thought when I crawled into that cockpit. The instructor told me to do a quick 'bump and go' around the landing circuit and then go fly, but not to be gone more than an hour. Someone else was waiting for the airplane.

"I got it started and taxied out to the head of the grass runway. Finally, I got the guts to open it up and by the time I got it airborne and got the wheels up and the propeller pitch squared away, I was halfway across the Channel at 10,000 feet!

"That was the way the whole thing went. We were there about five weeks, got 54 hours on the Hurricane, and shot the guns three times. It was pretty casual in a lot of ways, but surprisingly enough a fair percentage of us survived. Actually, we were pretty well trained compared to the average English pilot who was showing up with only about 140 flight hours at that time."

Ironically, after training on the Hurricane at Sutton Bridge, Campbell was briefly posted to 234 Squadron which was flying Spitfires in the southwest of England. He shrugged off the transition from the Hurricane to the Spitfire. "It wasn't that big of a deal. They flew a lot alike. The Spit had narrower landing gear and had a tendency on landing to glide with its nose quite high. They were both honest airplanes but the Spit was more of a lady. You had to treat it more carefully and it took more maintenance."

Campbell was with his new unit only a short time before receiving new orders on May 31, 1941. "I'm glad I was transferred," he said. "At the time 234 Squadron was operating from a very small strip on a plateau on the coast. And we flew at night." For a variety of reasons there was movement afoot at that time to gather all of the American pilots in the RAF into three fighter squadrons flying Hurricanes, and later Spitfires.

The units were dubbed Eagle Squadrons: 71 Squadron had already been formed to this purpose, and the second Eagle Squadron, 121, was in the process of being put together. Eventually three squadrons were formed. Campbell was pulled from 234 and sent to 121 at Kirton in Lindsey to fly Hurricanes.

"We were unfortunate in some ways," Campbell recalled. "The first squadron, 71, was taking some incredible losses—a lot of it due to stupidity, and weather, and other accidents. They pulled a lot of our experienced pilots from 121 Squadron to replace their losses, so we had a constant turnover in personnel.

"And we were doing a lot of convoy patrol," he remembered with a grimace. Desperate to protect the maritime lifeline that was its shipping, England employed every means to ensure its safety. These means included overhead fighter patrols that were sorely hated by the pilots. The weather over the convoys was quite often very foul with fog, low clouds, wind and rain. The water was inhospitably cold, and downed pilots quickly perished if a rescue boat wasn't immediately on the spot. Indeed, during this period there were more losses over the convoys due to weather and accidents than there were to enemy action. And too, the patrols were mostly exercises in boredom, as the Germans did not frequently attack.

"We had a surplus of pilots in England by that time—late summer." Campbell remembered that Fighter Command looked for different ways to keep its pilots busy. By the summer of 1941, the Germans had invaded Russia and had pulled a lot of their fighter units out of France and sent them east. "We flew a lot of rhubarbs [search and destroy missions] over the Continent. It was low flying, often under bad weather, shooting up targets of opportunity and trying to stir up trouble. From Kirton in Lindsey in the Midlands we went to the easterly bases south of London. There we fueled and flew missions into France or the Low Countries. After the mission we refueled, rearmed and did it again. Finally, we returned to base in the evening.

"The missions that scared me more than anything else were the attacks on the flak barges. The Germans used them to protect the ports," Campbell remembered. "They had about every type of antiaircraft gun possible on those boats. When you were in a strafing run against one of those things, every round they fired looked like it was coming in slow motion for that spot right between your eyes. I used to squeeze myself into a tiny ball right behind the windscreen. I was never as terrified in air-to-air combat as I was during those strafing attacks."

Campbell described escorting bombers against targets across the English Channel. "It wasn't much fun because our orders were that we were not to leave the bombers, no matter what. So, the Me-109s hung out above us. Then, if they thought they could catch us by surprise, they came down and tried to get at the bombers. Our job was to turn into them to try and keep them away. As soon as they broke off their attacks we were supposed to come back in close to the bombers again. The most unnerving part of that was flying through the trails of smoke that the German tracers left when they fired into the formations."

Still, the pace of the action wasn't quick enough for Campbell. "Most of our losses were due to accidents rather than enemy action," he recalled. "My roommate, Earl Tooty Mason, was killed doing slow rolls at low altitude on September 15. So I volunteered to go to the Mediterranean—to Malta—because things were happening there. Also, the English weather was getting me down and I was sick for several weeks with sinus infections. I figured the hot dry weather would cure me. The first time I asked to be reassigned my request was denied because our losses at 71 Squadron were too high. Well, later on, after I buzzed the base commander's car, they decided to honor my request.

"I transferred to 258 Squadron," he continued. "It was a New Zealand unit flying the Hurricane Mark IIC with four 20mm cannon in the wings." The unit was located at Debden, about forty miles northeast of London. To prepare for their eventual fly-off from an aircraft carrier onto the island of Malta, the squadron spent a short time practicing taking off from runways specially marked to resemble the decks of aircraft carriers. Finally, on

November 3, 1941—Campbell's birthday—with their aircraft carefully dis-assembled and loaded aboard the HMS *Athenia*, the squadron departed Glasgow, Scotland, for Gibraltar.

Campbell remembered that, with a celebratory hangover that would have killed most men, he left a slick of the residue of revelry in the water as the ship slipped its moorings and left the harbor. "I got sick over the edge of the boat," he said. Once in Gibraltar, Campbell recalled that 258 Squadron, along with two others, was supposed to embark aboard the British aircraft carrier HMS *Ark Royal*. That ship was to ferry them within flying range of Malta. The *Ark Royal* delivered portions of the units to Malta on November 10, 1941. Unfortunately, on November 13, the ship was torpedoed by the German submarine *U-81* while on its way back to Gibraltar to pick up and deliver the remaining elements. It sank the next day.

For the next month or so Campbell was stranded with the rest of his unit in Gibraltar. "They had us flying anti-submarine patrols," Campbell recalled. "We also flew up the Spanish coast to Cadiz. The Germans operated long-range, four-engine Focke-Wulf 200 Condor patrol bombers out of there and we hoped to catch one of them coming in or out, but we never did."

Campbell recalled an interesting incident which took place during this interlude. "I was out with Don Geffene when he had engine trouble and had to force land on the beach in Spanish Tangiers, across the Strait of Gibraltar. I saw troops coming over, and I told him over the radio to light that son-of-a-bitch off—to set his airplane on fire. Well, he didn't smoke and he didn't have any matches, so I told him to get out of the way. On my first strafing run all four of my cannon fired, but only about two rounds each. I came around again and ended up with one cannon that would shoot. Well, I finally set that damned thing on fire but I about used up all of my ammunition.

"Don was interned and found himself in a hot romance with the Governor-General's daughter. She helped him and he eventually got back. He later ended up in Ceylon and was killed by the Japanese on his first combat sortie on Easter Day [April 5], 1942.

"After the Japanese attacked Pearl Harbor and started their offensive against Singapore, they put us and our airplanes on a ship and took us to a place called Takoradi, on the Gold Coast of Africa." From there, after the aircraft had been assembled, Campbell and the rest of his squadron flew across Africa to Khartoum in the Sudan, and then up the Nile River to Alexandria, Egypt. "It was nothing but mud, flies, and camels," Campbell remembered. "We were based at a field just west of Alexandria where we flew a few strafing missions, but that was about all we did.

"On January 4, 1942, they took away our four-cannon Hurricanes and gave us Mark IIBs, which were Hurricanes with twelve Browning .303 machine guns—six in each wing. Then they sent us down to Port Sudan on the Red Sea and loaded us on board the HMS *Indomitable*. By this time we had our squadron and parts of others [232 Squadron]." The carrier set sail for the Far East on January 14, 1942.

Campbell remembered that the military intelligence provided to him and his fellow pilots during the voyage was poor. "They told us that the Japanese flew nothing but old biplanes and monoplanes with fixed landing gear. When we finally got close to Java on January 28, 1942, we flew from that carrier feeling about twenty feet tall. Here we were, finally going to get a crack at the Japanese who were flying a bunch of old wooden airplanes. We were all going to become instant aces!"

Java was nearly 300 miles to the north when the pilots of 258 Squadron and the other Hurricane elements launched from the *Indomitable* with long-range fuel tanks hung from their wings. After landing and spending the night at Batavia (present-day Jakarta), the pilots got airborne again and winged their way toward the beleaguered British bastion at Singapore, the "Gibraltar of the East."

By this time the Japanese had completed their conquest of the Malay Peninsula. All that remained was the British Colony on the island base of Singapore. Only partially completed, the defenses were manned by British, Australian, and Indian units which, as likely as not, were undermanned by recently-arrived, half-trained troops. Still, the defenders outnumbered the Japanese attackers. And their defenses, although only partially complete, were considerable. As the Japanese prepared to strike and the world looked on, Churchill urged the garrison to fight to the last.

"On the way to Singapore we stopped at Palembang, in Sumatra, to refuel and have our long range tanks removed," Campbell remembered. "The ground crews there told us that the RAF was getting the hell kicked out of it in Singapore. This surprised us, but when we learned that they were flying the Brewster Buffalo we brushed it off; it was no wonder they were having a hard time!" The F2A Brewster Buffalo was a near-obsolescent, single-engine American fighter that, although it performed quite well with the Finnish air force against the Soviets, was decimated by the Japanese wherever they encountered it.

In fact, the fighters already in Singapore were a mix of Buffalos and Hurricanes. The force, manned by a composite group of British, Australian and New Zealand pilots—among other nationalities—was never numerically strong, and the Japanese steadily wore it down during January 1942. Preparations were made to pitch 258 Squadron and the other air elements from the *Indomitable* into the fight. But ultimately, they would prove to be little more than a stopgap force.

Except for coming under intense antiaircraft fire by British-led Indian gunners, the well-traveled Hurricanes arrived at RAF Seletar in Singapore during the next several days. It was one of four airfields on the island. During a brief respite the aircraft were given much-needed maintenance that included cleaning the heavy anti-corrosion grease that had been applied to their guns prior to their long sea voyage.

They finally began operations on February 1, 1942. Campbell got airborne that morning on an alert during which nothing was sighted. His second sortie that afternoon developed to be much more eventful. "During my first combat in Singapore," Campbell recalled, "we attacked a formation of bombers. I got some hits on one bomber but am not certain that it went down. I dove away to pick up speed, and by the time I climbed back up again the bombers were too far away, and there was nobody else around.

"Then I looked down and saw two Japanese fighters—I think they were Imperial Japanese Navy Zeros. They had a Hurricane [flown by Bruce McAlister] boxed in. Every time he'd try to turn one way, they'd take a shot at him. So I pulled around and started down to help him. Well, he must have thought I was another Zero because he pulled to start taking lead on me. So I turned away and showed him the bottom of my airplane. With that duck-egg blue on the bottom of the airplane, the roundels were very easy to see.

"When I turned back," Campbell continued, "he had turned into the Japanese. Unfortunately, they nailed him. When I saw that there was no helping him, I looked for the sun, found it, and climbed up into it." From high above, hidden in the blinding tropical glare, Campbell dove on the two Japanese fighters. "Apparently they didn't see me. They sat down there doing regular search patterns, just weaving along. I opened fire at extreme range, about four hundred yards, without really expecting much. But I wanted to kill them. It was the only time I had that much time to think. I thought to myself that I needed to fire a little at nine o'clock because the Hurricane dived in a skid, and I needed to raise the nose a little bit because of the long range.

"I opened up with a short burst, and lo and behold, I hit him! Then I got buck fever and just held down on it and finally stopped firing as he turned into a great big ball of flame with a couple of wings sticking out of it.

"I pulled up and snapped over to the right as I passed over him," Campbell said. "When I came out of the roll I was sitting wing-to-wing, right next to his number two. He dove away, and I took a quick shot at him and got some hits, but that was it."

Campbell recalled that the situation at Singapore bordered on chaos. "Singapore, when we got there, was a disheartened place that had essentially already been given up. There were times during air raids when we couldn't even get our aircraft refueled. We'd have to bring people out of the air raid trenches at gunpoint."

Fighter operations were constantly shifting and difficult to control or coordinate due to a number of factors that included shortfalls in tools and parts, ground and air transportation, the air attacks and unreliable communications—among others. For these reasons, the fighter aircraft and their pilots were consolidated into two squadrons, 258 and 232. These operated from the various airfields on Singapore while staging, for the most part, from Palembang, in Sumatra.

There were two airbases at Palembang: P.1 and P.2. Campbell recalled the primitive conditions at P.2, which was a secret field carved from the dense, wet, tropical forest. "It was a jungle strip—grass—and the damned B-17s [heavy, four-engine American bombers] had been in and out of there and left big ruts in the strip. We lost several aircraft just in landing accidents. We broke propellers and busted wingtips because of those ruts and we didn't have any parts for repairs. In fact, I think that twenty to twenty-five percent of our losses were due to the B-17s!"

Campbell recollected the other difficulties that he and his comrades endured. "Our initial losses were terrible. We hadn't flown much together as a squadron. It was a great unit with five Americans, five New Zealanders, five Canadians, some Brits, two South Africans, and a Rhodesian, but we just hadn't trained much together. During an air raid, anybody who was there and had a flyable airplane took off and joined the formation. We staggered up to meet whole raiding forces with only six or seven airplanes."

Campbell also recalled that he and his fellow pilots were surprised at the quality of the Japanese aircraft and the skill of the Japanese pilots. "Our guys were trained to fight a hard-turning dogfight. In Europe we could out-turn anything out there." Unfortunately for Campbell and his comrades, the Japanese built their fighters with particular emphasis on maneuverability—few aircraft turned better than those of the Japanese. "At slow speed they could walk around you," Campbell remembered. "They were much lighter because they had no armor or self-sealing tanks.

"But the Hurricane was actually a better airplane than either the Zero, or the Japanese Army Ki-43. It was faster, it could out-climb them, and it had twelve machine guns and was more rugged. And," he added, "it could outturn them at high speeds. But not at slow speed. If you allowed them to fight you on their terms, they would chew you up. That's what they did to our guys early on. Most of the pilots we were up against were Japanese Army pilots who already had quite a bit of experience. They were good. By the time we got the know-how and experience, our numbers were pretty damned small."

It should also be considered that many of Campbell's comrades had no combat experience and that many of them had only just completed operational training prior to leaving England. After being stalled in Spain they had done little training whatsoever, but rather spent most of their time journeying across Africa, the Indian Ocean and part of the Pacific before arriving at Singapore.

As the situation worsened and the Japanese grip around Singapore tightened, human failings and shortcomings, normally held in check, manifested themselves. These came to the surface during preparations for a raid planned for February 3, 1942, against the Japanese-held airfield at Kluang, in Malaya. Nine Hurricanes from 258 Squadron were sent to Singapore where they were staged out of Tengah Airfield.

"The leadership had a big plan," Campbell recalled, "We were going to escort Blenheim bombers on a raid against a Japanese airfield in Malaya. We got up early and went to the planes and found that the gun panels hadn't been installed. It was a difficult panel with a locking device, not something you just slapped on." In fact, the panels couldn't be located and by the time they were found it was too late. The bombers flew unescorted. "It was almost like sabotage," Campbell said. "The mission was scrubbed and the next day the station commander shot himself."

Early during February 1942 with the fight for Singapore nearing its culmination as, in Winston Churchill's words, "The worst disaster and largest capitulation in British history," all fighter operations were withdrawn to Palembang, Sumatra. Palembang was important because of its immense refining facility which received and processed more petroleum than any other plant in the Far East.

Campbell operated primarily out of P.1. "There were the most fantastic thunderstorms I had ever seen," he remembered. "And the Japanese would come through and start strafing before we even knew they were there—our air warning system was just a bunch of towers with guys cranking klaxons. We often took off while they were strafing us. But we did score some successes.

"I got airborne during an air raid one day," he recalled. "I came back around and three Ki-43s saw me and started chasing me. Well, the Hurricane climbed very well, and could out-climb a Ki-43, so I tried to use that to my advantage. I wanted to get above them and then dive on top of them because I knew I couldn't mix it up with them.

"But I could only see two of them, so I started weaving to look for the other one, and they closed on me. I didn't have much of a choice so I turned into them and started firing. I saw big chunks come off of the cowling of one of them. I went over the top of him, then went into a cloud and hauled ass. When I turned around and came back there was nobody there."

Landing back at P.1, the ground crew greeted Campbell with cheers and congratulations. The Ki-43 he hit caught fire and plummeted into the jungle, scattering chunks of wreckage everywhere. Still not sure, Campbell was finally convinced when the ground crew pointed out the smoke and fire just outside the perimeter of the airfield.

Still, he wasn't always so lucky. "I got bagged once myself at Palembang. The Japanese kept to a pretty regular schedule, they typically raided us at ten and four just about every day. Well, our commanding officer had a problem. About 0930 every day he'd come up to me and say 'Red [Campbell's nickname], you take my airplane. I'm going into town to make sure that we're going to get some food out here for meal time.' It was unfortunate. He was a Battle of Britain guy, but he just lost it. Later—at the end— he got back to India and was sent home with an adverse report.

"So, on that particular day I took his airplane and scrambled with another fellow. We were told that there was a raid going on at P.2. There was cloud cover all over and on the way back I looked down through a hole in the clouds and it looked like a whole bunch of bees going around and around. I realized that it was an air combat, and we went screaming down in there. I don't remember everything that happened," he continued. "It was like the movies. There were airplanes all over the place and everyone was shooting at everyone else. From a head-on attack one of them pulled straight up into a hammerhead and I went up and nailed him at the top. He came apart and went in."

Unfortunately for Campbell, the fight didn't end on that high note. "Somebody came along and got some [bullets] into my engine. I damned near got back to the field though. As a matter of fact, I thought I was going to make it. But I ended up going in; I cleared about half an acre of jungle. But the Hurricane was like a bulldozer and I walked away from it."

The fighters making up the air defenses at Singapore were committed haphazardly and piecemeal. They were accordingly badly beaten. For example, four Hurricanes were lost on February 6, while claiming only one Japanese fighter. The following day, six Hurricanes, four Blenheims and a Hudson were destroyed in air and ground attacks; again, only one enemy fighter was downed. On February 13, nine reinforcement aircraft flying in from Batavia were caught by Japanese fighters as they tried to land. Only three survived. These types of losses were typical of the campaign.

Campbell recalled an incident from this period that illustrates the toughness of the Hawker-made aircraft relative to its more fragile Japanese counterparts. "One of our guys—his name was Scotty and he was a Canadian flight sergeant—was in the landing circuit with his wheels and his flaps down. Two Ki-43s saw him and came after him. The lead guy, instead of just dropping his nose and shooting Scotty, pulled up to attack him from above. Fortunately, on the way down he got too much speed up and when he yanked the stick back, his wings folded. From where we were, all we could see was the Hurricane and the Ki-43 merge together and one of them falling away. And we thought, boy, he sure nailed Scotty. But there was Scotty, still scooting along after all. Then the number two aircraft came down and took a shot at Scotty and left.

"Scotty started smoking," Campbell said, "and went down and that was the last we saw of him until about an hour later when he came walking back onto the field with his parachute under his arm. He was mad as hell that no one had come out to pick him up until I pointed out that no one had seen him bail out. 'Well,' he said, 'something shot me down. I pulled the canopy back, I jumped straight up, I pulled the ripcord, the parachute opened, and I landed.' I think he had the world's record for the lowest parachute jump!"

Notwithstanding Scotty's survival, it was a grim time for 258 Squadron. The Allied forces in Singapore and the Netherland East Indies were fast approaching collapse. On February 15, 1942, after a poorly executed defensive effort failed to repel the Japanese assault, Singapore capitulated. The loss of more than 80,000 personnel was the worst disaster in the history of the British military.

On February 14, Japanese paratroops were landed in an attack on P.1 and the refinery facilities at Palembang. Campbell was there. "I was on my way back from town to the airfield [P1]. There were quite a few British troops and they cornered me and asked 'What are we going to do, Sir?' So, I said to myself . . . shit. Then I realized that there was a Dutch armory nearby and that nobody was guarding it, so we broke in and armed ourselves.

"Now, I must say that I have a lot of respect for the British enlisted man. I told them that we ought to go get ourselves a Japanese paratrooper and they said 'right,' and off we went. Hell, most of those guys had never fired a weapon before. We ran into another bunch that had no weapons and they decided to join right in. They said, 'Well, maybe you'll kill a Jap and we can take his gun.'"

In the end, Campbell scouted ahead with another officer and faced a classic bayonet charge from a group of Japanese paratroopers. "Why the hell they didn't shoot us, I'll never know," Campbell said. A running gun battle ensued and Campbell downed one of his pursuers with his handgun. "If some Indonesian troops hadn't come by," he recalled, "I don't know what the outcome would have been."

The other airfield at Palembang, P.2, had not yet been discovered by the Japanese and received personnel and aircraft from P.1. The remaining aircraft—approximately 22 Hurricanes and 35 Blenheims—mounted attacks through the afternoon against the Japanese amphibious invasion force. Transports and their naval escorts were strafed through the day with considerable success.

Nevertheless, Dutch forces on Sumatra were incapable of stopping the advance and Campbell, along with what was left of the air elements that had been operating out of Palembang, finally retreated south to Java beginning the next day, February 15. Desperately needed supplies and aircraft components were destroyed or left behind.

Campbell recalled the dismal situation once the remaining fighter forces regrouped at Tjililitan Airfield near Batavia. "My squadron, 258, they cut us to the bone. The pilots that weren't actually flying, the sick and the wounded, they were shipped out. The commanders decided that six pilots from each of the two squadrons that were left would draw straws to figure out who would stay. Well, I was pissed off at my commanding officer so I said 'Hell, I'm going to stay.' John Vibert, a New Zealander, said the same. The rest were short straw types. So, there were six of us from 258 Squadron that stayed. Actually we were transferred over to 605 Squadron, but I only flew my last three sorties with them."

Campbell recalled his last combat sortie, which occurred on February 28, 1942, the day before the Japanese invaded Java. His was one of only four aircraft remaining to defend against a Japanese raiding force of 54 bombers and their fighter escort. He plunged headlong into the attacking aircraft and soon found himself in a whirling, World War I-type engagement. He spotted another Hurricane being harried by a Zero, and roared in to the rescue. "For some reason, when the Zero pilot saw me, he started doing barrel rolls and other aerobatics. I was just astounded. He rolled up on his back and I thought that he was going to try and dive away, so I rolled over as well."

The two aircraft hung suspended, upside down, for only a moment. Campbell remembered: "The Hurricane wouldn't run on its back for sour owl shit. Fortunately, he rolled back upright again and I let him have it. I put a whole burst right in the wing root and the wing just folded. I had never seen a Japanese pilot bail out. We found bodies in wrecks, but no parachutes, and I wanted to see what this guy did." The enemy flier failed to leave his destroyed aircraft as it fell to earth.

It was at this point, his attention diverted, that Campbell's own aircraft was ripped with gunfire from a different Zero. "Well, I really had my head up my ass. I could hear that damned 20mm cannon fire exploding against my armor plate. I shoved the stick over and put in full rudder to try and get away, but my old Hurricane was so slow by that time that it just sort of rolled while he blew the hell out of me. Part of the left wing and the aileron were gone and I couldn't pull out—it was very unstable. So I decided to get out.

"When I went to jump though, I had a problem. I always flew with the canopy open about four inches. But when this guy tore up my airplane, among other things, he damaged the track that the canopy slid back on. And it wouldn't come forward either. You could jettison the canopy on the Hurricane, but to do that it had to be fully forward. I fought with that damned thing and tore the handle completely off. When I last looked at the altimeter," Campbell said, "I was falling through 7,500 feet. Finally, I got up on the seat and shoved on the seat and the stick at the same time. The next thing I knew, the canopy, and me, and everything else went flying by the tail."

———————

The flying part of the war was over for Campbell. Nevertheless, the terror had only barely begun. Following the Japanese invasion of Java, Campbell and a band of remaining squadron personnel spent the next couple of weeks evading capture. This was made more difficult after March 9, 1942, when Java was surrendered and Dutch nationals were enlisted by the Japanese to hunt out Allied personnel still at large. Campbell was understandably bitter and angry: "We had a gun battle with the Dutch troops, who wanted to disarm us, and one Dutchman was killed." Finally cornered, they woke up on the morning of March 20 to find themselves surrounded. "One of the guys tried to make a run for it and the Japanese shot him. So I decided that there wasn't much of a future in that course of action."

Imprisoned for the rest of the war, Campbell and his fellow prisoners of war endured brutality and sickness and hunger and hardships of a type that cannot be adequately communicated. And during three-and-a-half years of imprisonment, he received only two postcards from home. Finally, one month after the Japanese surrender, he was liberated on September 15, 1945, by British paratroopers and sent home.

Kenneth Jernstedt poses next to an AVG P-40 at Kunming, China.
—*Kenneth Jernstedt Collection*

CHAPTER 2
TIGERS IN THE FRAY

The Flying Tigers name is history. Nearly every boy in America has had a model or picture of the iconic shark-mouthed P-40 flown by the famous group; virtually everyone is familiar with the image. But not everyone knows the story behind the 1st American Volunteer Group of the Chinese Nationalist Air Force—as the Flying Tigers were officially known. Although their exploits were a source of pride to the American people during the darkest days of the war, not many understood that they flew under the Chinese flag. Nor did they realize that they were paid not only a monthly salary but also a bonus for each enemy aircraft they destroyed.

Nevertheless, money was only a secondary inducement for most of the men. The chance to fly and fight against an immoral enemy was their primary motivation. In large part, it was this adventurous spirit that drove them to succeed and earn the reputation they deserved.

Ken Jernstedt

KEN JERNSTEDT WAS BORN IN CARLTON, OREGON, ON JULY 20, 1917, and grew up on a farm on the Yamhill River. "I always appreciated the fact that I was raised on a farm. It made me so I wasn't afraid of work. And learning to shoot stood me in good stead later when it really counted. We had everything—cows and pigs and horses. We grew alfalfa and cut wood for fuel. We raised barley and wheat and corn; you name it, we grew it."

Following graduation from Yamhill High School in 1935, Jernstedt attended Linfield College and studied business. He remembered the single incident that put him on the path to service as a Flying Tiger. "We had a student body meeting and a student got up to make a motion. Well, we all knew this guy was a communist. Anyway he made a motion against any type of military recruiting notices on the bulletin board. This was early in 1939 and he was hooted down. I wondered what pulled his string, and went out to the bulletin board to take a look. There was a recruiting notice that was entitled 'Be a Naval Aviator.'"

After deciding that he met the qualifications, Jernstedt applied to be a Marine Aviation Cadet; Marine pilots were trained as naval aviators and matriculated through the same syllabus. "After I was accepted, I got to wondering whether or not I'd even like flying. So, I hitchhiked into Portland, went down to a little airport called Swan Island, paid five bucks, and got my first airplane ride. That started me."

After leaving Linfield in 1939 with a degree in business administration, Jernstedt went through elimination training with the Navy in Seattle. He was subsequently sent to Pensacola, Florida, for flight training. His contract required him to serve as an aviation cadet for four years after completing flight training. Following that four-year commitment he was to be commissioned a second lieutenant in the reserves. However, the nation was readying for war. "About halfway through our training they changed the program," he recalled. "When my class—131C—graduated during July 1940 we were commissioned as reserve officers.

"After finishing my flight training at Pensacola I was ordered to the Marine air group at Quantico, Virginia. The Marine Corps had two air groups, one at Quantico, and the other at San Diego, California. I was with two other new second lieutenants and we all wanted to fly fighters. At Quantico they had a fighter squadron, a scouting squadron, a bombing squadron, and a utility squadron. It turned out that we all went to the fighter squadron, VMF-1."

Flying Grumman F3Fs, the service's last biplane fighter, Jernstedt deployed with VMF-1 to the Navy base at Guantanamo Bay, Cuba. "We didn't have much to do other than fly and play sports," he remembered. "We got up fairly early to fly then knocked off in the early afternoon, put on a pair of trunks and played volleyball or softball. I got into pretty good shape. I also got a chance to check out on the aircraft carrier *Wasp* [CV-7]. This was the first *Wasp* and it was practically brand new at that time. All in all, for a single guy, it was a wonderful experience. We were there for seven months though, and it was tough on my married comrades."

After returning from Cuba during the spring of 1941, Jernstedt continued to gain flying experience while also transitioning to the new Grumman F4F Wildcat. The Navy and the Marine Corps were busy fielding the little aircraft as their frontline fighter. Although it wasn't pretty, it was tough, maneuverable and easily maintained.

While Jernstedt was transitioning to the Wildcat, representatives of the secretive Central Aircraft Manufacturing Company, CAMCO, were recruiting pilots from all branches of the military. With the government's tacit approval, the company was readying pilots for combat service overseas. Specifically, CAMCO was sending the pilots to China.

Japan invaded Manchuria in 1931 and subsequently moved deeper into China during the ensuing years. Badly battered and increasingly isolated by the marauding Japanese, China was in danger of being cut off from the rest of the world. With its coastline secured by the Japanese, its only artery for military assistance and trade was the recently constructed Burma Road which wound through southern China and Burma. To help develop the road's aerial defenses, China contracted with Claire Chennault, a retired United States Army Air Corps captain.

Chennault was an irascible, outspoken and forward-thinking pilot who had served during World War I. As the head of the pursuit section of the Army Air Corps Tactical School during the 1930s he did much to influence the service's thinking on the future of its fighter forces. Nevertheless, Chennault's blunt nature did not ingratiate him with his superiors. His unpopular belief that modern bombers required fighter protection flew in the face of powerful bomber proponents. Those beliefs, along with hearing problems, contributed to his decision to retire during 1937 at the age of forty-seven.

Chennault went to China soon after as an air advisor to the Nationalist government. There, he helped organize a cadre of international pilots for service against the Japanese, but that effort was discontinued as Soviet flying units arrived to augment China's own feeble air force. Soviet aid notwithstanding, the Chinese were still desperate to field more aircraft units against the Japanese.

But Chennault was unable to quickly build a credible air force using only Chinese pilots and equipment. Consequently he turned back to the

United States for help. After a plea from China's leader, Chiang Kai-shek, President Roosevelt allowed CAMCO to recruit American military pilots for service in Burma and China. Additionally, the president helped smooth the way for Chennault's acquisition of a hundred Curtiss P-40 fighters.

"The recruiters," Jernstedt remembered, "made a pitch for a unit that was being organized in great secrecy. Chuck Older, Tom Haywood and me—and a Navy pilot and comic artist named Bert Christman—thought we'd at least look into it. We made an appointment during the first part of June 1941 and went to the Chrysler building in New York City to interview with the Central Aircraft Manufacturing representative. The more we heard, the more interested we became."

The recruiter did his work well. On July 1, 1941, Jernstedt was out of the Marine Corps and a few days later he and Older and Haywood, together with a group of others, headed to Burma. After an exciting trip through some of the world's more exotic ports, the men arrived at Rangoon, Burma, on September 17, 1941. "They took us to Toungoo, up the road toward Mandalay. The RAF had a base there, and that's where we did our training."

It is also where Jernstedt first encountered the legendary Chennault, head of the American Volunteer Group, or AVG. "I liked him very much," Jernstedt said. "Of course he was very formidable looking in a way, but he had a heart of gold. He was a competitive man and believed very much in what he was doing. I didn't have a lot of contact with him except for early in the morning. We all met for classes at 0700 during which he lectured us on what we would be up against, the tactics we would use, and so forth. His tactics differed from what we had been taught."

And appropriately so. Chennault had observed first-hand the capabilities of the Japanese fighters and knew that his pilots would fail if they used traditional dogfight tactics against the light and very maneuverable Japanese aircraft. Accordingly, he developed fighting schemes which pitted the strengths of the P-40 against the weaknesses of the enemy planes. He pounded home the point that the American pilots should not try to turn with the Japanese aircraft. Instead, he instructed his men to gain an altitude advantage and make a quick, high-speed, diving attack. They were then to use the airspeed they gained during the dive to zoom back up to altitude, and set up for another attack.

The aircraft he secured for his fledgling air force was the Curtiss P-40. Although it wasn't the best fighter in the world it was certainly a capable one. It was the result of Curtiss's successful mating of the Allison V-1710, liquid cooled, 12-cylinder engine, with its earlier-developed P-36A air-frame. In 1939 the War Department ordered 524 P-40s; it was the largest American aircraft contract since World War I.

Although not particularly nimble, and lacking in high altitude per-formance, the aircraft was sturdy, reasonably fast, easy to fly, and well-armed and protected. Importantly, the P-40 was the only Army fighter being mass produced in 1940 that had any chance of succeeding against the best Japanese and German fighters. In production until 1944, and widely exported among the Allies, nearly 14,000 were produced.

Chennault's men flew uniquely configured P-40Bs originally intended for Great Britain's Royal Air Force as Tomahawk IIBs. They carried a mix of .50- and .30-caliber machine guns and had armor protection for the pi-lots. And most of the aircraft had self-sealing fuel tanks that lessened the chances of fire or explosion if hit by enemy fire.

It was the American Volunteer Group of the Nationalist Chinese Air Force, as Chennault's flyers were officially known, that secured the P-40's place in history. "I liked it from the word 'go,'" Jernstedt said. "It kind of purred—it had a different sound to it. Of course it was the first liquid-cooled engine I had flown. I was used to the air-cooled radial of the Wild-cat. But I didn't have any trouble checking out in it at all. It was easier to fly than the Wildcat."

The people he flew and served with were an odd mixture of pilots and ground crews from all the different services; they had flown and serviced a broad spectrum of aircraft. The group was divided into three squadrons, the 1st was the *Adam and Eve* squadron while the 2nd and 3rd were the *Panda Bears* and *Hell's Angels* respectively. Jernstedt, who was assigned to the *Hell's Angels* with his friends Older and Haywood, remembered that the flyers came together very well. "The 3rd Squadron," he recalled, "got along beautifully. And I think the others did too. There were a few dissi-dents of course, but they were in other squadrons, not mine."

Living conditions for the Tigers varied, depending on the period and where they were stationed. Sometimes their situation was comfortable, with fresh laundry service and other perks such as houseboys who ran errands and attended to other duties. "I particularly liked being able to get a shave and a haircut at Kunming for less than a dime," Jernstedt recalled. "That was real luxury." At other times, particularly when sent to outlying airfields, the men had little more than a roof over their heads.

Although they came from military backgrounds, the men did not rigidly follow military protocols. "We adhered to it to some extent," Jernstedt said, "but not anything like what I was used to with the Marines. It was a strange situation. I think we worked well together because of the comradeship we developed. Also, we received wonderful service from our ground crews and our radio people in the boondocks. I would compare them most favorably with any group in the world. Their work was outstanding."

From September 1941 until the attack on Pearl Harbor on December 7, Chennault's men trained hard, flying almost daily. "We had the spare parts and the gas to do it," Jernstedt recalled, "especially before the war. Chennault wanted us to be ready."

After the Japanese attacked Pearl Harbor on December 7, 1941, in response to a British request, Chennault sent the *Hell's Angels* to Rangoon on December 12 where they flew out of the airfield at Mingaladon. At the same time he moved the other two squadrons to the main base at Kunming, China. "Chennault figured that Rangoon, because of its port and its position at the end of the Burma Road, would be one of the first cities targeted," Jernstedt remembered.

The Flying Tigers first saw action when the 1st and 2nd squadrons downed three of ten unescorted Japanese Ki-48 bombers on December 20 as they raided Kunming. Jernstedt's 3rd Squadron, far to the south at Rangoon, didn't score until a few days later. "We had a lot of false alarms and were up and down all the time.

"Finally on December 23, we got into it for keeps," he remembered. "I was flying on Neil Martin's wing with one other pilot, Bob Brouk. Neil Martin was one of the best pilots in the squadron; he was well-liked and a great athlete. We took off and climbed to altitude and then, here they came. There were two squadrons of bombers and at least a squadron of fighters. We had about twelve P-40s and the Brits had about seven Brewster Buffaloes.

"Neil Martin went down first," Jernstedt remembered. "He went through the tail-end of the bomber formation and then pulled up. I don't know if they killed him when he went through and the plane just came back up on its own, or whether he made a horrendous mistake; he pulled up right in front of the lead bombers. Then all of a sudden he fell off on a wing, smoking, and down he went.

"As I said," Jernstedt recounted, "he was one of the best in the squadron, and to see him get it on the first pass was very disconcerting." Still though, Jernstedt dove into the attack as he had been taught. Coming down onto the left side of the formation of twin-engine Mitsubishi Ki-21s, he pressed home his attacks again and again. "I kept pecking away at them, and one blew up all of a sudden. I came in fairly close and it just caught fire and went down.

"I had used that same approach on a couple of other bombers earlier," he said, "but I don't think I was close enough. One slowed down momentarily when I knocked some metal off, but it didn't leave the formation." That day, despite being heavily outnumbered, the Flying Tigers lost three aircraft and two pilots while downing at least eight of the Japanese bombers.

The Japanese returned two days later, on Christmas. "When I took off I was with two other aircraft and then I started having engine trouble," Jernstedt recalled. He weighed his options as his comrades climbed away from him. "I thought I was going to have to go back to base, but I didn't want to do that because it seemed the airfield was going to be under attack. Then the engine settled out so I started climbing again."

It was then that Jernstedt spotted an enemy fighter—a Ki-27. Smaller and more maneuverable than the P-40, the Ki-27 had fixed landing gear and was not as fast. Importantly, it was not nearly as heavily armed or well protected as the P-40.

The enemy fighter was ahead of Jernstedt and headed in roughly the same direction but crossing slightly from left to right. Jernstedt added power to close the distance. "He saw me and turned toward me at the same time. I didn't want to get in a dogfight with him so I tried to shoot him down in a head-on pass."

Jernstedt fired his two cowl-mounted .50-caliber machine guns, and his four, smaller, wing-mounted, .30-caliber machine guns. The little Japanese fighter went up in flames before the fight really began. The novice

Jernstedt's introduction to combat was off to a good start; he had been in combat only twice and scored during both engagements.

Following the Christmas engagement over Rangoon, the *Hell's Angels* saw no more action and were rotated north to Kunming. Combat for Jernstedt was hit-and-miss during this period. "We rotated between day and night duty. Night duty was kind of a cinch because all you had to do was be ready. Daytime duty got to be kind of boresome because nothing happened. Soon, though, we started flying offensive missions. On one day we escorted some Chinese bombers on a mission to Hanoi. They were Soviet-built, twin-engine bombers [probably Tupolev SBs] that were so cock-eyed slow, and so obsolete, that I couldn't believe it. We couldn't fly slow enough to stay in the sky and escort them without flying circles over them." Fortunately for the Chinese, the Japanese defenses that day included only some light antiaircraft fire.

By March 1942, offensive missions against the Japanese were more common. Jernstedt recalled the mission of March 19. The night prior, he and Bill Reed flew from their base at Magwe to Toungoo, which had already been evacuated in the face of the Japanese advance. "It was the first time I ever saw bodies in a pile," he said. "There were about two hundred of them. The Japanese had hit a Buddhist temple which was full of Burmese."

The next morning, March 19, they took off in the predawn darkness for an armed reconnaissance mission of the Japanese airdrome at Moulmein, near the border between Thailand and Burma. "We were just going to go down there and look around," he remembered. "We didn't even know for sure that there were any airplanes there. Anyway we got south of Moulmein a little bit and let down from 20,000 feet through a bit of cloud cover and I'll be darned if there wasn't a little airfield sitting out there. Just a single strip with airplanes lined up wingtip-to-wingtip on both sides of the runway." The airstrip they found was the Japanese auxiliary field at Mudon.

The two Americans immediately started strafing the enemy aircraft. "It was just like shooting ducks in a pond," Jernstedt said. "Bill would go up one side and I'd go in the opposite direction on the other side. Then we'd just make a turn and come back. We shot up quite a few airplanes there, but we kept a little ammunition and headed up toward Moulmein."

Surprised and pleased at destroying a number of Japanese aircraft at an airfield they hadn't even known existed, Jernstedt and Reed raced up to Moulmein, their primary target. "I guess by that time they were awake," Jernstedt said. "One plane was taking off and we got him just as he got up in the air. We messed around there for a while and I dropped a fire bomb on a transport that was being refueled.

"I'll never forget that mission," Jernstedt remembered, "because Chennault sent us a radiogram: 'Congratulations, you have set a world record for destruction.' We got credit and were paid for destroying fifteen airplanes."

Jernstedt was nearly killed two days later on March 21, 1942, while flying out of Magwe. After getting airborne with fellow Tiger Parker Dupouy during a Japanese raid, he climbed to altitude and attacked the enemy bombers—K-21s—as they headed away. "I think they were headed for Hanoi," he remembered. "Anyway, I made high-side passes from above and got two of them. On what turned out to be my last pass, a bullet from one of their gunners came through my windshield, passed by the side of my neck and hit the armor plating behind my head. Well, like a darned fool, I had put my goggles up because I wanted better peripheral vision—I didn't want anyone to sneak up on me. Glass from the windshield hit me smack in the left eye.

"I disengaged right then—dove out and headed for home. I had to keep my eye shut and fly with just the other. By the time I got back to Magwe I was nearly out of gas and the place had been pretty badly shot up. I was lucky. When I landed I just barely missed a bomb crater in the runway that I didn't even know was there." Jernstedt was indeed fortunate. Timely medical attention and evacuation to a hospital at Kunming saved his eye. A week later he was sent back to Magwe for flying duty.

Although the Tigers continued to score dramatic successes in the air, they could not win the battle alone. The Japanese air and ground effort was enormous and Chennault's relatively tiny group consequently found itself retreating from base to base in the face of the enemy advance. By the middle of April 1942, the Japanese were in control of the Burma Road, and virtually all the material the AVG needed had to be flown over the Himalayas from India.

Spare parts and fuel became increasingly scarce. The AVG mechanics performed wonders as they manufactured needed parts or cannibalized them from damaged or grossly unserviceable aircraft. Nevertheless, mechanical miracles aside, the number of aircraft ready for combat steadily decreased.

Illness also took a toll on ground crews and pilots alike. "Early on I had a streak of dengue fever," Jernstedt recalled. He wasn't alone. Working under austere conditions with limited supplies and equipment, the AVG's tiny medical staff treated exotic diseases they had never before encountered.

The group sustained losses from other causes too. "We lost some pilots to their own darned foolishness," Jernstedt said. "Accidents. Or navigation—they'd go flying down and around the hills and get killed—stuff like that."

Although Chennault's flyers sometimes escorted Chinese bombers, one escort mission that Jernstedt recalled in particular didn't involve bombers. "Chiang Kai-Shek and Madame wanted to go down to Burma to tour some bases there. So, six of us escorted their DC-3 for a couple of days to different bases. I liked them both," he said of China's leader and his charismatic wife and champion, Madame Chiang. "He was very quiet and she was an exuberant, beautiful, woman. They were both very nice. Sometimes they ate lunch with us.

"One time, they held a huge banquet for the AVG at Kunming. It was quite an affair as his whole cabinet was there. You know when you're the age I was at that time, you're not too impressed. But looking back at it, there was the leader of a nation of 750 million people, and the rest of his government, and I was in the same room eating with them!"

Soon after Jernstedt's eye injury healed and he returned to flying at Magwe, the airfield was hurriedly evacuated as the Japanese approached. The *Hell's Angels* fell back to the Chinese base at Loiwing near the border with Burma. It was there that Jernstedt scored his final aerial victory. He remembered the frantic scramble when word came that a Japanese attack was imminent. "It was one of those instances where there were a lot of people scrambling and looking out for themselves. The Japanese came in with nothing but fighters to strafe the field. Fortunately I got off before they arrived and got some altitude."

Jernstedt engaged a single Ki-27. "We started making passes at each other. He would turn to get on my tail, but I would pull up each time and get an altitude advantage before he could align himself on me." Flying the perfect fight against a better-turning adversary, Jernstedt maintained his cool and used his aircraft's superior power and speed until he was in a position to score. "I was finally able to come down on him from above and behind," he said, "and I got him."

By early summer of 1942, the AVG's exploits were legendary and were a boost to Allied morale across the globe. Having been credited with the destruction of nearly three hundred Japanese aircraft for a loss of only fifty aircraft of their own, and having lost only twenty-two pilots to all causes, the AVG's record was unequaled at a time when Allied air forces elsewhere were taking a beating.

Nevertheless, the nature of the war was changing and the United States government wanted to assimilate the AVG's personnel into the Army Air Forces, the USAAF. The date for the disestablishment of the AVG was set for July 4, 1942.

Unfortunately the Army was too heavy-handed at a time when many of the AVG's men were exhausted and in ill health. "I was in the hospital at the time with diarrhea and a series of nasty boils," Jernstedt remembered. "I was down to 135 pounds." Although many of the pilots were offered commissions and generous promotions, most of them wanted time off in the States to rest and recover before they committed to another lengthy combat tour in China. Afraid of losing so much talent at once, the Army officials threatened the pilots with the draft if they returned to the States.

The threats backfired. Most of the Flying Tigers turned their backs and only five men agreed to a commission. Chennault himself, committed to see his mission through, accepted a colonelcy and was quickly promoted to brigadier general. Another seven pilots agreed to stay on for a short time to help ease the transition as new Army Air Forces pilots were brought in as replacements.

The American Volunteer Group was officially disbanded on schedule and its operations were taken over by the newly-formed 23rd Fighter Group. Although the new fighter group continued to use the Flying Tigers name, the true group, the one that made it famous, was no more.

At the end of June 1942, still recovering from boils and gastrointestinal disorders, and unable to fly, Jernstedt asked Chennault for permission to leave for the United States before the unit was officially disbanded. A grateful Chennault granted his request. Considered persona non grata by the Army Air Forces, the bedraggled flier, credited with destroying 10.5 Japanese aircraft, was forced to find his own way across the globe to get home.

Once back in the States, Jernstedt was offered a commission as a major with the U.S. Army Air Forces. And the Marine Corps offered to take him back as a captain with the same seniority he had when he left the service. Ultimately, having seen all the combat he desired for a while, he signed on as a test pilot with Republic Aviation. He stayed with the airplane manufacturer until the end of the war. While there he flew and tested combat-bound P-47s.

Following the war he returned to Oregon where he operated a Coca-Cola bottling business and served a total of 22 years in the state legislature. His political career also included two elections to the mayor's office in Hood River.

It was 1996 before the pilots of the AVG were belatedly recognized by their own country for their service in Burma and China. Jernstedt, probably the only pilot in history to do so, was led to the podium by his seeing eye dog, Driscoll, and awarded the Distinguished Flying Cross.

CHAPTER 3

DIVE BOMBERS AT GUADALCANAL

Although the Japanese were dealt a stunning defeat at Midway during June 1942, American dominance in the Pacific was still well more than a year away. The United States Navy, not yet fully recovered from its losses at Pearl Harbor, the Coral Sea, and Midway, was still compelled to tread carefully. Indeed, it wasn't until August 1942 that America felt strong enough to attempt its first offensive in the South Pacific.

Jesse Barker

JESSE T. BARKER WAS BORN IN NEWTON, UTAH, ON FEBRUARY 1, 1918. "I grew up on a farm—dry farming," he recalled. "I didn't realize until years after I got an education that we were actually subsistence farming; we were able to produce only just enough to get by. I went to the local county schools as I grew up, and took jobs on other farms where I made two dollars per day pitching hay onto a wagon. After I graduated from high school in 1934 I joined the old Army Air Corps as an enlisted man.

"I made $21 per month. That was a lot of money to me. When I enlisted they promised me that I would get trained as an aircraft mechanic but all they let me do was wipe grease off of the cowlings and change spark plugs and that sort of thing. I could see that it was going to be a dead end. That's why I decided to buy out my contract—you could do it in those days. I think it cost me about 85 dollars to get out of the Army."

After taking a job and saving some money, Barker attended the Utah State Agricultural College at Logan, Utah. "I had two years of college when the Marines came around looking for candidates for flight school in Pensacola. I was very interested because I had always wanted to fly. But they were only taking college graduates. Later, I left school and took a job in Ely, Nevada, as a mechanic. I was the foreman of a five-man shop. During 1940, Ely started its first class in the Civilian Pilot Training Program and I was in it. I soloed in four-and-a-half hours and did well enough that the guy who was running the school asked me if I wanted to be an instructor."

Barker was sent to Scott Flight Services at Long Beach, California, to be trained as an instructor. While there he became friends with three other young instructors-in-training. Over the course of a couple of weekends, enamored with the idea of military flying, they all applied for service with the Navy, the Army, and the RCAF—the Royal Canadian Air Force. "The others were all picked up by the RCAF and were sent to Canada for training and then later on to England," Barker remembered. "One of them was killed just after arriving in England. The other two ended up transferring to the Army Air Forces and were killed later in the war.

"I never heard from the RCAF. A couple of weeks later I got orders to report to the Navy by 13 April, 1941. I had about 200 hours of flight time when I reported to Pensacola, so they started me at the 30-hour check. I had no trouble at all and went right on through and finished up in September 1941. After that I went to Opa-Locka, Florida, for advanced fighter training. I flew the little F2F and F3F biplanes and the Brewster Buffalo.

"In October 1941 I reported to San Diego, California and was assigned to the Advanced Carrier Training Group. There were about 150 of us there waiting for transportation to our assigned carriers out in the Pacific: *Lexington, Saratoga, Hornet, Yorktown,* and the *Wasp.*" It was during this time that Pearl Harbor was attacked. In the confusion that followed, Barker and most of the other pilots waiting in San Diego were stranded as the aircraft carriers undertook wartime operations.

"I had orders to Fighting Two aboard the old *Lexington,*" Barker recalled. "But after Pearl Harbor everything was in turmoil. After a few months they decided they needed dive bomber pilots more than they needed fighter pilots and I was dragged away from fighters—kicking and screaming—into a dive bombing unit. Anyway, we trained for several more months until May 1942, when they put us in a sort of composite air group, Air Group 3, aboard the *Saratoga.*"

The USS *Saratoga* had been torpedoed by a Japanese submarine several months earlier on January 11 and had consequently missed action in the

Pacific, including the Battle of the Coral Sea. Nevertheless, she underwent extensive repairs while receiving significant upgrades and was ready to return to combat by the end of May. At San Diego, the ship was loaded with a detachment of fighters from VF-2 as well as Barker's dive bombing squadron, VS-3, or Scouting Three. Replacement fighters and dive bombers were additionally loaded and *Saratoga* departed San Diego on June 1, 1942, ready to fight. Barker remembered the voyage: "They rushed us out to Pearl Harbor, and then up toward Midway for the big battle there, but we got there a couple of days late."

The aircraft Barker flew with VS-3 was the Douglas SBD Dauntless. A two-seat dive bomber, the type was first delivered to the Navy and the Marine Corps during 1939. Crewed by one pilot and one rearward-facing gunner who fired two .30-caliber machine guns, the SBD was critical to the early successes of the Navy and Marine Corps. Although its performance figures were modest—it cruised at about 130 knots—its stability, its ability to take punishment, and its bomb-carrying capability, combined with a respectable range, proved equal to the tasks it was assigned.

Armed with two cowl-mounted .50-caliber machine guns, along with the rear-mounted .30-caliber guns, the Dauntless carried a respectable bomb load, up to a single 1,000-pound bomb under the belly and two smaller bombs hung under the wings. Ultimately it was credited with sinking more enemy tonnage than any other U.S. aircraft type.

It wasn't until two months after the battle at Midway, during the American invasion of Guadalcanal, that Barker first saw combat. "By that time I had been assigned to Scouting Five, VS-5, which was an old *Yorktown* remnant [*Yorktown* was sunk during the fighting at Midway]. We ended up on the *Enterprise* and sortied out of Pearl Harbor on July 15, 1942, for Guadalcanal."

Part of the Solomon Island chain, and located roughly 500 miles east of New Guinea and 1,000 miles northeast of Australia, Guadalcanal's location made it of particular strategic value. An airbase and garrison on the island could support the Japanese plan to advance south and sever the lines of communication between the United States and Australia. With that goal in mind, the Japanese landed on the island in May 1942, and were busy constructing an airfield when American Marines stormed ashore on August 7, and captured the unfinished airstrip the following day.

Barker was flying a mission as part of that invasion force on the morning of August 7. "North, across the strait from the invasion force, was a Japanese radio station on the island of Tanambogo. That was my target. Even though it was my first mission I wasn't particularly frightened. At the time, we didn't know enough to be scared. Anyway, I dropped my bomb. I'm not sure if I hit the damned tower or not, but there was a huge secondary explosion—a bomb blast and an enormous fire. The Japanese must have had fuel oil and ammunition stored all around that tower because the blast was terrific!"

The Japanese reacted quickly to the American invasion. By that same afternoon, Japanese aircraft based at Rabaul attacked the American warships that made up the invasion force. The attacks continued during the next two days but achieved nothing noteworthy; two ships were damaged and aircraft were lost on both sides, but otherwise the American invasion was a marked success.

Nevertheless, the Japanese air raids had an effect. Frank Jack Fletcher, the American admiral in overall command, was concerned that his fleet might be pinned down while supporting the landings. Fletcher, who had lost the aircraft carrier *Lexington* during the engagement at Coral Sea, and the *Yorktown* at Midway, was fearful that another of his precious aircraft carriers might be sunk. At the end of the day on August 8, Fletcher's Task Force 61, which included the carriers *Enterprise, Wasp,* and *Saratoga,* was sent away from the island.

There were a number of valid factors, including the fuel states of the carriers, which played into Fletcher's decision. But ultimately, the American transports, without the carriers for protection, were compelled to leave Guadalcanal after unloading only parts of their cargoes. Consequently, the Marines were left alone and without much of their supplies and equipment.

Over the next couple of weeks Task Force 61 maintained a position southeast of Guadalcanal. Out of the range of Rabaul-based aircraft, they were still able to cover the supply routes to the island. In the meantime, patrol aircraft searched for signs of a Japanese task force. The Japanese were expected to reinforce their units on the island to expel what they still believed was only a small American garrison.

On August 23, 1942, elements of a Japanese task force, which included three aircraft carriers and troop transports, were discovered. By the next day,

Fletcher had his forces in position to launch strikes. The Japanese carrier *Ryujo* was found in the morning, badly damaged, and later sunk. In the meantime, the Japanese located the American carriers *Wasp* and *Enterprise*.

Barker was on the *Enterprise* on August 24. "The position reports for the other two Japanese carriers were incorrect," he recalled. "No one really knew where they were. We manned our planes about three different times. Each time, they cancelled the strike and we went back down to the ready room. Finally, around five o'clock in the afternoon they started to launch us. In the meantime, the Japanese found us and dove on the ship and bombed us as we took off.

"Eleven SBDs were launched before the *Enterprise* was hit and flight operations were stopped. I was flying as wingman to Lieutenant Turner Caldwell, the commanding officer of our squadron, VS-5. We had been briefed that the Japanese carrier we were supposed to go after was beyond our range. The plan was for the *Enterprise* to steam up toward the target so that she could meet us on our way back."

As it happened, no part of the plan came together. The *Enterprise* took three bomb hits that killed nearly eighty men and wounded a hundred more. With her steering damaged, she careened badly out of control. In the meantime, Caldwell led the SBDs, a mixture of aircraft from VS-5 and VB-6, nearly 300 miles from the *Enterprise* and 60 miles beyond the reported position of the enemy. "We searched," Barker remembered, "until after dark. We were low on fuel and finally just dropped our bombs into the water." In the dark, his search now hopeless, and without enough fuel to return to the *Enterprise,* Caldwell turned his flight toward Guadalcanal.

Although Barker's combat career was only just getting started, the Battle of the Eastern Solomons was over. It was not a decisive clash, but still it was an American victory. The enemy carrier *Ryujo* was sunk and Japanese aircraft losses exceeded American losses by a considerable margin. The *Enterprise,* although damaged, was not mortally hit.

"We barely had enough fuel, but we finally landed late that night at Henderson Field on Guadalcanal," Barker recalled. "From that point forward our little group from the *Enterprise* became known as Flight 300. That was what our mission, or flight, from the ship on that particular day was called."

The Marine airmen, who had only just arrived a few days previously on August 20, were operating on a shoestring. Supplies and equipment were exceedingly scarce. "The situation was pretty bad when I got to Guadalcanal," Barker remembered. "The first night there they gave me a blanket that had blood on it. A man had been killed in it the night before. I had to spend the night on the ground in that bloody blanket.

"The Marines had an SBD squadron there, VMSB-232, commanded by Lieutenant Colonel Richard Mangrum. They kind of adopted us and took us in. From that point on, until we were evacuated, we operated quite closely with them."

The importance of the accidental diversion of Caldwell's flight cannot be overstated. At the time, the Marines had only about fifteen F4F fighters from VMF-223, and a dozen SBDs from Mangrum's VMSB-232. The addition of the flight of eleven more SBDs from the *Enterprise* nearly doubled the offensive capability on Henderson Field, and made a telling difference in the weeks to come.

In fact, Flight 300's operational association with the Marine dive bombers started immediately. After being shelled by five Japanese destroyers during the same night that the Navy fliers arrived, the Marines of VMSB-232 launched two missions into the darkness. Their strikes were unsuccessful. Finally, at first light, VMSB-232 tried again with three aircraft of Flight 300 in tow. "After the Marine crews struggled in the dark to fuel and arm our aircraft," Barker recalled, "Caldwell, myself, and Ensign Chris Fink, took off with Mangrum and four other Marine SBDs. We went after a Japanese task force that was reported to be coming down to reinforce the island. This was the morning of August 25, 1942."

The enemy force was composed of the light cruiser *Jintsu*—flagship of Rear Admiral Raizo Tanaka—three troop transports, four old destroyers, and the five destroyers, only recently joined, which had shelled Henderson Field the previous night. "We climbed to about 12,000 feet before we found the ships," Barker recalled. "The five Marine pilots dove on the cruiser and got one hit. The pilot who got the hit was named Lawrence Baldinus. I remember his name because he was killed when shellfire hit our tent a couple of weeks later." As it developed, the bomb that Baldinus put into the *Jintsu* knocked Tanaka unconscious.

"We Navy boys dived on the transports. The antiaircraft fire wasn't particularly heavy and I only got one hole in my plane. Anyway, we got two hits on the transports." One transport, *Kinryu Maru,* with its 1,000-man landing force, was left dead in the water and sinking. The destroyer *Mutsuki,* which pulled alongside to evacuate survivors, was hit and sunk by a later flight of B-17s. The Japanese task force was forced back without landing any reinforcements. *Jintsu* limped away and did not return to combat until repairs were completed in Japan during January 1943.

The tiny and mixed force of Marine and Navy dive bombers returned to a base that had little to recommend it, particularly where food was concerned. "It was pretty bad," Barker said. "All we had to eat for a while was captured Japanese rice. That morning the Marine cook was standing next to a big pot of water which was boiling over a fire. He had a big shovel-full of rice and was trying to be funny. He kept pointing out that we were going to have fresh meat with our rice. When I looked closer I could see that the rice was just crawling with maggots. I couldn't eat for several days after that.

"We had very little support for our aircraft during this time. We were kept going by the Marines and a detachment of Navy personnel, but they were spread pretty thin. We had to fuel our aircraft by ourselves. It was me and my gunner, a great little Irishman from Boston, named E. J. Monahan. They'd drop off a fifty-gallon drum next to our aircraft along with a three-gallon bucket. We'd bucket the fuel out of the drum and strain it through a chamois cloth into the aircraft by hand. It was very primitive."

The next day, August 26, Barker was back in action. "I was on a patrol in the morning with Ensign Hal Buell as my wingman. We found two destroyers, one bigger than the other. We dived into an attack. Buell said I got a hit—he said that there was a flash and a fire on the starboard side, amidships. I personally am not sure whether it was a hit or a near-miss. Anyway, I didn't claim it, because I wasn't sure."

Barker remembered the dive bombing technique that he and his comrades used in their venerable SBDs. "Usually we tried to get to about 14,000 feet. Then we simply rolled inverted, right into a near-vertical dive of about 75 degrees. The SBD had perforated dive flaps that we extended to slow us down. As we came down we lined up the target in our sight. It was a telescopic sight about eighteen inches long and about two inches around. The trouble with the sight was that it fogged over as we descended from the cold air at altitude, into the warm, moist air of the tropics. So, we adapted by looking over the top of the thing, just like sighting over a rifle barrel.

"Finally, we released our bombs at 2,500 feet, pulled out of our dives at about four Gs, and leveled off over the water at about 500 feet. The SBD wasn't a very fast airplane, but it was a very reliable and steady dive bomber."

While there was considerable aerial combat above and around Guadalcanal during this period, Barker encountered enemy aircraft only once. "It was the same day that I was returning from the attack with Buell on the Japanese destroyers. We were down on the water at about 500 feet. Our route took us by the little island of Gavutu, north of Henderson Field. As we cruised past this island I came head-to-head with a Japanese Zero on floats, an A6M2-N. It was painted kind of a basic white. Anyway, he was right on my altitude and we were both just looking at each other's eyeballs. I guess we were both surprised because we passed each other before we knew what to do. I made a hard turn and he made a turn to come back around. I started firing and only got off three rounds from one of my .50-caliber machine guns before it jammed. The other one wouldn't even fire. What saved me, I think, is that this little Japanese boy was as scared of me as I was of him, because he just took off in the other direction."

Henderson Field's codename was Cactus, and the collection of aircraft and personnel from all the services based there soon became known as the Cactus Air Force. "We settled down into a kind of routine," Barker said. "Late in the morning the Japanese came down and bombed the airfield. We usually took off just beforehand so that our aircraft wouldn't be destroyed, and then we'd get out of the way while the Marine fighters shot them down. Then, in the afternoon, we would take off to try and catch the Japanese destroyers on their way down from Rabaul with troops. Finally at night, Japanese ships would come in and shell the field. That was pretty much the routine.

"On August 28, I was assigned to the afternoon search again. We took off at about four o'clock. Only about 80 miles out we came upon four Japanese destroyers coming down at high speed, in line, really putting out a wake. So I climbed up because we normally conducted these searches down low over the water. At the same time I called back to Henderson field and reported what I saw. As I waited for them to launch a flight from the airfield, I climbed up to about 10,000 feet and made my own attack.

These ships didn't try to circle, or turn, or evade at all. They just stayed in line. I got a hit right on the stern of one of them. There was an explosion and a fire and the ship went dead in the water, trailing oil. I went back to base and Mangrum and Caldwell and some of the others came out and got hits on two more, and confirmed that the one I had hit was trailing oil and down in the stern."

In fact, after receiving Barker's report, the Cactus Air Force sent out a flight of eleven SBDs. Ensign Chris Fink struck the *Asagiri* amidships with his bomb, and Caldwell hit the *Shirakumo* with another. The *Asagiri* exploded and sank, while the *Shirakumo* was taken under tow. The ship that Barker hit was most likely the *Yugiri,* which remained out of service until mid-January, 1943.

The Japanese Navy, in order to escape air attacks from the Cactus Air Force, soon began operating almost exclusively at night. Their surface forces were adept at night operations and were successful at delivering reinforcements in the darkness—right under the noses of the Americans concentrated near Henderson Field.

Still though, the Cactus Air Force sometimes risked the dangers inherent to night flying operations. "One night," Barker recalled, "the Japanese were landing supplies and troops in barges on the beaches to the west of Henderson Field. The weather was miserable—misty and foggy—and it was a very dark night. But the decision was made to send us out anyway. I was loaded with bombs, and went in at low altitude, about 2,500 feet. My dive was very shallow—it was a glide bombing attack—and I got some pretty good hits on those barges. But it was very dark, no horizon to speak of, and we lost one pilot. I think he probably just got disoriented and flew into the drink."

As the weeks went by, the wear and tear of the constant aerial attacks together with nightly shelling by enemy warships—and poor diet and disease—took their toll. "After we were moved into a tent with the Marine pilots, Chris Fink and I dug a slit trench outside between a pair of palm trees. Everyone made fun of us. One night, September 12, Japanese warships came in to shell us again. As soon as the shelling started Chris and I got into the trench. The tent took a direct hit. When it was over and we crawled out, some of the tops of the palm trees nearby were shot off. That was the same night that Baldinus was killed."

By the end of September the members of Flight 300 had been drastically reduced by combat and disease. And they had few aircraft that were flyable. The decision was made to relieve them from combat duty and they were flown out of Guadalcanal. "By the time we were evacuated on September 27, 1942," Barker said, "Chris Fink and I were the only two out of the original eleven pilots who were still flying. Everyone had dysentery and malaria—and the trots. It was really bad."

When the Navy fliers departed, they had reason to be proud of their accomplishments. It is arguable that without the extra punch they provided to the early campaign, the outcome of the fight for Guadalcanal might have turned out quite differently.

Following his tour at Guadalcanal, Barker said good-bye to the trusty SBD and retrained in night fighters—F6F-5N Hellcats. By the summer of 1944 he was back in the Pacific aboard the Independence *as part of VF(N)-41. During this period his unit was instrumental in protecting the fleet against both day and night raids, particularly kamikaze attacks. His last combat assignment was with a day fighter unit, VF-18, aboard the* Intrepid. *He finished the war with three Distinguished Flying Crosses, a host of Air Medals, and official credit for destroying 1.25 enemy aircraft.*

Barker's subsequent career was just as remarkable. During 32 continuous years of service he flew more than 117 aircraft types and amassed nearly 13,000 flight hours. Highlights of his career included service during the Korean Conflict flying F4U-4Bs, and two tours as a squadron commanding officer. While serving as the projects officer of the Service Test Division at Naval Air Test Center, Patuxent River, he stewarded John Glenn's record-setting transcontinental dash (Project Bullet) across the United States on July 16, 1957. His final assignment was as the commanding officer of the Naval Air Maintenance Training Command. Captain Jesse Barker retired in 1973 after 32 years of service.

CHAPTER 4

ARMY FIGHTERS OVER GUADALCANAL

Although the Imperial Japanese Navy was staggered at Midway, 1942 was a year during which American forces were still doing their best simply to hold the line against Japanese expansion. The Imperial Japanese forces were still dominant through most of the Pacific, and ranged virtually at will across the vast expanse of water and island groups.

During this period the United States Army Air Forces were still fielding a mixture of barely adequate fighter types, particularly the P-40 and P-39. It was mostly these aircraft that were used at New Guinea and elsewhere to guard the approaches into Australia. Indeed, the fighter that would ultimately down more Japanese aircraft than any other Army type, the Lockheed P-38 Lightning, did not draw first blood in the South Pacific until the very last month of 1942.

Julius Jacobson

JULIUS "JACK" JACOBSON WAS BORN ON SEPTEMBER 27, 1916 IN San Diego, California. He was always an adventurer. At age seventeen he told his parents that he was going to visit with a relative. Somewhere along the way he zigged when he should have zagged and stowed away aboard a freighter out of Long Beach. He was in the Philippines before he was able to cable his parents that he was safe and in good health.

From the Philippines he worked his way back home the long way around. Serving as a cabin boy, he passed through Ceylon and Bombay, pushed on through the Suez Canal and the French city of Marseilles, and finally reached New York City where he was promptly fired. "The ship's stewards had a scam," Jacobson remembered. "The rich fathers came down to the docks and paid the crew to hire their sons. The boys would get hired, then after the ship went through the Panama Canal and arrived in Los Angeles all the cabin boys were fired and the crew hired new ones all over again."

From New York, young Jacobson was bilked and cheated in a series of misadventures as he made his way across the country. Finally, ninety days after leaving home, while hitchhiking through the desert town of El Centro, California, he was picked up by his father's business partner in an "it's a small world" fluke. His long and capricious trek ended with a ride directly to his own front doorstep.

He was twenty-four and still without any clear career goals in early 1940 when he accompanied his father on a visit to a nearby dairy farm in the low-lying area that abutted the San Diego River. "I didn't really have any direction as far as what I wanted to do with my future. The farmer we were talking with pointed up at some Army training airplanes that were flying low overhead. He said that I ought to give flying a try."

He did. Researching the Army requirements to become an aviation cadet, he discovered that if he could pass a two-year college equivalency test, the Army would accept him for flight training. "At that point," Jacobson recalled, "I was working in a clothing store. I was a pretty big clothes horse—I liked to dress well. And although I had been pretty good at math in high school, I had only a half year of college." Jacobson's approach was a deliberate one; he enrolled in a school that specialized in preparing its students for various accreditations, and batteries of tests. After a few months of study, he took the Army's equivalency exam, passed it and was accepted for flight training.

Jacobson stayed relatively close to home during his tenure as an aviation cadet. He reported to Ontario, California, in March 1941, and graduated from Stockton, California, with his wings and a commission as a second lieutenant in December of that same year. "I graduated during the same week as Pearl Harbor," Jacobson recalled. "And I was selected to be a flight instructor, which I thought was a great honor until war was declared. Then I rushed right down to the administration section and pleaded for a change of orders. I wanted to be a fighter pilot for the war, not an instructor!"

He was sent to Hamilton Field in northern California to join the 35th

Pursuit Group flying P-40s. Unfortunately, the squadrons were gone on exercises when he arrived and there were no aircraft to fly other than the advanced trainers he had flown as a flight student. "At the time, I was nothing but a hot-shot AT-6 pilot," Jacobson recalled. "They had four P-40s down at Alameda Naval Station in Oakland, so they sent a bunch of us down there and gave us blindfold checks and let us fly. When I sat in the cockpit for the first time the nose of that airplane looked like it was thirty feet long!"

Jacobson recalled his first flight: "I took off without any problems," he said. "I didn't touch a thing. By the time I leveled off and figured out what was going on, I was damned near all the way to Mexico." The flight continued uneventfully until it came time for him to land. "I couldn't complete an approach safely. The first two times I came in much too fast. I was going about 150 miles per hour and I should have been at about 90 miles per hour. After the third try the tower finally called me on the radio and said that maybe they would just have to *shoot* me down." Finally, Jacobson got some expert advice over the radio from a seasoned pilot who suggested that he climb to altitude and practice slow flying the fighter in the landing configuration. That exercise seemed to do the trick. On his next attempt he landed without incident.

After collecting only a few more hours in the P-40, Jacobson was sent overseas. "We left for Fiji on January 20, 1942. By this time I had been assigned to the 70th fighter squadron but still had not gotten a lot of flight time in the P-40. We sailed on one of the Dollar Line steamships, the *President Monroe*. This was before rationing and we were treated like first-class passengers. The waiters wore tuxedos and there was fine linen and crystal. We had a wonderful time." Squadron mate Doug Canning recalled, "We drank and partied all the way across the Pacific."

Their wonderful time was short-lived. They were surprised when they reached their destination—Suva, Fiji. "When we got to Fiji we unloaded the aircraft crates. Instead of P-40s," he remembered, "the crates had P-39s in them."

The Bell P-39 Airacobra was a sleek, handsome, yet tiny fighter with an unusual mid-mounted engine arrangement. It is remembered as an unusual and mediocre aircraft at best. Produced without a supercharger, it performed poorly at altitudes above about 15,000 feet. The unusual mechanical arrangement, which mated the airframe, engine, and armament in a fashion never before operationally fielded, presented unique and frustrating maintenance challenges. Too, its short range limited its reach in both the attack and escort roles. In air-to-air combat it was only competent and not nearly as nimble as the Japanese Zero.

Despite the type's limitations, which he readily acknowledged, Jacobson remembered the P-39 as an easy and fun aircraft to fly. "It fit like a glove. I felt like I was wearing it and that I could have flown it just by thinking about it. And it had a tricycle landing gear which made it easy to land. The squadron really didn't have a lot of problems learning to fly it."

Still a relative neophyte who had flown only a small number of hours in the P-40 during the previous few months, Jacobson honed his aerial combat skills at Fiji. "Fiji is where I really learned to fly," he recollected. Assigned to "B" flight headed by then Captain John W. Mitchell, Jacobson continued to build flight time and experience. "Mitchell was an aggressive leader, and we had a tight-knit and aggressive group."

During this time Mitchell selected Jacobson as his wingman. Doug Canning recalled this period: "In Fiji, John Mitchell tested each one us, unknowingly to us, to see who he wanted as his wingman in combat. Jacobson won. Unfortunately, as a wingman, this deprived him of opportunities to score aerial victories later on. I was glad that Mitchell didn't pick me."

During October 1942, after months of training and preparations on Fiji, Jacobson, Mitchell, and a cadre of ten others were transferred from Nandi Field on Fiji to the 67th fighter squadron at New Caledonia. From there they were sent north to the cauldron of miserable jungle rot and combat that was the island of Guadalcanal.

American Marines had been on the island for two months when Jacobson arrived on October 7, 1942. During the intervening period, control of the surrounding sky and sea—and of the island itself—was hotly contested. The Japanese were determined to retake the island and reacted swiftly and powerfully to the American seizure of their base.

Although the Japanese had only 2,000 defenders to meet the 10,000 American invaders on August 7, 1942, they quickly reinforced their garrison using a mix of troop transports and destroyers dubbed the Tokyo Express. By early October, the Tokyo Express had been making deliveries for nearly two months, and the number of Japanese soldiers on the island equaled the number of Americans—roughly 20,000. Furthermore, control of the skies was still contested, and at night the Imperial Japanese Navy ruled the waters around the island. The outlook was grim and the Marines were pressured to very near the breaking point.

In the air, the mostly Marine forces—nicknamed the Cactus Air Force after the code word for the airfield—fought stubbornly. Augmented by aircraft from the Army and the Navy, the small and beleaguered Cactus Air Force was desperately short of everything but hardship. Aircraft, fuel, ammunition, food, and personnel were scarce. Diseases, including dysentery, diphtheria, and malaria, were rampant. Still, through a monumental effort by the ground crews, pilots and other support personnel, the Cactus Air Force was a critical factor in holding the line against the tenacious Japanese.

"Our operations at Henderson Field on Guadalcanal were still very primitive when I arrived," Jacobson said. "We were there to replace and augment pilots of the 67th Fighter Squadron who had been there since August 22, only a couple of weeks after the Marines landed. They were flying P-400s; the P-400 was a cheap, export version of the P-39 originally intended for the British. By that time the aircraft were in poor shape and many of the pilots were sick. Some had already been lost.

"They had been shelled by ships or bombed or both nearly every day," Jacobson continued. "Many of the planes were barely flyable, but every day they were still launching those that could get airborne. They had shot down some Japanese planes and also helped out the Marines on the ground with strafing and bombing. But by the time I got there, the P-400s had been pretty much relegated to the ground attack role—they weren't much of a match for the Zero. The P-39s that we brought with us weren't much better.

"My first mission was on October 9, 1942. I took off with Mitchell and three others to escort Marine SBD dive bombers to New Georgia. Unfortunately, my belly fuel tank wouldn't transfer and I had to turn back. They found some Japanese vessels, and the SBDs got some bomb hits, and Mitchell and a couple of others shot down some Japanese biplane float jobs. With that sort of action happening I decided that I definitely wasn't going to miss the next mission. As it turned out, I flew twice more that day, mostly patrol, but we did bomb and strafe some ground positions out past Cape Esperance."

Although it was constantly under air attack, the airfield remained operational, but only barely. Moreover, rain often turned the place into a muddy quagmire and it was not unusual for an aircraft to get stuck so badly that it couldn't move. Consequently, normally routine activities were often quite difficult, or even hazardous. For instance, on October 9—the day of Jacobson's first mission—a flight of P-400s was stymied before it even got airborne as the nose gear of one was sheared off by the rough terrain, another suffered two flat tires and a third was simply stopped in place by the airfield's sticky, sucking mud. A few days later on October 12, two P-39s from the 67th were lost in a crack-up on the muddy airfield during takeoff. One pilot was badly burned.

That same day the difficulties on the airfield were compounded when Japanese field artillery pieces—nicknamed Pistol Pete—lobbed shells into the perimeter. "We were going to launch the P-400s to find the guns, but they called off the mission," Jacobson recalled. "The airfield hadn't been resupplied in a while, and the supply of aviation gasoline was simply running too low to justify the effort."

What Jacobson didn't know at the time was that a historic naval engagement, the Battle of Cape Esperance, had been fought north of the island the previous night. Task Force 64 under Rear Admiral Norman Scott defeated a group of Japanese cruisers and destroyers. This marked the first time the American navy scored a significant victory at night against the Japanese. Despite the victory, a group of Japanese ships slipped past the American force and landed reinforcements along with artillery pieces and badly needed ammunition and other supplies.

And although the American Navy had won the battle, they were not yet close to controlling the sea surrounding Guadalcanal. During the night of October 13–14, the Japanese battleships *Haruna* and *Kongo* slipped into New Georgia Sound, just north of Henderson Field. The two ships readied a heavy gun bombardment that would never disappear from the memories of the men who lived through it.

The drone of a small spotter plane grew audible just before midnight. Next, three flares pierced the darkness. Men shaded their eyes as they looked overhead at the bright green, red, and white points of light. A moment later a dull roar rumbled in from the sea followed by the sound of large caliber shells shredding the air overhead. The first shells exploded and the men scrambled for cover across the eerily lit airfield.

Thus started the night of terror. "The shelling was horrible," Jacobson recalled. "Men screamed, cried and prayed. I spent four hours in the coconut groves with eight other guys in one miserable foxhole. We were near the airfield, which of course was the main target. The ground shook—I'll never forget the sound of the shrapnel ripping through the trees and whatever else wasn't protected. It was a helpless, terrifying feeling to not know where the next salvo of shells would land. Finally, when we were able to get out the next morning, we found that only two of our aircraft had survived the bombardment and that the aviation fuel supply had been destroyed."

What Jacobson survived that night was the worst bombardment of the entire campaign—one of the most intense naval bombardments in history. Nearly a thousand 14-inch shells from the two battleships were augmented by aerial bombs and by artillery fire from the hills around the airfield. All of it was directed at the airfield and it destroyed more than half of the Cactus Air Force's 90 aircraft; moreover, 41 men were killed. Through it all, the American Navy was absent and the Tokyo Express landed another 4,500 troops. The Japanese wanted the island badly.

The men on the airfield, dazed and sleepless, sick and injured, got on as best they could. "There was no mess tent—no place to eat." Jacobson recalled. "We raided what was left of the pantry and ate what we could find right out of cans and cartons. I found several cans of Vienna sausages that I ate for the next few days. On the airfield our ground crews salvaged parts and siphoned fuel from wrecks, and we managed to get a few missions airborne against the Japanese transports." As it turned out, the aircraft from the Cactus Air Force sank three Japanese transports that day.

Jacobson flew several missions against Japanese shipping during this time. In the early afternoon of October 15, 1942, he was airborne as part of a mixed flight of P-400s and P-39s. The target was a group of transports offloading troops and supplies only a few miles away at Tassafaronga. "My oxygen system wasn't working so I dropped down low and strafed the transports, and the patches of jungle along the beach where the Japanese were taking cover."

The various air, naval and ground artillery bombardments wore at the men. By late afternoon, October 15, Jacobson had had enough. "I guessed that the ships were going to be back that night. I took off walking before it got dark and just worked my way back into the jungle area behind the airfield, perpendicular to the beach. Finally I came upon an abandoned Japanese bunker facing away from the ocean. I crawled in there and spent the night while they shelled the field again." That night the Japanese cruisers *Chokai* and *Kinugasa* poured eight hundred rounds of 8-inch naval gunfire into the Henderson Field complex.

It wasn't the last time Jacobson had to take cover against enemy shelling. In fact, the Japanese ships returned each night during the following week and kept the pressure up for months to come. But during the day, the pilots of the Cactus Air Force, Jacobson among them, struck back. The Japanese warships and troop transports, under constant harassment, suffered serious losses.

The pilots at Henderson were able to inflict those losses only because brave pilots shuttled unprotected C-47 transports back and forth between Espiritu Santo and Guadalcanal, often under fire, to bring in drums of aviation gasoline. On their return trips the pilots of the twin-engine transports fulfilled an equally important and vital mission as they evacuated the sick and wounded.

"During this time, aside from hitting transports, we also flew a lot of strafing and bombing missions against targets in the jungle that we couldn't see," Jacobson said. "We were told about particular areas where the Japanese were hiding which we subsequently worked over pretty good. But still, it was impossible to see down into the jungle and much of the time we never really found out how effective we were."

Records show that these and other strikes were, in fact, very effective. The attrition that the American fliers inflicted on the Japanese reinforcement and supply efforts played a critical role in an imminent ground engagement. Over the course of two weeks, the newly-landed Japanese troops, whose objective was Henderson Field, marched to a point less than ten miles away. But beset by fatigue, hunger, and disease—and bloodied from constant air attacks—they were exhausted before the battle was joined.

This particular action reached a bloody climax during the two days beginning on October 24, 1942. With the goal of breaking through to the airfield, the Japanese launched their final attack with typical ferocity but were repulsed at the Matanikau River by devastating fire from American ground forces. The victory was decisive, and marked a turning point in the campaign. The success of the defense was due in part to the aerial pounding the Japanese received in the days before the battle.

Although Jacobson was frustrated by his inability to see the effects of his attacks against hidden jungle targets, such was not the case during a strike against an Imperial Japanese Navy cruiser on October 25, 1942. He was the last aircraft in a flight of five P-39s sent to dive-bomb the *Yura*—a light cruiser.

The previous four aircraft dropped their bombs and missed the big ship by the time Jacobson was established in his dive. "I misjudged my dive before I was ready to drop my 500-pound bomb. So I had to do a half-roll and pull back around to get pointed at the ship again. Well that was just plain stupid. I was much too low." Diving nearly straight down, Jacobson watched the big cruiser quickly grow larger through his windscreen. Finally, he released the bomb and hauled back on the aircraft's control stick.

"The cockpit filled with condensation as I leveled off right on the water," Jacobson recalled. The thick fog developed when the cold, moist air in his cockpit warmed as the aircraft plummeted to low altitude. He struggled to see outside through the mist that shrouded his vision. "I was so low that the altimeter actually read below sea level." With the speed he had built up in the dive, Jacobson escaped the torrents of gunfire the cruiser directed at his aircraft. As he cleared the enemy fire, his flight leader called out that his bomb had struck the ship. "My bomb hit it in the stern and stopped it dead in the water."

The cruiser, which had been hit by other American forces earlier in the day, was badly damaged by Jacobson's bomb and suffered further from other airstrikes through the day. Finally, with no hope of saving the ship, the *Yura*'s crew evacuated her and she was scuttled. "While I didn't get full recognition for sinking that ship, I did get credit for a pretty big assist," Jacobson remembered.

He also recalled that while the conditions on the island were primitive, he and his fellow Army fliers took great pride in the fact that they were a part of the Marine Corps team which, at great cost, was driving the Japanese Army from the heavily-jungled island. "We thought very highly of the Marines. They were the ones who were feeding us and keeping us in clothing and other gear. We were proud of the fact that we were part of the First Marine Division, and as such were awarded the Presidential Unit Citation."

Following his first tour at Guadalcanal in P-39s, Jacobson and the rest of the cadre was rotated to New Caledonia for a break from combat operations. From New Caledonia he made his way to Sydney, Australia, for a well-deserved rest period. Jacobson recalled that he enjoyed Australia immensely. Through the war, American servicemen were enthusiastically welcomed by the Australians, and women and liquor were readily at hand. "When they finally sent a C-47 to pick us up," Jacobson recalled, "we convinced the pilot to have some 'engine problems' for a few days. Finally, under the threat of disciplinary action, we went back."

Once back in New Caledonia they were surprised when the unit was assigned new P-38Gs. The twin-engine, twin-boom, Lockheed aircraft was the fastest fighter in the Pacific theater. Heavily armed and maneuverable, with good range, the Army Air Forces finally had a fighter that could compete successfully with the Japanese Zero. "We did like the fact that it was a twin-engine aircraft," Jacobson recalled. "Especially because we did so much flying over the water. And it had great armament, with four .50-caliber machine guns and the 20mm cannon. The tricycle gear was nice too, and it was easy to fly."

Their checkout in the new aircraft was cursory. The outcome of the war in the Pacific during late 1942 was still very much in doubt and the new aircraft were needed in combat immediately. After only one familiarization flight in the P-38, Jacobson and the newly formed squadron—the 339th Fighter Squadron—were sent back to Guadalcanal on November 12, 1942.

Jacobson's recollection of his first mission in the P-38 illustrates how unfamiliar with the aircraft he still was. "We had only been back on Guadalcanal for a day or two when I flew my first mission in the P-38. There was a radio call that radar had picked up Japanese fighters in the area. We took a vector and started getting prepared." Jacobson recollected how he fumbled around the cockpit trying to complete his combat checks. "It was frustrating. I couldn't even figure out where the switch was to turn on the gunsight!" Fortunately for Jacobson, the Japanese aircraft never materialized.

Indeed, Jacobson remembered that the P-38s saw little air combat over Guadalcanal. "We flew escort missions, but by that time the Japanese fighters weren't showing up too often. It wasn't like it was during October when they were coming over almost every day. Then, the Marines were knocking them out of the sky like you wouldn't believe."

One of the most famous Marine flyers on Guadalcanal was Captain Joe Foss. Foss was the first American aviator in World War II to equal Captain Eddie Rickenbacker's score of twenty-six enemy aircraft shot down during World War I. Jacobson remembered that Foss was a likable and ebullient man who was also imbued with a good amount of luck. "On one mission I was on Mitchell's wing and we were on our way back after looking for some Japanese destroyers. It was getting near dark and we looked up and saw a couple of Marine F4Fs crossing our nose. Mitchell called out and asked who it was. Turns out it was Joe Foss. Mitchell said 'Hey, you're going the wrong way,' and Foss said 'No, *you're* going the wrong way.' Well, it wasn't that hard to navigate around there. Each island had its own set of clouds that sat right on top of it, and all you had to do was follow the clouds to Guadalcanal. Well, Joe Foss ended up in the drink!" Fortunately the Marine flyer was rescued soon after and returned safely to Guadalcanal.

Although the Guadalcanal-based P-38s were tasked primarily with countering the Japanese aerial threat, they also proved to be devastating attack aircraft. Jacobson's squadron mate, Doug Canning, recalled how the 339th's P-38s made a unique attack on a Japanese vessel. "On the afternoon of April 2, 1943, I was on standby alert with my squadron mates. We were called together and briefed that six Marine Corsairs had found a small freighter moored along a wharf in Kokolope Bay on Vella Lavella Island. They strafed it repeatedly and were unable to sink it. Our mission was to go up there with seven P-38s and see what we could do to it."

It was suggested that the flight try hitting the enemy freighter with its external belly-mounted fuel tanks. Soaked with aviation gasoline from the shattered tanks, subsequent gunfire from the aircraft ought to be able to set the ship afire. Accordingly, with their plan set, the seven aircraft got airborne in the late afternoon. Captain Tom Lanphier led the first flight of three aircraft and Canning led the second flight of four.

"After an uneventful flight of about an hour-and-a-half, we found the target nestled up against the island and moored to a wharf. Tom made his attack and was successful in hitting the ship. When it was my turn, I came in extremely low over the water and to my amazement my belly tank hit the bridge of the ship. My wingman, Del Goerke, came in firing at the gasoline-drenched ship and immediately it began to burn fiercely.

"We then flew back to Guadalcanal and reported our success," Canning remembered. "The Marines sent a PBY back to the scene to see what was happening. Near midnight they saw the ship explode in a tremendous fireball. Evidently it was laden with a considerable amount of munitions."

On April 14, 1943, U.S. Naval Intelligence learned that Admiral Isoroku Yamamoto, the Commander-in-Chief of the Imperial Navy's Combined Fleet, and the architect of the attack on Pearl Harbor, was scheduled to visit the Japanese airfield at Buin, on the island of Bougainville, on April 18. Buin, located 350 miles northwest of Guadalcanal, was beyond the reach of every American fighter on Guadalcanal except the P-38. Accordingly, P-38 pilots from the 339th Fighter Squadron—as directed by Secretary of the Navy, Frank Knox via a top secret message—were ordered to ambush Yamamoto's flight.

"John Mitchell, the C.O. of the 339th, was assigned to lead the mission," Jacobson said. After briefing with Admiral Marc Mitscher, Commander Air Solomons, on April 17, Mitchell made the pilot assignments. He selected eighteen pilots although virtually everyone volunteered. Jacobson was to be his wingman. Even though their early P-39 flying days at Fiji were long past he still occasionally flew as Mitchell's wingman.

That night Mitchell overviewed the mission with the rest of the flight, and with help from select pilots worked out the details. The expected disposition of Yamamoto's aircraft and escorts was discussed while the route was precisely plotted. The weather forecast was reviewed as were the distinct roles of each pilot. All of this was covered carefully during the pre-mission briefing that began at 0600 on the morning of April 18.

"We were divided into two different groups," Jacobson recalled. "There was a four-plane killer group whose job was to attack the transport carrying Yamamoto, and another top-cover group that was to provide protection from enemy fighters for the killer group. On the morning of the mission there were eighteen fighters available. The ground crews had worked through the night to get every airplane they could into the air."

Desperate to get as much range as possible out of the P-38s, each was hung with an asymmetric load of one 310-gallon external fuel tank (these had been rushed to Guadalcanal from New Guinea), and one 165-gallon external fuel tank.

Mitchell led the P-38s airborne at about 0715 that morning. Flying them were pilots not only from the 339th Fighter Squadron, but also the 12th Fighter Squadron. Almost immediately there were problems. "One P-38 blew a tire before takeoff and another couldn't get fuel out of its external tanks, so the pilot had to abort," recounted Jacobson.

Jacobson also had problems with his aircraft: "After takeoff I had trouble with the supercharger on one engine. Normally the engine pulled about sixty inches of manifold pressure. The engine was only pulling about fifty, but there was no way I was going to miss that mission!"

It was known that Yamamoto was fastidious about adhering to timetables. If Mitchell could manage the difficult navigational challenge of bringing the flight across the water by a circuitous route without the aid of any landmarks—thereby avoiding Japanese coast watchers—the mission stood a good chance of intercepting Yamamoto. But he had to be on time.

It wouldn't be easy. The P-38's heading indicator was sometimes inaccurate. Using only a borrowed Navy compass and his watch, Mitchell had to navigate via dead reckoning—using only heading, airspeed, and timing—to determine his position. Wave tops could give him a notion of which way the wind was blowing, and how hard, and how he might adjust his course.

Flying no higher than fifty feet above the water and in radio silence, Mitchell navigated the five legs of the planned route flawlessly. "On the last leg of the flight we were flying perpendicular to the intercept point," Jacobson recalled. Nearing Bougainville, the pilots test-fired their guns.

"As soon as we saw the island, our twelve-plane top-cover group started climbing to fourteen thousand feet," said Jacobson. At almost the same time Doug Canning broke radio silence and called: "Bogies, ten o'clock high." It was 0934 and Yamamoto was exactly on time. The pilots shucked their drop tanks and readied for combat.

Rather than a single large aircraft to transport Yamamoto and his staff, the American pilots spotted two Mitsubishi G4M "Betty" bombers. They were at approximately 5,000 feet and were escorted by two flights of three Zero fighters, each. The Zeros were stacked a couple of thousand feet above the bombers in a protective umbrella. The Japanese did not immediately spot the twin-boomed P-38s.

The four-plane killer group led by Tom Lanphier included Rex Barber, Besby Holmes, and Ray Hine. "When we got to about twelve thousand feet," Jacobson remembered, "we heard someone calling for help. Mitchell and I left the top-cover and started down. There was a Zero chasing a P-38." Jacobson recalled that Mitchell pulled in behind a lone Zero but was able to fire only a few rounds because he was overtaking the enemy aircraft too quickly. "I also only got off a short burst. Then we both headed for home."

Down low, the killer flight engaged the Bettys carrying Yamamoto and his staff. Lanphier and Barber approached the two bombers from a ninety degree angle. As they closed within firing range they were attacked by three of the six escorting Zero fighters. Lanphier turned back into the enemy aircraft. Barber continued the attack and poured fire into the engines and fuselage of the lead bomber.

Watching the bomber smoke and subsequently erupt in flames, Barber overshot it and, chased by enemy fighters, headed toward the water. The enemy fighters were scattered by a pair of P-38s; Barber was consequently free to chase the second bomber which turned over the beach and was being attacked by Holmes and Hine. Barber made his own firing run on this second, already damaged bomber, and watched it break apart, flame, and crash into the sea.

In the meantime, Lanphier, who was no longer under fire from the Zeros, executed a wingover and attacked a Betty that was turning over the trees. He saw a wing come off and watched the big aircraft crash into the tangled snarl of jungle below. Although Lanphier didn't know it at the time, this was the first bomber that Barber had attacked earlier.

The mission was over. Missing was Ray Hine; his fate would never be known. That sad fact notwithstanding, Yamamoto was dead.

But the controversy surrounding the mission continues. Upon returning, the flight claimed the destruction of three Betty bombers and three Zeros. The Japanese fighter pilots, it was later learned, claimed the destruction of seven P-38s. In reality, there had been only two Bettys in the flight.

Both were destroyed. Interviews long after the war with a surviving Japanese pilot indicated that all of the Zeros landed safely and subsequently returned to their home base.

It is possible, but not certain, that the Zeros claimed as aerial victories were based at Kahili. The sole P-38 loss was Ray Hine of the low, killer flight. The conflicting claims on all sides illustrate how difficult it was, even immediately after a mission, to accurately reconstruct, verify, and record what actually occurred in the twisting, terrifying, three-dimensional maelstrom that was aerial combat in World War II.

Adding further confusion to the issue was controversy over who actually shot down the aircraft carrying Admiral Yamamoto. "Lanphier landed and told everyone that he shot down Yamamoto," Jacobson remembered. "There wasn't a big argument, but Barber wanted to know how Lanphier was so sure that Yamamoto had been in the bomber he had shot down. There was no way of knowing for sure."

Barber had a point. For all that anyone knew at the time, Yamamoto could just as well have been in the aircraft that Holmes and Hine had attacked—the same one that Barber later fired on and watched crash into the sea. Jacobson recalled that the flight members were never gathered for a debriefing to determine what had happened. "It was just Mitchell, Lanphier, and Barber who debriefed with a Marine intelligence officer. Actually there were only six of us who even fired our guns—Mitchell and me and the four aircraft in the killer flight." Jacobson recalled that Lanphier probably helped write the official report on the mission.

Since that time books have been written, controversy and arguments have flared, and wartime friendships have been shaken. Statements from the participants have been recorded and expeditions have been sent afield to examine the wreckage of Yamamoto's bomber, which was in fact the aircraft shot down over the jungle. In 1988 a symposium was held at the Admiral Nimitz museum in Fredericksburg, Texas, which heralded the mission and examined the evidence surrounding it. Despite the engagement of many of the key participants the issue was not conclusively settled and the controversy goes on.

Ultimately, the Thirteenth Air Force, the parent command of the 339th Fighter Squadron, credited both Lanphier and Barber with half-credit each for Yamamoto's aircraft. Through the years and until the present there have been attempts—in light of compelling evidence—to take that half-credit from Lanphier and give sole credit to Barber.

Jacobson was bothered by the debate, which took on a bitter edge. "It wasn't as if we were sitting up there in a big amphitheater," he said. "The mission will never be reconstructed absolutely perfectly. There are people who are trying to take credit away from Lanphier, and that's not right. He's dead and can't defend himself. Who shot down Yamamoto's aircraft simply cannot be positively proven."

Indeed, those who would attempt the impossible seem to have lost sight of what is truly important: against the odds, the flyers of a newly resurgent America pulled off a stunning upset. They skillfully struck down the mastermind of Japan's war in the Pacific, and in so doing dealt the enemy a telling blow to its collective morale and psyche. The mission was a harbinger of America's unbreakable will and boundless power. They were the tools with which Japan was crushed.

———————

Jacobson's third combat tour on Guadalcanal was fairly short and unremarkable. "They wanted us back in the States for war bond sales after the Yamamoto mission." Upon his return to the States he married, then served for a short time as the commanding officer of a B-29 maintenance squadron. During late 1943, again reunited with Mitchell, he was assigned to Muroc Flight Test Base. While there he took part in the development of the early jets and was only the fourth pilot to fly the prototype of what would ultimately become the P-80. By war's end he had served as the commanding officer of one of the first jet squadrons, and had still somehow found time to complete a three-month exchange tour with the Navy, flying F6F Hellcats, which included carrier landing qualifications on Lake Michigan.

CHAPTER 5

NORTH AFRICA AND THE PACIFIC

As 1942 drew toward a close, the awesome power of America's manufacturing and military muscle was just becoming apparent. Exercising skill and enjoying a certain amount of luck, American forces scored some successes against the Japanese and were holding the line in the Pacific. But the United States had contributed little other than material to the fight against Germany and Italy. That changed during November 1942 when American troops went ashore to fight in North Africa. Supporting those troops was a cadre of Navy fliers who gained valuable experience before departing to fight in other theaters against other enemies.

Hamilton McWhorter

BORN IN ATHENS, GEORGIA, ON FEBRUARY 8, 1921, HAMILTON McWhorter spent a good deal of time with his father hunting the woods and fields of that part of the state. This time afield, much of it spent shooting game birds on the fly, proved to be invaluable to his future success as an aerial marksman flying Navy fighters.

McWhorter's flying career began at the University of Georgia in his hometown of Athens. He enrolled in the Civilian Pilot Training Program during 1940 and earned a Private Pilot's License, while logging about seventy-five hours of flying time paid for by the United States government.

This flying experience, like his hunting outings, stood him in good stead when he entered the Navy's Aviation V5 flight training program during August 1941. The flying and academic regimen of the intensive syllabus presented him with no great problems. "Everything went along very smoothly until late in the flight training program," McWhorter recalled.

"I was out on a solo aerobatics flight, and an instructor happened to fly by and catch me and another student having a wonderful time in a dogfight. Unauthorized dogfighting was forbidden and my punishment included many evenings drilling and marching with a rifle."

Nevertheless, McWhorter's aggressiveness belied a character that typified the Navy's most successful fighter pilots. He remembered that in December 1941, after completing basic flight training and "having done quite well in air-to-air gunnery while flying the SNJ advanced trainer," he was one of the lucky few selected to train in fighters at Opa-Locka, Naval Air Station Miami.

The aircraft used for fighter training at the time was the Brewster F2A Buffalo. The Buffalo was considered a frontline fighter and was even then being operated by the Navy as well as the British, the Australians and the Finns. Although it was butchered by the Japanese while flown by both American and British pilots, the Finns used it effectively, especially against the Red Air Force. However, the airframe, much of it handcrafted, was plagued with quality problems both in its design and construction. The issues became so blatant and outrageous that Brewster never recovered from government investigations into the company's poor practices.

It was while completing advanced fighter training that McWhorter fell victim to the F2A's abysmal reliability. "One day I came in for a landing after cranking the wheels down. The gear indicator showed that they were down. But as I landed on the grass field I was almost immediately enveloped in a very large cloud of dust as I slid across the ground on the bottom of the fuselage—the landing gear had collapsed." Fortunately he suffered no injury other than shock and surprise.

This exact sort of landing gear malfunction had occurred a few times before and no blame was attached to McWhorter. He was designated a naval aviator after completing fighter training and was subsequently commissioned an ensign in the Naval Reserve on February 9, 1942. Later that month he received orders to Fighter Squadron Nine (VF-9) at recently completed Naval Auxiliary Air Station Oceana, near Virginia Beach, Virginia.

At this time VF-9 was flying the Grumman F4F Wildcat, the Navy's newest fighter which had been in operational service only since 1940. If the Wildcat were a child, its appearance might politely be described as "husky," or "sturdy." Fat and round, it was not an attractive aircraft, and was slower than many of its contemporaries. But it did have decent range and high altitude performance for its time, and was relatively maneuverable. These attributes, together with its extraordinarily sturdy construction, and heavy armament of four or six .50-caliber machine guns, enabled it to hold the line for the Navy until better types were available.

McWhorter remembered Oceana's early days: "The facilities were rather primitive. We lived in Quonset huts, eight pilots to each hut. Because it was a marshy area, boardwalks connected all of the huts and other facilities so that we didn't have to walk in the mud when it rained. Still, we had a great time since we were the only squadron assigned to the airfield. We underwent rather intensive training in combat tactics, gunnery, strafing, bombing, night flying, and carrier qualifications. We were under pressure to get combat-ready as soon as possible."

By the fall of that year, they were. On October 3, 1942, VF-9 was embarked aboard the USS *Ranger* (CV-4), along with VF-4, and a dive bombing squadron, VB-4. They were deployed in support of the Allied invasion of North Africa, codenamed Operation TORCH. A joint Anglo-American effort, TORCH consisted of three separate task forces under the command of the American general, Dwight D. Eisenhower. The invasion was intended to thwart Rommel's efforts to take control of the coast from the British. Moreover, and importantly, the operation would finally put American ground troops into combat with the Germans.

TORCH presented considerable unknowns of an ironic sort because the forces defending the initial objectives were French. Previously allied with the British against the Germans, these forces were now controlled by the Vichy French government. The Vichy treated with Hitler following France's capitulation and he sanctioned them to govern unoccupied France in addition to the French possessions in North Africa. Although the Vichy government had declared war on the United States, it was unknown whether the French in North Africa would oppose the Allied landings. Consequently, considerable clandestine political energy and subterfuge was exerted to convince the Vichy military leadership to lay down their arms upon the arrival of Allied forces.

To facilitate scheduling and operations for the upcoming strikes, the two fighter squadrons aboard the *Ranger*, VF-4 and VF-9, splintered off nine aircraft each to form a third squadron which was unofficially dubbed

VF-49. McWhorter was selected to fly with the new squadron and at dawn on November 8, 1942, he was airborne as the last aircraft of an eight-plane fighter sweep. "The Vichy French had a battleship, a heavy cruiser, and several destroyers in the harbor at Casablanca. Our job was to prevent those warships from leaving the harbor to attack the invasion forces. On this, our very first combat flight," McWhorter recalled, "we saw Vichy French destroyers leaving the harbor at high speed and heading up the coast."

At this point McWhorter's flight leader pushed over into a strafing attack on one of the speeding destroyers. "He was about half-way down in his firing run when his plane was hit by antiaircraft artillery. He started yelling that his aircraft wasn't flyable and that he was going down. And there I was watching it all and I hadn't even started my dive yet. It was a real eye-opener for my first combat sortie!"

McWhorter and his squadron mates overcame their apprehension and made several strafing runs against the destroyers. They put so many holes into the thin-skinned vessels that they turned and ran themselves aground on the beach. Meanwhile the flight leader landed his damaged aircraft on the beach where he was captured by Vichy forces. "I watched him crash," McWhorter said. "He was so excited that he fired his guns as he landed; there was smoke streaming back over his wings."

Although his squadron scored a few aerial victories against the French during the TORCH landings, McWhorter personally never saw any of the enemy aircraft airborne. "I didn't see any Vichy aircraft in the air, but on my second mission that day, I strafed and burned several on the ground, including a large seaplane. I had just strafed some planes parked near the eastern edge of the airbase at Port Lyautey when I saw a large hangar across the airfield. It looked like a huge Quonset hut and sheltered an enormous seaplane. I flew across the field about fifty feet above the runway and fired directly into the hangar, setting it on fire." Some of the aircraft he wrecked that day were, paradoxically, American-built Curtiss P-36s—or Hawk 75s—a type which had been sold to the French and had seen considerable action against the Luftwaffe.

For three days, the fighters and bombers from the *Ranger* hammered at the Vichy forces. McWhorter described one of the most vivid and terrible episodes he experienced during that period of the war. "Our squadron commander, Lieutenant Commander Jack Raby, spotted a small fuel truck traveling along a road and strafed it, setting it on fire. The driver tumbled out of the truck with his clothes afire and rolled on the road to try and put the flames out."

During that same flight, while strafing a command post, McWhorter's own aircraft was hit. A bullet smashed through his windscreen just to the left of the bulletproof center panel, and passed only six inches from his head. "Much too close!" he recollected.

Perhaps because the action was so small in scale when compared to the colossal engagements of the Pacific, the aerial action in support of the TORCH invasion is remembered as little more than a curiosity. Still though, the fighting was furious and losses were suffered at a rate that could not have been sustained for very long. "The antiaircraft fire from the many ground batteries, and from the Vichy warships, was fierce," McWhorter recounted. "Four of our pilots were shot down and killed in three days. Two other planes were badly damaged and lost when their pilots ditched next to the task force. All-in-all we lost twenty-five percent of our aircraft in just three days." On November 11, after three days of ferocious fighting, the French forces finally capitulated and the pilots who had been captured were freed. The *Ranger* departed for home and shortly before Thanksgiving arrived back at Norfolk, Virginia, for a very meaningful holiday.

The next six months were busy ones for McWhorter and the fighter pilots and support personnel of VF-9. Originally slated to be reequipped with the Vought F4U Corsair, plans were changed and the squadron was one of the first to become operational with the new Grumman F6F Hellcat. While retaining some of the family attributes of its older sibling, the Wildcat, the F6F was greatly refined and not quite so unattractive. Although it was bigger and heavier, it was more aerodynamic and was faster and climbed better. It had greater range yet was still robust and well-armed with six .50-caliber machine guns. Moreover, it was easier to fly.

One of McWhorter's first experiences with the new fighter occurred during January 1943, "I was in the initial group that flew up to the Grumman plant at Bethpage, New York, to pick up our squadron planes. When we got there, they only had one aircraft ready to go. So, as I was the junior ensign, I was 'volunteered' by our skipper to fly that plane back on the same day. The others got to enjoy a night in New York courtesy of Grumman. But I'll admit that when I stopped at the Naval Air Station at Anacostia to refuel, I thoroughly enjoyed the envy shown by the pilots there who had not seen the F6F before."

After several months of training, and a shakedown cruise on the newly commissioned fleet aircraft carrier USS *Essex* (CV-9), McWhorter and his squadron sortied aboard the new ship to Pearl Harbor during May 1943 via the Caribbean and the Panama Canal. While in Hawaii, VF-9 continued its training and waited for other forces to join them so that they could begin striking the Japanese.

During this period in the Pacific war, bases that could service the carrier task groups were limited. Typically the carrier groups sortied out of Pearl Harbor. The transit from Hawaii to the Japanese bases was long and much more time was spent underway than in combat. It was inefficient, but without good forward bases, it was the best way to strike out.

VF-9 embarked back aboard the *Essex* on August 23, 1943. The *Essex* was joined by the *Yorktown* (CV-10) and the two ships and their escorts headed for Marcus Island. The strike against Marcus Island, planned for September 1, was intended to be a warm-up for the new crews that made up the little task force. McWhorter recalled that the predawn launch and rendezvous, with aircraft groping about in the dark, was probably the most stressful part of the one-day strike. "After we finally got all of the strike force rendezvoused and on the way toward Marcus, some idiot toward the rear of the group accidentally fired all six of his .50-caliber machine guns, which sent a *huge* arc of tracers over the top of us. In the dim light of dawn a .50-caliber tracer looks to be about the size of a basketball. More than a few planes took rather violent evasive action!"

VF-9 came out of the action in fine fashion, losing only one aircraft whose pilot managed to ditch alongside the task force and was subsequently rescued. The task force returned to Pearl Harbor on September 8; it had taken seventeen days to launch a one-day strike.

On September 29, the *Essex* and VF-9 departed Pearl Harbor for their second combat sortie. This time the target was Wake Island, which the Japanese had seized from the United States during the weeks following the attack on Pearl Harbor. Again McWhorter was part of the first launch. "As we neared Wake Island, I looked down from my escort position above and to the rear of the strike group, and there, about a thousand feet beneath the bombers, and flying in the opposite direction, was the first Zero I had ever seen. Since the Zero pilot had not pulled up and blasted the bombers from below as he could have easily done, I knew that he would probably execute an Immelmann and end up right behind me.

"I immediately rolled into a hard right turn in order to meet him head-on," McWhorter said. "I had only completed about one-half of my turn when I looked over and there was the Zero. He had already completed his Immelmann and there were red tracers coming toward me from the two machine guns in the cowl of his aircraft." Reacting quickly, McWhorter rolled over into a dive and escaped the enemy aircraft.

But the mission had barely begun. After escaping the Zero and rejoining the strike group, McWhorter prepared for the attack on the island. "Wake Island is shaped like a 'V,' and the attack was down one of the legs, right into the apex. As we pushed over into our strafing run in front of the bombers," he remembered, "an incredible amount of antiaircraft artillery erupted from both legs. The red tracers formed an almost solid arch over the island—and we had to dive down into it and then climb back through it! Somehow my plane was not hit and as I was climbing out, I ended up behind and beneath a Zero. I fired a short burst and it exploded."

McWhorter had scored the first of his eventual total of twelve aerial victories. Nevertheless his action over Wake was not yet over. "After a few more strafing runs, I spotted another Zero ahead of me and started after him. I hadn't quite reached firing range when suddenly, a stream of very large tracers passed just above my plane from behind." Just as when he had been attacked at the start of the mission, McWhorter flipped over into a dive to the right in order to evade the fire. "But when I looked back as I rolled over," he remembered, "there was an F6F way behind me firing at the Zero that was still well out of *my* firing range. Needless to say, neither one of us got that Zero."

McWhorter's aerial successes continued. On November 11, 1943 during a strike on Rabaul he added two more Zeros to his tally. His fourth aerial victory came on November 18, in support of the invasion of Tarawa Atoll. There, at a catastrophic price, the Marines were clearing Betio Island of Japanese. McWhorter was escorting strike aircraft back to the *Essex* when he spotted a biplane with floats, above and to his left, passing in the opposite direction. It was a Japanese observation aircraft, a Mitsubishi F1M1, codenamed "Pete."

"None of the other pilots in front of me took any action, apparently thinking that the aircraft was one of ours. I immediately applied full power and pulled up. As I did so he started a steep dive toward some clouds below and to my left. Then several other F6Fs started after him but I had a head start. The Pete dived down at about a forty-five degree angle ahead of me from my right as I commenced my run. I had it in my sights and was just waiting to get close enough. Before I reached firing range though, the Pete made a hard turn to the right to reverse course away from me, and dived toward the clouds below. This changed my run from a port quarter attack from about his seven o'clock position, into an overhead type run. Just as I was reaching firing range for a full deflection shot, he disappeared into the clouds."

At this point McWhorter thought he had lost the enemy aircraft. "I continued my run and maintained the intercept path that I had established. And then the Japanese pilot's luck ran out. For just an instant the clouds thinned barely enough for me to see a very faint, blurred, shape through my gunsight. I fired just as it disappeared again. Since the Pete was in the clouds when I fired, I didn't see whether I hit it or not. But after I passed through the clouds I looked back and saw it spinning down in flames."

The following day, November 19, 1943, McWhorter was flying Combat Air Patrol as the section leader—the number three aircraft—of a four-plane division. The flight received a vector from the ship's fighter director to intercept an unidentified aircraft about twenty miles distant. "When we got to the area," McWhorter recounted, "I spotted it, a Mitsubishi G4M Betty twin-engine bomber, very low on the water. It was about three miles or so ahead and going away from us. My division leader started his run, diving down from directly astern the bomber. I knew that the Betty had a 20mm cannon in the tail and so elected to make a flat-side run from the starboard side."

Pushing over into a steep dive at full power, McWhorter set himself up for a full deflection shot from the right side of the enemy bomber. As he descended he watched the tail gunner blaze away at his division leader with the 20mm cannon. Moving much faster than the rest of the pilots in his flight, McWhorter closed on the enemy bomber.

"I came in on the starboard beam of the Betty which was flying so low, only about ten feet above the water, that the propwash was making a wake.

I only had time for a short burst, firing at a range of about four hundred feet or so, and I observed many hits in and around the wing root area. The port engine burst into flames and the Betty immediately crashed into the water and burned. This was my fifth kill, and so I became the first ace in the squadron.

"This victory also made me the first pure F6F ace," McWhorter said. "I was the first pilot to score five aerial victories with the Hellcat." When he landed back aboard the *Essex*, the armorers found that he had fired only eighty-six rounds from all six guns combined—and these included the rounds fired during a test burst prior to the engagement. It was a fine testament to McWhorter's aerial marksmanship as the six guns had a combined rate of fire of sixty rounds per second.

Through the rest of his first combat tour in the Pacific, McWhorter continued to add to his score. During raids throughout the Central Pacific, to include actions at Roi, Kwajalein, Truk, and Saipan, he added five more Zeros to his tally and became the first Hellcat pilot to reach the double-ace mark. McWhorter's achievements aside, VF-9 posted a superb record during this period: "We were in the Pacific for ten long months. Of that time, 127 days were spent at sea, with 21 days in actual combat during eight separate combat actions. Our squadron shot down 120 enemy planes and destroyed 159 on the ground, while losing four pilots killed and two declared missing in action."

After leaving Hawaii, VF-9 arrived back in the United States on March 10, 1944. Following a well-deserved leave period, McWhorter was sent to Melbourne, Florida, where he was assigned to build a combat team for a newly forming squadron and eventual deployment back to the war in the Pacific. Now a wizened and savvy combat veteran, at the ripe old age of twenty-three, McWhorter was assigned a new batch of recently-winged youngsters. "Six of the seven new pilots that I had to train were just kids— high school graduates. The seventh was a lieutenant commander, also just out of flight training and with no previous combat experience."

Following training at Melbourne, the group was moved to San Diego, then to Naval Air Station Astoria, in Oregon. While there, they were consolidated with other similar teams of fighter pilots to form VF-12, as part of Air Group 12. During November 1944, the group was moved back to San Diego. Finally, following combined training exercises between the fighter, torpedo, and dive bombing squadrons, Air Group 12 was slated to go to the western Pacific aboard a small escort carrier as a replacement air group.

There was still a war on, however, and orders were often changed. "We received surprise orders and departed San Diego on January 16, 1945," McWhorter recounted. "We were ordered to Naval Air Station Alameda where we replaced another air group aboard the USS *Randolph* (CV-15)." From there, the *Randolph* sortied into the Pacific and after a short stay at Pearl Harbor, arrived at Ulithi Atoll. The ship was just in time to join the task force which sailed on February 10 for the first aircraft carrier raids on Tokyo.

McWhorter recalled his first mission over the Japanese home islands. "On February 16, 1945, we were launched from a point about 135 miles east of Tokyo. As we neared our assigned sector which was north-northeast of the city, I spotted a Zero about two miles away at my seven o'clock position, and at about the same altitude, heading toward us." McWhorter turned into the enemy fighter for a head-on gunnery run. The enemy fighter pilot apparently reconsidered his tactics in the face of the American fighter's aggressiveness and started a shallow dive for a deck of clouds below. "As he came nearer beneath me, I rolled over into an overhead attack," McWhorter recounted. "This was my first opportunity to use the new gyro-stabilized gunsight."

The new gyroscopically stabilized gunsights had been in service with the Navy for less than a year. They automatically computed the correct lead required for firing at a non-maneuvering target. "I only had to keep his wingspan framed in the circular gunsight reticle by twisting the throttle and keeping the pipper on his nose. From that point, all I had to do was wait until I got into firing range." Inverted through most of the run, McWhorter came in range of the enemy aircraft just as he was pointed vertically downward. It was a full deflection shot of ninety degrees—the most difficult shot in aerial gunnery. "When I fired, I immediately saw a bunch of bright flashes as the Armor Piercing Incendiary rounds hit all around the nose, cockpit, and wing-root area; it was exactly where I was holding the pipper."

McWhorter was surprised when, unlike the Zeros he had flamed during his earlier Pacific tour, this aircraft didn't explode immediately. Unknown to him, the Japanese had started manufacturing their fighters with self-sealing fuel tanks that made them much less likely to catch fire when under attack. "But just before reaching the clouds, a long flame appeared from the engine area and the Zero was burning as he disappeared into the clouds. Someone from the air group down below the clouds spotted it when it passed very near them, spinning out of control."

Despite a break in combat of nearly a year, it was obvious that McWhorter hadn't lost his touch. Still though, things were different on this combat cruise. By now, Japan was reeling under the weight of the colossal forces fielded by America's industrial might. Huge flotillas of U.S. warships stretched across the ocean from horizon to horizon.

Warplanes were innumerable, easily replaceable, almost throw-away commodities. McWhorter recalled an incident from this second combat tour that underscored the point. "We had just received five brand new F6Fs. During a *kamikaze* attack, the ship's 5-inch guns fired at a depressed angle, right over the top of the new airplanes. The concussion from the guns popped every rivet and we just pushed them overboard."

This practice was not uncommon, particularly during enemy attacks when carrier decks, often crowded with damaged aircraft and wounded personnel, were transformed from orderly models of efficiency into scenes of near pandemonium. In order to recover aircraft back aboard the ship there was often no other recourse than to push perfectly serviceable aircraft into the water in order to make room.

Japan's desperate counter to the overwhelming military might of the United States was the *kamikaze*. A monstrous concept, *kamikaze* pilots were often ill-trained youngsters put into obsolescent aircraft loaded with fuel and bombs. They were ordered to crash into American warships and were difficult to defend against. In essence, the *kamikaze* was a thinking, decision making, flying bomb. The skill required to fly an aircraft into a warship was much less than that required to accurately deliver a bomb or a torpedo into the same target. Ultimately the strategy failed, but not without tremendous losses in lives and equipment on both sides.

While aboard the *Randolph*, at anchorage in Ulithi lagoon, McWhorter felt and witnessed the terror of the *kamikaze* firsthand. The ships at Ulithi came under attack from a flight of twelve, Yokosuka P1Y, *kamikaze* T-At-tack Corps aircraft loaded with 800-kilogram bombs. The twin-engine bomber type was codenamed "Frances." The attack force numbered 24 aircraft when the group launched from Kanoya, Japan, more than 1,360 miles distant, but half of the aircraft lost their way.

"I was working in our squadron office on Sunday evening on March 11, when the *kamikaze* hit," McWhorter remembered. "It was a Japanese twin-engine Frances bomber and the damage was incredible. An entire 40-foot by 40-foot section on the aft side of the starboard quarter of the ship was blown away. The explosion knocked us out of our chairs from 250 feet away. I ran up to the flight deck and the entire aft end of the carrier was blazing with huge clouds of black smoke. I then went down to the hangar deck and the aft end of it was also on fire. There were bodies all over the deck, some badly mangled. From there I went forward to the bow of the ship to get away from the fire and smoke."

The fire and smoke and heat, the cries of the wounded, and the pieces of the dead made a terrible specter that the men remembered all their days. These suicide attacks were difficult for the Americans to understand, and many men were frightened—rightly so—of being hit. Through the end of the war, the *kamikaze* attacks caused more damage to the American Navy than did conventional bombing or torpedo attacks.

During the three-week period that the *Randolph* was being repaired, the air group was based at Falalop Island. From there, McWhorter and the rest of the air group flew patrols over the fleet, in addition to conducting strikes against the nearby Japanese-held island of Yap. These strikes against Yap were more or less intended to help the squadrons, "keep their heads in the game." The Japanese garrison was nearly starved but it still possessed formidable antiaircraft defenses.

On March 31, 1945, with repairs to the *Randolph* newly finished and the air group back aboard, McWhorter was part of a last strike back to Yap. "During this mission, I strafed an antiaircraft artillery position ahead of the bombers. As I pulled out of my dive at about fifty feet or so above the island, I looked down at my right wing and saw a veritable blast furnace burning away, and a stream of flame reaching past the tail." Near panic, McWhorter opened the canopy and unstrapped preparatory to bailing out.

"Fortunately, considering where I was, commonsense prevailed over the panic of the moment. Since the wing had not yet burned off I decided to stay with the aircraft and continued climbing out. I was lucky that the fire burned itself out." After McWhorter brought the damaged aircraft back to the ship, it was discovered that an antiaircraft round had ruptured the gun charger lines, which had caused the hydraulic fluid to burn. The fire caused the .50-caliber ammunition in his wing to explode.

On April 8, 1945, the *Randolph* and Air Group 12 arrived on station in the waters off Okinawa with the mission of supporting the invasion forces that had landed on April 1. McWhorter's first mission was a Target Combat Air Patrol (TARCAP) over the airdrome on Wan—a small island north of Okinawa and south of Japan. The Japanese were using it as a staging point prior to launching *kamikaze* attacks against the fleet. "We orbited over the area for most of the flight but no Japanese planes showed up and there were none visible on the airfield. Our plan was to strafe the antiaircraft artillery positions around the field just before we departed.

"The weather was ideal for a strafing attack. There was an overcast layer at about ten thousand feet. I briefed the flight to approach the pushover point just up into the base of the clouds and commence the attack on my radio command." As briefed, McWhorter gave the command and rocketed down on the enemy positions. He fired on a large gun emplacement where, as he streaked by from only a hundred feet overhead, he could see the Japanese crewmen hunkered down against his attack. "I proceeded toward the planned rendezvous point and looked around in vain for the rest of my division. It turned out that I had just made a solo run against the Japanese battery!" McWhorter climbed back up to altitude, and using the threat of bodily harm among other things, corralled his flight back together for another strafing run.

"After our final strafing run, my wingman, Jay Finley, failed to join up at the rendezvous point." McWhorter and his flight continued to call for Finley as they searched the area for signs of a crash. No one had seen Finley go in. McWhorter himself was in some distress as his aircraft took a 37mm hit and had a two-foot wide hole in the right horizontal stabilizer. After a fruitless search, the flight, minus one, returned to the *Randolph*.

"Six days later we learned that Finley was picked up by a PBM search-and-rescue seaplane a few miles north of Kikai Shima. He had been adrift in his life raft for five days. As it turned out, Finley's aircraft had been hit during the final strafing run. During his pullout the tail section broke off of his aircraft. He had bailed out at only a few hundred feet, his parachute opening just before he hit the water. He was worried that the Japanese might have marked his position so he turned his inflated life raft upside down—it was painted blue for that purpose—and hid underneath it until the wind and tides blew him away from the island. From there he drifted for five days until the seaplane picked him up."

McWhorter and VF-12 spent most of the rest of their combat tour flying ground attack missions in support of the offensive on Okinawa. Their load was typically either bombs or 5-inch High Velocity Aerial Rockets (HVARs) which they often delivered in close proximity to friendly troops. The flying was a dangerous, fearful grind; there was almost always heavy and accurate antiaircraft fire from the Japanese positions. During three months of operations, McWhorter lost twelve squadron mates. It was during this period that he also scored his last aerial victory; it was against a high-flying single-engine, Nakajima C6N Myrt, a reconnaissance aircraft.

One of McWhorter's last significant recollections of his wartime service was also one of the most stupid and senseless. After departing the *kamikaze*-plagued waters off Okinawa, the *Randolph* dropped anchor in Leyte Gulf in the Philippines for a well-deserved rest. The ship had survived fifty-one days in support of the invasion without suffering so much as a scratch from the enemy attacks. McWhorter recalled the incident which occurred on the afternoon of June 7, 1945. "An Army P-38 [actually an F-5 photo reconnaissance version of the P-38] dove down and attempted to show off by doing a slow roll over the *Randolph*. Tragically, he fouled it up and fell out of the roll, crashing into the planes parked on the forward part of the flight deck." The grim mishap—reminiscent of the actual *kamikaze* attack at Ulithi earlier in the year—took several lives and destroyed twelve F6Fs while causing considerable damage to the ship itself.

McWhorter and VF-12 saw no more action. After boarding the escort carrier USS *Makassar Strait*, the unit passed through Pearl Harbor and finally arrived back in San Diego on July 11, 1945. The Japanese signed surrender documents less than two months later.

McWhorter received many decorations for his service, which spanned a greater period and more theaters of combat than most. However, the accomplishment of which he was most proud had its origins in the fields and forests of eastern Georgia from the time when he learned to wing-shoot game birds. "Every plane I ever shot at," McWhorter said, "went down."

Hamilton McWhorter's many decorations for his wartime service included five Distinguished Flying Crosses. He continued his career in the Navy after the war and served in a variety of billets while logging more than 8,000 hours of flight time. One of his proudest achievements was flying as part of the first crossing of the Pacific by propeller-driven fighter aircraft. Flying an F8F Bearcat, he was part of a mixed flight of Bearcats, Skyraiders, and F4U Corsairs to Hawaii, which stopped to refuel and replenish engine oil on two different aircraft carriers that were staged along the route. Additionally, he served as the squadron commander of his old wartime unit, VF-12, equipped with the jet driven F2H Banshee. He ultimately retired as a commander in 1969.

Jack Walker in front of his P-38, *Elaine II*. —*John Walker Collection*

CHAPTER 6

THE EARLY FIGHT

Although the United States eventually produced a fighting force that was staggering in terms of its size, equipment, and talent, the nation was woefully ill-prepared for a global conflict at the start of the 1940s. When war broke out in Europe in 1939, the American army was smaller than that of Portugal. Its air force was one-hundredth the size it would be at the end of 1944.

While the nation girded itself to produce the massive amounts of material and the trained men needed to destroy the Axis, the forces it deployed early to hold the line were not nearly so well-trained or equipped as those that would come into play during the last years of the conflict.

John "Jack" Walker

JOHN "JACK" WALKER WAS BORN ON JULY 7, 1920 IN SASKATOON, Canada, and moved with his family to West Hollywood, California, when he was a small boy. He grew up during the Great Depression as did all his peers, but the proximity of the great Hollywood movie studios gave his childhood a perspective that few others shared. "My friends and I sneaked onto the movie lots quite often and watched a lot of films being made. And we saw a number of stars from that time, close up." For Walker, it was a golden experience from a golden age.

Flying was another glamorous notion that appealed to him. Not long after starting studies at Pasadena Junior College, he enrolled in the Civilian Pilot Training Program. Started in 1938, the program—despite its name— was intended to create a large pool of pilots trained to at least basic standards from which military pilot candidates could be drawn. It developed to be a huge success with more than 400,000 participants trained by more than 2,000 different schools; it was terminated during 1944 when it became apparent that it was no longer required to help win the war.

"I wanted to fly with the Navy," Walker said. "I loved those white uniforms and the idea of being at sea and flying from a ship. The whole idea was very exciting." Unfortunately, reality short-circuited his dreams. "Sometime during 1940 I went to the naval facility at Long Beach, California, for my flight physical; they disqualified me because of an old ankle injury. The flight surgeon there noticed how upset I was and told me that I ought to go to Glendale and take the Army flight physical. And he told me to make sure I kept my socks on. So, later, we were all lined up at the Army physical in Glendale. All of us were stark naked except for me—I had my socks on."

The Army didn't care about his ankle. Rather, he was failed for blocked nasal passages. "My dad knew a doctor who arranged an operation to fix the problem. I went back for another physical after I healed and was accepted by the Army as an aviation cadet during the summer of 1941."

The Japanese attack on Pearl Harbor occurred during the middle of Walker's training. "Oh, it was chaos," he remembered. "We were issued rifles even though a lot of us had never held one before. Most of us didn't even know where Pearl Harbor was. Anyway, during that time we stood guard duty on the aircraft at night and then flew during the day. It was pretty stressful."

As part of the first cadet class groomed specifically for flying Lockheed's P-38 Lightning, Walker graduated during March 1942, and was later sent to McChord Army Air Field, in Washington. There he was assigned to the 55th Fighter Group. The character of his training was indicative of the nation's desperation at that point in the war to get pilots trained and into combat as quickly as possible. "It was pretty disorganized," Walker recalled. "None of us had any experience with the P-38. We showed up for flights and figured out on the spot who had the most time in the aircraft so that we could make flight leader and wingman assignments. It was crazy."

Lack of experience with the new aircraft and a consequently high accident rate made many of the new P-38 pilots apprehensive. "We had two test pilots from Lockheed with us and they said that the P-38 on a single engine during takeoff was deadly. A lot of the guys—me included—were scared." With the lack of training and a poor understanding of the handling characteristics of the complex aircraft, accidents on takeoff and landing were not infrequent, and were often fatal. The runways at McChord were bounded by trees which exacerbated even more the danger of dealing with an engine-sick P-38 on takeoff or landing.

One mishap that Walker remembered vividly occurred during this period. Unlike most accidents in the P-38, this one was totally unrelated to the handling qualities of the twin-boomed fighter. "I was number three in a flight of four aircraft and we started a tail chase over the water off the Washington coast. The lead aircraft started a turn around a towering cumulus cloud and plowed head-on into a Navy PBY Catalina flying boat. They both disintegrated in a huge explosion that killed the PBY crew and our flight leader." Air traffic control was virtually nonexistent at that time, and as America's skies filled with unprecedented legions of warplanes, accidents of this nature became more common.

From McChord, Walker was assigned to the 97th Fighter Squadron of the 82nd Fighter Group. At this time the 82nd was made up almost exclusively of flying sergeants led by officers. The three squadrons of the 82nd were assigned to separate bases in the Los Angeles area—the 97th operated out of Long Beach Airport. Walker was among the first new officers to be assigned to the 97th. "I thought to myself, oh my God, what did I screw up to end up with all these sergeants? I talked with the adjutant and he told me not to worry about it. The Army was getting ready to commission the sergeants and I was part of a group of new lieutenants that were being brought in to ease the transition."

What the sergeants lacked in rank, they made up for in flying skill. "Those guys were good," Walker remembered. "Some of them already had several hundred hours in the aircraft and knew how to fly it well. On my first flight, a technical sergeant grabbed me and took me out. No brief, no checking of the magnetos, nothing. By the time I got my aircraft started, he was already airborne and circling in the landing pattern and shouting over the radio at me to hurry up!"

Walker's technical sergeant flight leader took him on a sortie that included a formation loop over Pasadena's Rose Bowl, a tree-top tour of the surrounding communities, and a wave-top dash to and from Catalina Island. "I was exhausted by the time we landed. When we got back to the squadron area he pointed back over his shoulder at me and said 'This one's okay, I guess.'"

During September 1942, the 82nd Fighter Group was sent to Camp Kilmer, New Jersey, and from there was embarked aboard the *Queen Mary* for the trip to the British Isles. "We were met by two Royal Navy light cruisers as we approached the Irish coast on October 2, 1942." Walker recalled. "As they tried to fall into our zigzag pattern, one of them, the HMS *Curacoa*, ran right in front of us and was cut in half. It sank in just a few minutes and we didn't stop to rescue any of the survivors. Only 99 of its crew of 430 survived."

The 82nd's pilots were staged at RAF Maydown in Northern Ireland, near Londonderry. There, they waited until Lockheed put together enough P-38s at their assembly depot at Belfast. To maintain their proficiency, the Americans were lent a handful of Spitfires which they took turns flying. "The Spitfire and the P-38 had just about nothing in common," Walker recalled. "We were used to flying the P-38, which had a tricycle landing gear arrangement whereas the Spitfire was a tail dragger and was more difficult to handle on the ground. We wrecked all of those Spits in just a few weeks. I only got one flight.

"The RAF pilots also came to talk with us about tactics and such," Walker recollected. "They had been at war for more than three years by that point and knew their business pretty well. I was a little disappointed by the way some of our guys treated them. The Brits had accents, of course, and dressed more formally than we did. They also gave the Germans credit for being pretty good pilots. For those reasons some of our pilots thought that they were sissies and discounted much of what they told us. I reminded them that the RAF had done a lot more fighting than we had."

The last of the 82nd's P-38s were finally assembled and ready for operations during December 1942, and the group was ordered to North Africa. The American army was finally engaged in actual fighting against the German army, and air support was desperately needed. For their part, Walker and his comrades were happy to be on their way; they watched the ground crews as the aircraft were readied for the long flight south. Those preparations included hanging large, external fuel tanks from the wings, inboard of the engines.

Walker left for North Africa as part of an eight-aircraft formation on

December 27, 1942. It wasn't long after he got airborne that he discovered that his aircraft had fuel-transfer problems. "Over the Welsh coast I got a red fuel light and made a call that I was going to have to land." The weather was horrible and the majority of the route to that point had been flown through heavy rainstorms. Through a break in the clouds Walker caught sight of a small grass airfield on an island near the coast. "I nosed over, dropped through the clouds and put down on the field which was absolutely water-soaked. I came in a little bit too fast and because my aircraft was heavy it hydroplaned on top of all that water. I had no brakes at all."

Nearing the end of the short, grass strip—which at that moment resembled a neatly groomed marsh—Walker worked the brakes frantically but to no avail. "I hit a raised embankment at the end of the airfield and continued to slide toward the ocean. The landing gear and the left propeller were ripped off while the aircraft spun around. I skidded for a while before stopping in the middle of a minefield on the beach. As I sat there in shock with the landing gear warning horn blowing in my ears, a British soldier made his way over to me and climbed up on the airplane and started banging on the canopy. He said, 'Hey, Yank, get out of there before it burns.' He helped me get out of the airplane then led me off the beach with a mine detector."

A Polish unit operated out of the small airfield towing practice targets for antiaircraft gunners. They were happy to see Walker and quickly welcomed him into their little community. "I even flew a few missions with those guys in their Lysanders. I was with them for a few days before I got ordered to Land's End, Wales. They put me up in an old castle with a bunch of other guys like me who had gotten lost, or crashed or otherwise separated from their units."

Finally, during January 1943, he was assigned to fly an F-5—the photo reconnaissance version of the P-38—to Algiers. "A couple of guys had flown these F-5s to Lands End and then gone into town. Well, I wanted to get back with my unit so I grabbed one of them. I didn't have any charts or anything and the bomber guys told me to just stick with them." The flight was a large and unusual formation made up of B-24s, B-17s, B-25s, P-38s and P-39s; the aircraft were being ferried to combat units as replacements. Aside from the fact that the eight hour and twenty minute flight was the longest of Walker's life, the trip was unremarkable. Walker landed at Maison Blanche Airport in Algiers and taxied his aircraft to where the 3rd Photographic Group's aircraft were parked. The unit was commanded by Elliot Roosevelt, the son of the President of the United States.

Walker was surprised and panicked when he was told that he was to be reassigned to the photo reconnaissance unit. "I didn't want any part of that," he said. "So, I sort of slipped over to a nearby hangar where I saw some French Dewoitine twin-engine aircraft. I ran into a French pilot who delivered mail to the different Allied airfields in the area; the 82nd was on his route. I crawled into the back of his aircraft and settled in among the sacks of mail. It wasn't long before he had me back with my unit. They acted like they saw a ghost—they had been told I was dead!"

Assigned to the Twelfth Air Force, the 82nd Fighter Group was based at Telergma, Algeria. After only a month in theater, the group had already lost nearly ten percent of its pilots. "The guys told me that I was fresh meat. By that point they had come to respect the German Me-109 pilots. Anyway, I hadn't had any real training in months but I was scheduled for a combat sortie the very next day." It was an indication of the desperate mindset of the time.

Walker was assigned as wingman to one of the squadron's few captains for a bomber escort mission. "I thought that I wouldn't have much to worry about because the captain would take care of me. Sure enough, the Germans showed up and we got into a big, twisting, turning dogfight. I didn't know what was going on and was so desperate just to stay with my flight leader that I never saw a thing. The only thing I saw was shell casings coming from his aircraft as he fired his guns. I never saw a single German aircraft. I thought to myself afterward that I needed to get my head out of my ass if I was going to last very long."

Walker did learn as he gradually logged more missions and combat time. On his sixth mission on March 7, 1943, he was part of an early morning bomber escort. "Just off the Tunisian coast, my flight leader and I spotted an Italian three-engine seaplane, a CANT Z.506 B," Walker recalled. "They used it for bombing and reconnaissance."

The awkward Italian aircraft crossed in front of the P-38 formation, from left to right. "This guy had no business in the world being where he was, just off the coast like that," Walker recalled. "I followed my flight leader down to the deck in a sweeping right-hand turn and watched as he fired. He didn't take enough lead and his rounds fell into the water behind the seaplane.

"I made sure I didn't make the same mistake." Walker pulled the nose of his P-38 well in front of his target before pulling the trigger. His rounds found their mark; the enemy airplane caught fire and shed pieces under the effects of his gunfire. "Just before it hit the water, I saw a guy jump out the side of the airplane. I have no idea whether or not he lived." It was Walker's first confirmed aerial victory.

The working conditions in North Africa during this time were primitive, yet the mechanics and pilots kept the aircraft flying. "The ground crew for my aircraft lived right next to it in a little shack they made from a belly tank crate," Walker recounted. "It was primitive, but they did a good job."

Walker scored again the following month when he flew as part of a low-level sea-sweep escorting B-25s on April 5, 1943. "As we crossed the coast of Tunisia and headed toward Malta, someone called out, 'Good God, look at twelve o'clock.' I took a look and saw what looked like a swarm of bees. It was a huge flight of Ju-52s bringing gas to Rommel."

The B-25s turned to get out of the way, and the P-38 pilots tore into the enemy formation; it numbered more than one hundred aircraft. "I took one look and wondered how we were going to handle this," Walker recalled. "The belly tanks from the 1st Fighter Group came right down through us—it's a wonder no one was hit. And the radio chatter was horrendous. The radio was essentially useless. Everyone simply chased after whatever they wanted and I lost my flight leader almost immediately.

"I dove and turned after the gaggle. It seemed to me that everyone was going too fast, so I put out a bit of combat flaps to slow myself down. The Germans in the Ju-52s fired out of every opening through which they could stick a gun. I fired on one of them and it exploded in a big ball of fire and went right into the water."

The air battle swirled around Walker. "I saw another flight of P-38s barreling through the Ju-52s and again, I thought they were going much too fast. I was still alone and made a complete circle before starting another run on the transports. Just as I was going to fire, another P-38 cut me off. I came very close to blowing him out of the sky. In front of him was a Ju-88 medium bomber sitting in the middle of all the Ju-52s. The rear gunner was firing and I wanted to shoot at him but I couldn't get the other P-38 to move over. I finally fired a burst and saw strikes on it before I had to break away.

"I turned to follow a different Ju-52 that was trying to get away," Walker continued. "But my guns quit. And by that time a bunch of Me-109s had shown up so I got out of there as fast as I could." Walker was joined by two P-38s from the 1st Fighter Group and—short on fuel—he led them to the British airfield at Bone where a number of other P-38s had also diverted. There, Walker and the other pilots made their victory claims via telephone.

Confirmation of aerial victories was an imprecise science that varied in its practice throughout the war, depending on the theater, service, and time-frame. During the North Africa campaign gunnery cameras were uncommon. Consequently, aircrew debriefs were the primary means of determining the validity of claims. In this particular action there were very nearly more claims submitted than there were enemy aircraft airborne. Nevertheless, Walker received official confirmation for the destruction of one Ju-52. He was additionally credited with probably destroying one Ju-88.

During the spring of 1943, even though the German ground forces in North Africa were nearing capitulation, the German airmen were still skilled and formidable foes. And although Walker had enjoyed some success against Axis aircraft, he had yet to best an enemy fighter. "In many respects, North Africa was a disaster early on," he recalled. "We got our asses kicked from time-to-time because no one knew anything. For instance, as wingmen we still flew too close to our flight leads and had no room to maneuver. The Germans were smart. They simply stayed high above our formations, then dived down in slashing attacks and zoomed back up to where we couldn't get them. It didn't matter anyway because at that time General Jimmy Doolittle, the Twelfth Air Force commander, wouldn't let us leave the bombers to go get the enemy fighters.

"And quite frankly, a lot of the German pilots were better than us; they were more experienced. Many of them had seen a couple of years or more of combat. On the other hand, we had been in combat only a couple of months. Our leadership still wasn't that good. Our commanding officers didn't have any more experience than we did and we lost a lot of pilots and aircraft."

Late in April 1943 as the fighting in North Africa was drawing to an end, Walker got involved in a scrap with enemy fighters while escorting B-17s on an attack against German positions at Bizerte. Separated from his flight leader and the rest of the escorting P-38s, Walker found himself on the wrong end of four Me-109s. "I just went straight down. And they weren't getting any smaller!" During the dive his canopy cracked and the rapid change in the air pressure ruptured an eardrum. After finally outdistancing the enemy aircraft, he returned to base and a month of non-flying duty while his eardrum healed and the Allies forced the Germans in North Africa to surrender.

Following his recuperation and return to the 97th Fighter Squadron, Walker was ordered to Casablanca. At this point in the war, Casablanca was a major logistics depot and personnel staging point. As the huge aviation training complex in the United States began to flex its muscles, replacement pilots were received in North Africa faster than they could be handled. Arrangements were made to give them advanced training in theater before they were sent to operational units. Walker was sent to serve as a combat-seasoned instructor.

"It was a wonderful way to gain experience for myself," he recalled. "I logged a lot more flight time while I was there and continued to learn while I taught. And I got to check out in several other types of aircraft, including the P-40 and the P-39. In fact, I spent a month teaching French airmen to fly P-39s. Those guys never learned about overheating the engine in that aircraft. I'm not sure if they didn't understand or didn't care."

But Walker's training assignment included mistakes. On one gunnery exercise he stayed airborne too long with his students. After a couple of navigational miscues he realized that his flight didn't have enough fuel to return to base. "We finally landed on a wide stretch of beach, and pretty soon this French official of some sort came down in his staff car and asked us what we were doing on his beach." Ultimately they spent the night while fuel was trucked from their base. Upon safely returning the following day, Walker was directed to report to the commanding officer. "Oh man, did I catch hell. I was the talk of the town for a while after that stunt."

Walker was promoted to first lieutenant and sent to Lecce, Italy, to rejoin the 82nd during October 1943. He was immediately designated a flight leader and fell into the routine of bomber-escort missions. "These were fairly easy sorties in that most of them were short so we didn't have to worry too much about gas." The caliber of the German fliers, under the constantly increasing pressure of the Allied aerial offensive, seemed to have deteriorated as well. "These guys weren't as good as the ones in North Africa had been."

Still, some things hadn't changed. "We flew in our weave with the bombers and watched the Germans high above us. We still weren't allowed to go up after them. Then, down they would come in those same slashing attacks. The radios would start crackling and guys would start chattering. A lot of it was just garbage that didn't help anybody. Some guys went so far as to just unplug their radios."

Walker scored his third confirmed aerial victory while escorting B-24s to the railroad marshalling yards at Sofia, Bulgaria, on December 10, 1943. "The weather was horrible, lots of cloud layers. I was more worried about running into someone than I was about enemy aircraft. Well, we got into a couple of big fights. One was going on above a cloud layer high over the top of me. I was involved in another fight down lower. Anyway I got a shot off against an FW-190," Walker recalled. "I'm not even sure I hit him. I thought that I was shooting low and underneath him, but he popped his canopy and bailed out." Walker remembered that his wingman almost flew into the German pilot as the enemy airman jumped clear of his fighter. Although the German pilot escaped being hit by the big P-38, his luck turned from bad to tragic. "We watched him fall all the way to the ground. His parachute trailed behind him and never opened."

Walker scored again on January 24, 1944, while covering the Anzio beachhead near Rome. He was part of a fighter sweep cruising the coast for targets of opportunity. With his wingman, he spotted a flight of two Me-109s low over the water. Sweeping down, he opened fire on one of the enemy aircraft as it cranked around in a hard turn for the beach. Caught in Walker's gunfire, the Messerschmitt dropped down to the wave tops until its lower wingtip dipped into the sea and sent the aircraft cartwheeling into the water.

Walker made interesting observations about the P-38 as a gun platform. Although the four .50-caliber machine guns and single 20mm cannon—all concentrated in the nose—packed a deadly punch, they weren't easy to employ in a turning fight. "All we had at that time was an illuminated Christmas-tree type of sight." This required the pilots to calculate their own firing solutions. In a twisting aerial melee this required a great deal of skill.

"Almost every type of firing solution in aerial combat calls for leading the target—shooting in front of it," Walker recalled. "When you did that with the P-38 you had to lift a wing up and frequently the engine on the high wing blocked the target from the pilot's view. You often had to fire blind. A lot of guys missed out on kills because they'd drop their wing to make sure they didn't run into the guy they were trying to shoot down."

Near the end of his fifty-mission tour, on April 2, 1944, Walker was caught up in a whirling engagement with German fighters over Dubrovnik, Yugoslavia, while escorting B-24s. Walker spotted a P-38 being dogged by a gaggle of German fighters. Rushing in with his wingman to rescue his harried brother-in-arms, Walker opened fire and tore pieces from an Me-109. The two Americans continued their attacks against the enemy fighters and finally drove them away. Scanning the airspace about him, Walker spotted a crippled B-24 that had fallen out of its protective formation. He attached himself as close escort to the big, wounded bird and saw it safely home.

Unfortunately however, his claim for the Me-109 from the mission was officially denied. This would have been his fifth victory, the one that would have made him an ace. For whatever reason, witness accounts to back his claim were not collected and properly filed. However, his squadron put him in an awkward situation when it released information crediting him with a fifth victory. The news was picked up and carried by Walker's hometown paper, which hailed the local boy as the region's newest ace. This was embarrassing for him when he returned to the States a few weeks later. "I got tired of explaining about that when I finally got home," Walker said.

Decades later, following a review by the United States Air Force that stripped some aces of their aerial victories and credited a few others who had been earlier denied, Jack Walker was vindicated. It was a gratifying twist. At a ceremony in El Cajon, California, on October 10, 1998, he was officially credited with his fifth aerial victory.

═══════

Following his combat tour, Walker served as a P-38 instructor and ensured that his young charges had a syllabus of instruction that prepared them for the challenges of combat. It was a far cry from his own indoctrination to Lockheed's twin-boomed fighter.

Walker joined the California Air National Guard in 1948 and flew T-6s, P-51s and C-47s. He additionally checked out in the P-80 Shooting Star jet fighter, and was recalled to active duty in 1950 for the Korean War. He subsequently served in a variety of capacities, including studies at the Air Force Command Staff School, and as an ROTC instructor at UCLA. After leaving active duty a second time he rejoined the California Air National Guard and retired as a colonel in 1967.

Colonel Walker's personal decorations include the Distinguished Flying Cross, the French Croix de Guerre, and the Air Medal with multiple Oak Leaf Clusters.

Above: John Campbell's Hawker Hurricane at Batavia, Java, February 28, 1942. —*John Campbell Collection*

Right: Censored photograph of nineteen-year-old Pilot Officer John Campbell in RAF uniform shortly after arriving in England, April 1941. —*John Campbell Collection*

AVG P-40E in China, March 1942. —*San Diego Aerospace Museum Collection*

An unusual tail-on view of an F-5 on an airfield in Italy. —*USAAF*

This England-based F-5 is a reconnaissance version of the P-38. Willard Caddell flew the F-5 during 1944 from bases in Italy. —*USAAF*

Right: Kenneth Jernstedt recovering after his eye was struck by flying glass during air combat. —*Kenneth Jernstedt Collection*

Below: Air and ship bombardments destroyed many aircraft at Henderson Field on Guadalcanal during Jesse Barker's tenure there, late summer of 1942. Here is the smoking wreckage of an SBD Dauntless. —*USN*

This photo shows the attack on the USS *Enterprise* that was underway on August 24, 1942, when Jesse Barker flew from the deck at the controls of his SBD Dauntless. —*USN*

Scouting 5, summer 1942. Jesse Barker is standing, third from left. His gunner, E.J. Monahan is standing, fourth from left. —*USN*

Japanese installations at Tanambogo burn immediately after being bombed
by Jesse Barker on August 7, 1942. —*USN*

The Me-109G was the German fighter type most encountered by USAAF
pilots over Europe. —*San Diego Aerospace Museum Collection*

The P-38 wasn't produced in numbers as great as the P-47 and the P-51, but it was an important type through much of the war. —*USAAF*

Hamilton McWhorter in the cockpit of an F4F Wildcat, 1942. —*Hamilton McWhorter Collection*

Hamilton McWhorter flew the Grumman F4F Wildcat over North Africa from the USS *Ranger* during November 1942. Modest in performance, but exceptionally rugged and sturdy, the Wildcat also helped hold the line against the Japanese early during the war. —*San Diego Aerospace Museum Collection*

A captured example of a Japanese Mitsubishi A6M3. The vaunted Zero was exceptionally maneuverable and had tremendous range. Nevertheless, its very light construction made it quite susceptible to the concentrated firepower of Allied machine guns and cannons. —*San Diego Aerospace Museum Collection*

Quartering front view of a Grumman F6F-3 Hellcat. The Hellcat, which followed the Wildcat into service during 1943, was clearly superior to the Japanese Zero.
—*San Diego Aerospace Museum Collection*

F4F Wildcats aboard the USS *Ranger* testing their machine guns en route to North Africa for the TORCH invasion, November 1942. —*USN*

The USS *Randolph* following the *kamikaze* attack of March 11, 1945. —*USN*

F6F-5 Hellcats of McWhorter's VF-12 aboard the USS *Randolph* during early 1945. —*USN*

The Me-262 jet outperformed Allied piston-engine fighters.
—*San Diego Aerospace Museum Collection*

B-24s of Kaestner's 308th Bomb Group over China, 1944. —*Walter Kaestner Collection*

Kaestner's bombs explode in an attack on a Japanese held bridge near Vinh, French Indochina. —*Walter Kaestner Collection*

Kaestner described how this P-40 dove straight into the ground at Kunming. —*Walter Kaestner Collection*

Donald Whitright in full flying gear, England, 1945. Note the Mae West life preserver around his chest and the rubber dinghy and parachute slung beneath his hips.
—*Donald Whitright Collection*

Donald Whitright (standing, second from right) and the 5th Emergency Rescue Squadron. Note the P-47 has had two guns removed from each wing to lighten it and increase its endurance. Also, note the droppable life raft mounted under the wing.
—*Donald Whitright Collection*

A damaged F6F being jettisoned from the *Yorktown*. It was not uncommon to dump damaged aircraft overboard in order to make room for flight operations during combat. —*San Diego Aerospace Museum Collection*

A Kawanishi H8K *Emily* goes down. This is the same type aircraft shot down by Rudolph Matz during the prelude to the great air clashes of the First Battle of the Philippine Sea. —*USN*

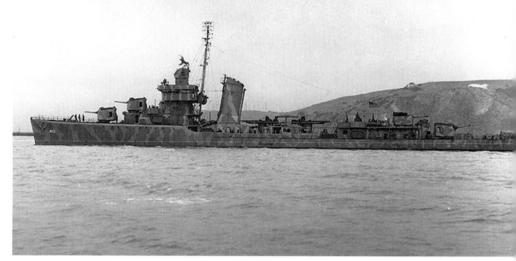

Rudolph Matz served in the fire control section of the USS *Hughes* from before the war until the Battle of Midway during June 1942. —*USN*

An F6F-5 Hellcat from Rudolph Matz's VF-1. —*USN*

"The Frame." Richard Deitchman (on right) during his trek back to the USS *Manila Bay* following the Second Battle of the Philippine Sea. He is posing in front of a damaged Japanese Zero on the contested island of Peleliu on November 14, 1944. —*Richard Deitchman Collection*

A crew struggles out of a ditched TBM-3 Avenger. Both Ray Crandall and Richard Deitchman experienced the same misfortune. —*San Diego Aerospace Museum Collection*

Above: Ray Crandall at the controls of a TBM Avenger aboard the USS *Manila Bay.* *—USN*

Left: Ray Crandall and Richard Deitchman, stateside, January 1945. *—Richard Deitchman Collection*

CHAPTER 7

HEROES AT HOME

For every aviator deployed to a combat theater there were many more servicemen in various support roles back in the United States. For example, during mid-1944, out of every three officers in the Army Air Forces, roughly two were stationed stateside. Many of these were pilots. Their duties, although less glamorous than fighting the enemy, were absolutely essential to the successful conduct of the war. Their tasks included flight instruction, industrial liaison, administrative work, training support, ferrying of aircraft and flight testing, among many others.

In effect there were many men who would never become great fighter aces and bomber leaders simply because they never had the opportunity. Commanding officers of support units were often reluctant to give up their best officers to combat units. Many pilots tried fervently to get orders to combat only to be turned down time and time again. They were too valuable.

These men were the ultimate Unsung Eagles.

Mort Blumenfeld

"I GLANCED INTO THE REARVIEW MIRROR AND COULD SEE THAT the crash trucks and the ambulance were already roaring down the runway. Further back, men were donning asbestos firefighting suits. I depressed the mike button on my throttle and spoke into the throat microphone which was pressed against both sides of my larynx: Mayday! Mayday! Mayday!"

Mort (Alfred M. to the Army) Blumenfeld was born on June 7, 1919. His father, Max, was a veteran of President Theodore Roosevelt's Great

White Fleet and was busy clearing the North Sea minefields in the wake of World War I when his son was born.

Blumenfeld grew up in Philadelphia. Fascinated with airplanes, he doodled World War I bombers in school, built model airplanes and a one-tube, shortwave radio from scratch. He followed the exploits of early aviation pioneers such as Charles Lindbergh, Amelia Earhart, Wiley Post and Jimmy Doolittle. After graduating high school in 1937, an interest in commercial illustration led him to the Philadelphia College of Art and subsequently to the Pratt Institute in Brooklyn, New York. During this time he learned to fly through the Civilian Pilot Training Program at Floyd Bennett Field.

Inspired by his father's Navy service he applied for naval flight training during the spring of 1941 but was turned down. A few months later he was accepted by the Army as a flying cadet and was sworn in on Friday, September 13, 1941. "It was Friday the 13th," he recalled, "and there were thirteen of us there to be sworn in. A reporter from the Philadelphia *Inquirer* showed up with a ladder, a mirror to break, and a black cat. All of the mothers kept in touch during the war. Frank Green and I were the only two out of the thirteen to survive the war. We both came home as majors."

Four months after Pearl Harbor, in April 1942, Blumenfeld finished his flight training and was commissioned as a second lieutenant. "Of course I was ready to save the world for democracy," he remembered. "Instead, I was ordered to Lawson Field at Fort Benning, Georgia, to join a new special observation squadron supporting the Infantry Officer Candidate School. Apparently someone up near the top thought it was important because several of us were frozen in that job for the next two-and-a-half years."

He was assigned to the 3rd Composite Squadron of the 3rd Reconnaissance Command, Third Air Force. Like many of the stateside units which served in supporting roles, Blumenfeld's squadron was low on the priority list when compared to those units preparing for imminent combat operations overseas. Consequently, aircraft, spare parts, and personnel were always in short supply. As a result, the stable of aircraft in the 3rd Composite squadron was constantly changing. "I was the operations officer, and later the maintenance officer, of a rag-tag complement of 35 aircraft that we scrounged in ones and twos. They were usually late-model aircraft left behind as 'hangar queens' by combat units that shipped overseas. At one time we had six P-39s, six P-40s, two A-36As—which were a dive bombing variant of the early P-51—six B-25s, an A-20, and a litter of various oddball observation and utility types." One perk of Blumenfeld's assignment was that he flew a wide variety of different type and model aircraft. "One day in my logbook shows flights in a Cub, a P-40, an AT-6, and a B-25.

"One aspect of our mission at Fort Benning—as part of the Infantry School Troops Brigade—was flying various scenarios for the officer candidates: Enemy air attack, air support, liaison with ground forces, etc." Nevertheless, the mission of the 3rd Composite Squadron evolved over time. "Someone at the Pentagon got this great idea of creating 'Dog and Pony' shows; these were airpower demonstrations for noncombatant-type troops who were slated for deployment to the war zones. These guys were medics, signal corpsmen, supply types, and so on who had never seen airpower in action.

"We typically assembled a flight of about four medium bombers and six fighters," Blumenfeld recalled. "Aside from a normal five-man crew on the B-25s, we carried one good brake mechanic, one propeller specialist, one crew chief for each two fighters and a slew of armament men to load ammo and bombs. In all, it worked out to about fifty men and ten planes.

"We went on the road for a week or two out of every six weeks and performed two or three shows at widely separated camps. At the different camps, usually in the artillery impact areas, soldiers constructed realistic looking enemy tank convoys from wood lath, burlap, and crankcase oil. About a half mile away, ideally on a parallel hillside, seating was arranged for several thousand troops and occasionally, invited guests from nearby towns, and families of the servicemen.

"We flew rehearsals the day before to get everything safely aligned and coordinated. Then on show day we armed up and went. We strafed, put down smoke screens, dive bombed and skip-bombed. For the finale we sent two bombers across the target at 2,000 feet and dropped sixteen 500-pound high explosive bombs." These demonstrations gave their audiences a real sense of the destruction that airpower could cause.

Although Blumenfeld's service was not in combat, it was not without danger. Weather, old and tired aircraft, lack of parts and support personnel, and the relatively rudimentary development of the science of aviation conspired to lay potentially lethal traps for the airmen of the day.

"October 13, 1944, was almost the last day of my life," Blumenfeld remembered. "I stayed on the line working when most of the pilots went to lunch. Just as I was about to leave, the operations officer called and asked me to take a P-40 on a school mission that had just come up.

"I put on my flight suit, helmet, goggles, and calfskin gauntlets and climbed into the aircraft." After starting the fighter's engine, Blumenfeld wasted no time in getting it taxied to the end of the runway for takeoff. Even in late autumn the liquid-cooled V-12 engine of the P-40 was prone to overheating. By the time he reached the end of the runway, Blumenfeld had completed his pre-takeoff checks and the control tower cleared him for takeoff.

"This particular aircraft," Blumenfeld recalled, "was one of six RP-40Rs acquired from Olmsted Air Depot as restricted use aircraft. They were modified to use 91 octane fuel to save 100 octane fuel for the war zones. We were directed to operate these aircraft at reduced power settings in order to save the engines. Those reduced power settings were considered adequate for our mission at the Infantry Officer School.

"I took off to the northwest on the longest runway at Lawson [Army Airfield]; it was about 7,000 feet long. At the far end of the runway, the ground dropped off to a perimeter dirt road, then sloped down again to the banks of the Chattahoochee River. Across the river in Alabama the land rose in a long, gradual, stump-covered incline for about a mile or more.

"I smoothly poured on the power and fought the torque from the engine as I began my take-off roll. Just after I got airborne the engine quit cold and then roared back to life. It continued to do that at five-second intervals. My heart pounded, my mind raced and my sphincter bit into the seat cushion of my parachute."

Blumenfeld looked into the rearview mirror mounted at the top of his aircraft's windscreen and saw emergency vehicles and crews speeding down the runway after him. He made a Mayday call to the control tower and then turned his full attention to staying alive

"I was less than forty feet above those stumps and was barely going 120 miles per hour. The engine coolant gauge showed the temperature at 120 degrees centigrade—well above normal operating limits. Turning back to the airfield when an engine quits is normally a bad option. In trying to stretch the glide, pilots often stall the aircraft and crash. Normally I would have held my airspeed and just bellied it in. But those stumps would have crumpled the fighter and put that big Allison V-12 right into my lap. So, I decided to turn back toward the runway.

"The engine was still misbehaving; it alternately roared to life and then stopped. Anxious to avoid a stall, I made a very shallow turn because the stall speed increases as the turn increases. I guess my guardian angel stayed on my shoulder, because the plane completed the turn. When I was finally safely pointed down the runway and certain that I could clear the hundred feet or more of grassy area on the approach to the pavement, I eased back on the stick at about ten feet of altitude, and hit the landing gear lever. I heard and felt the downlock pins go into place just an instant before I heard the twin chirps of tires touching down on the runway.

"I decelerated to a stop and cut the engine. With barely enough strength to get out of the aircraft, I fell down to my knees and kissed the runway. Then I asked for a cigarette. When the jeep dropped me off at the flight line my commanding officer was there. He grinned and told me to go up to the officer's club, have a drink and take the rest of the day off."

An investigation revealed that running the engines at reduced settings with the 91 octane fuel caused a build-up of lead on the engine's spark plugs. This buildup caused the fuel to pre-ignite in the cylinders, or it melted, ran like solder and shorted the spark plugs. The prescribed fix was simple; the pilots were to briefly run the engines at increased power settings and lean mixtures every twenty minutes or so in order to burn off the lead buildup.

━━━━━━

At war's end Blumenfeld was in the Pacific as a member of the 417th Light Bomb Group flying A-20 light attack bombers. The group was based on Okinawa in preparation for the invasion of Japan. Although the war ended before he saw combat, his contributions to the victory—like those of tens of thousands of others who never fought the enemy—were considerable.

Following the war, Mort Blumenfeld returned to the profession he trained for—industrial design. He became a noted design specialist in plastics product development and shared his expertise through writing and lectures in the States and abroad, and as a college adjunct professor for materials and processes.

Ruldoph Matz (center, kneeling) and his fighter training class in front of an F4F Wildcat.
—*Rudolph Matz Collection*

CHAPTER 8

CIVILIANS IN UNIFORM

The colossal transformation of the armed forces of the United States cannot be emphasized enough. The Navy alone grew from a force of 161,000 in 1940 to one of nearly 3.5 million by war's end; it was more than a twenty-fold increase. Its air component grew from just under 11,000 men to nearly 440,000—a forty-fold increase. This meant that less than one in twenty of those in the service at the end of the war had more than five years in uniform. The overwhelming majority were men only a couple of years removed from civilian life. Few among the Navy's ranks were the men who could claim to have taken part in nearly every epic battle for the Pacific.

Rudolph W. Matz

RUDOLPH MATZ WAS BORN IN NEWARK, OHIO, ON OCTOBER 21, 1919. The son of immigrants—his father was German and his mother was Austrian—he grew up with six siblings on a farm during the hard years of the Great Depression. "We were very poor," Matz recalled. "My father wanted me to go into the Navy as a machinist, so when I graduated from high school on a Friday, he took me down to the recruiter the following Tuesday." However, because there was a backlog to begin training, the elder Matz had to wait more than a year before his son finally left for boot camp in the summer of 1939.

"I got to boot camp at Newport, Rhode Island, and two months later the war started in Europe. They hurried up and kicked us all out of training and into the fleet. I never did get to go to aviation mechanics school. I ended up in the fire control section of a destroyer."

Assigned to the USS *Hughes*, Matz took part in the Neutrality Patrols in the Atlantic which protected American interests and Allied shipping— particularly merchant vessels carrying desperately needed war material to England. This was a particularly delicate period for the United States. Although many of the nation's leaders were certain that entry into the war was imminent, there was still a strong isolationist sentiment among much of the population. Nevertheless, if the United States was to enter the war in Europe, the survival of England was paramount. The Neutrality Patrols, which eventually escorted shipping well beyond the eastern shores of Iceland, were essential to that survival.

Although America was still not at war with Germany in May 1941, the breakout into the North Atlantic of the deadly German dreadnought *Bismarck* was an event that threatened all shipping, non-belligerent or not. Matz remembered that the *Hughes,* as part of a naval task force that included the aircraft carrier *Yorktown,* the cruiser *Nashville,* and the battleship *New Mexico,* among others, was alerted to watch for the fearsome ship. "Yes, they sent us out to look for the *Bismarck*," he recalled. "And I'm glad we didn't find it."

Matz regularly applied to be an enlisted pilot since shortly after joining the Navy. "The fire control ensign onboard the *Hughes* knew that I had been trying to get into flight school," Matz remembered. "But you had to serve three years on a newly commissioned destroyer, which the *Hughes* was, before they'd let you off. Anyway this ensign had a brother who was a yeoman who worked on the aviation cadet selection board. He told me to go see him." Wasting little time, Matz made his way to Boston and met the ensign's brother. By another stroke of good fortune, a medical officer who conducted the application physicals had a brother-in-law who served on the *Hughes* with Matz. Things looked promising.

Pearl Harbor was attacked soon after and the first few months of the war were a blur for the young sailor. "We pulled into port at Bangor, Maine, on December 7, 1941, and didn't even drop anchor. We picked up the *New Mexico*, then joined with the *Yorktown* and went through the Panama Canal to San Diego." Matz remembered that the *Hughes* left San Diego for Samoa on January 10, 1942 as part of an escort force for Marines bound for Samoa. Later, during early February, the *Hughes* was part of the task force which conducted the first offensive operations against the Japanese; these were attacks on Japanese installations in the Marshall and Gilbert island chains.

During early May 1942, the *Hughes* was part of a task force deployed to the Coral Sea under Rear Admiral Frank Jack Fletcher. Fletcher was charged with thwarting a Japanese landing at Port Moresby in New Guinea. Losses were significant on both sides, yet the men of the *Hughes* were lucky. "Our fire control director jammed," Matz remembered. "At the time we were escorting the *Neosho,* which was a tanker. My division officer and twelve enlisted men were transferred to another destroyer—the *Sims,* which replaced us with the *Neosho.* We went back to Pearl." On the next day, May 7, 1942, Japanese naval aircraft sank both the *Neosho* and the *Sims.* A bare thirteen survivors were recovered from the *Sims* but none were among those transferred from the *Hughes.*

The Coral Sea fight was the first battle in history during which the opposing fleets never gained sight of each other. It was fought solely from the air, and was a portent of things to come. The Americans won and stymied Japanese designs on Port Moresby, but it was barely a month later that the United States Navy found itself committed to a battle that marked the turning point of the Pacific war.

Again, Matz and the *Hughes* were there. This time the Japanese were trying to trap and destroy the American aircraft carriers at Midway. Only 1,300 miles northwest of Pearl Harbor, Midway's bases and location made it strategically invaluable. It had to be defended.

The Battle of Midway was fought from June 4–7, 1942, and developed to be one of history's most important and decisive victories. The United States, owing to the fact that its code breakers could read Japanese message traffic, was ready for the trap that Admiral Isoroku Yamamoto and his staff prepared. Once the fight was joined, the Navy exercised great audaciousness and skill—and enjoyed a good deal of luck—to sink four Japanese aircraft carriers. These ships, the *Kaga, Hiryu, Soryu* and *Akagi,* had all launched aircraft against Pearl Harbor seven months earlier. Moreover, hundreds of difficult-to-replace airmen were killed and several smaller ships were destroyed. Not only did the victory mark the shift of power in the Pacific toward the Americans, but also helped to avenge the sneak attack that compelled the United States into the war.

The one significant American loss at Midway was the aircraft carrier *Yorktown.* Matz was a participant in the action during which the big ship was lost. "We were there when the *Yorktown* was hit," he recollected. After picking up survivors, the *Hughes* stayed with the stricken ship while the rest of the task force continued after the retreating Japanese. "The *Yorktown* was listing and we stayed there all night circling it. In the morning at about 0500 we saw splashes in the water. There was a kid still aboard the *Yorktown* and he started firing a 20mm cannon to get our attention. We put the whaleboat in and went over there and picked him and a few others up. I'll never forget his name—Norman Pichette. He was from Pennsylvania, and he was holding his guts in with one hand. He died on our ship. I was a sideboy for the burial detail.

"That morning at about 1000, some of the other destroyers came back. There were about six of us altogether." A tug had also been dispatched out of Hawaii and the *Hughes* tied up alongside the *Yorktown* later that day to help with the salvage effort. Later the *Hughes* stood off from the *Yorktown* while the *Hammann* moored alongside to transfer hoses and other fire-fighting equipment. "We had just pulled away after the *Hammann* moved in," Matz remembered, "and completed about a third of a circle around them, and . . . BOOM!" The *Hammann* and the *Yorktown* were hit by torpedoes from the Japanese submarine *I-168*. The *Hammann* went down immediately with few survivors. "What happened," Matz remembered, "is that the *Hammann's* depth charges started going off and everyone in the water was killed by the concussions.

"So we took off and started searching for the submarine," Matz continued. *Hughes*, along with the other destroyers, damaged *I-168* with depth charges but failed to sink it. "The Japanese submarine surfaced at about 2030—it was just getting dark. I was in the director so I knew all of the ranges; the maximum range we could fire was 17,000 or 18,000 yards. Well, we fired but it was too far out." Safely away and with darkness descending, *I-168* slipped away from the American destroyers.

Yorktown sank at 0701 on the following day, June 7, 1942. The Japanese submarine, *I-168*, was ultimately destroyed on July 27, 1943, during an engagement with the American submarine, *Scamp*.

Following the battle at Midway, Matz returned to San Diego aboard the *Hughes* via Pearl Harbor. Since joining the ship's crew in 1939 he had been a busy man. "Out of three years, I got fifteen days of leave," he remembered. Once back in the States he checked on his request for flight training. To his surprise he was very near the top of the list, but there was a problem. "I told the guy that my ship was getting ready to leave the next day for a six-month stint in the South Pacific."

The two enlisted men conjured up some administrative wizardry. Personnel policies and guidelines were researched and modifications were typed. The end result was that the *Hughes* departed the following day without Matz. Orders sending him to pilot training arrived soon after, but the deal with the devil didn't come cheap. "I was stuck with a seven-year service obligation," Matz remembered.

Flight school posed no real problems for the battle-seasoned sailor, though his initial training started a little slow. Itching to do more, Matz exercised some initiative that would have gotten him in real trouble had he been caught; he partnered with a fellow student for some "extracurricular" training. "I'd never been flying before flight school—I'd never even been around it," he recalled. "Being from the farm, I didn't know diddly about it. Well, there was this enlisted kid named Herbie Hecht who had been around aviation and who was also an enlisted flight student. I was just getting ready to solo, and he had already soloed. He took me flying with him, which was illegal, but I learned more with him in that one hour, than I had with my instructor after fifteen hours." Matz smiled as he remembered, "If I had been caught I would have been kicked out."

Following his completion of flight school during late 1943, Matz was held back a short time before being commissioned and sent to fly fighters. "I finished fighter training at Lee Field, near Jacksonville, Florida, in December 1943. I had about 115 hours of flight time in the F4F Wildcat." Following carrier qualifications aboard the *Wolverine* on Lake Michigan that same month, Matz was sent to San Diego for assignment overseas. After a brief stay in San Diego, where he was billeted in the zoo's converted horse barn, he made his way back to the Pacific on a PBM-3 flying boat. He arrived at the Navy's huge complex at Espiritu Santo in January 1944.

While at Espiritu Santo waiting for a permanent assignment, Matz was bounced from squadron to squadron while he picked up a few odd hours in the Navy's frontline fighter, the F6F Hellcat, which he had never flown. His travels carried him as far as Guadalcanal where, bored and tired of doing nothing, he ferried SBD dive bombers to Vella Lavella for the Marines. He remembered his few days at Guadalcanal: "They put us up in the Hotel De Gink. It was full of Marine officers and there was a lot of drinking and carrying on. It was very wild."

Finally, back in Espiritu Santo, he was assigned to VF-5 which was flying F6F Hellcats off of the new *Yorktown*. "Those of us who were newly assigned to VF-5 were very fortunate. They had been in combat for several months and had a lot of combat experience. This proved to be very helpful for us green 'know-it-all' ensigns."

Afloat in the Pacific once more, this time as a fighter pilot, Ensign Matz remembered his first day of aerial combat: March 30, 1944. "They woke me up in the morning at about 0400 and told me that I was going to be a replacement pilot for a strike on Palau. Now, I was pretty confused. It was my first flight with the squadron—a combat flight—and I only had about fifteen hours in the F6F."

Inexperienced, overwhelmed, and briefed in only a cursory manner, Matz watched from the rear of the ship where he sat in the spare fighter. There in the predawn darkness, tucked amongst the strike group's TBM torpedo bombers, he nervously tracked the progress of the launch as he waited his own turn. As the last of the torpedo aircraft got airborne, he was launched as an extra to fill in where other fighters dropped out.

"I joined up with the TBMs," Matz remembered. "But I didn't like it with them because they were so slow, so I went up to the SBD dive bombers. After I got settled in with them I saw some fighters so I flew over and joined up with two of them.

"Our targets had been briefed as the airfield, the radio station, and the seaplane ramps. But we were specifically told not to hit the brewery at the north end of the island. The two guys I was with turned out to be wild," Matz recalled. He and the two other Hellcat pilots dove with the rest of the strike group through the murderous antiaircraft fire and turned their .50-caliber machine guns onto whatever target presented itself. "We went down and strafed the seaplane ramp, and then the radio station and the airfield," Matz remembered. "Then we hauled ass on a heading of 355 degrees. Well," he said smiling, "that heading would have taken us up past the Philippines instead of back south where the ship was."

Uncertain because it was his first combat mission, Matz kept quiet and maintained formation as he followed his ad-hoc flight leader north—away from the *Yorktown*. "Hell, I thought maybe we were going to go shoot up the brewery." Finally, beyond Palau and with his fuel quantity steadily decreasing, he couldn't stand it anymore. "Breaking radio silence was forbidden, so I pulled out my plotting board and pointed to it." There was no response from his flight leader. "So I waved it at the other guy. He was only an ensign though, just like me, and he just shrugged.

"Finally, I got it out again and really waved it at him. Well, we finally turned around, but right about the time we got back over Palau he turned around again and left us!" It wasn't until several minutes later, his head finally cleared, that the flight leader appeared again and sheepishly rejoined the two youngsters for the flight back to the task force.

After picking up the *Yorktown's* ZB homing beam, Matz and the other two fighters arrived overhead long after they should have. Scrambling to prepare the deck for landing because Matz had only twenty-five gallons of fuel remaining, the *Yorktown* was just barely able to make room in time to recover him. The other two pilots landed aboard the *Bunker Hill.*

Matz had been airborne more than five hours. "The VF-5 administration shop already had my confidential folder out. They thought I was missing in action. Anyway, I hadn't been back two minutes," Matz recalled, "when there was a call over the intercom: 'Ensign Matz report to the bridge!' Well, Captain [Ralph] Jennings started raising hell with me. Finally, I told him what had happened and that this had been my first combat flight. After a minute he looked at me and said, 'Okay, Ensign Matz, I'll give you a gold star for navigation. Now get off of my bridge.'

"As it turned out," Matz remembered with irony, "the two pilots I was actually supposed to join with ran into Japanese fighters. One of them got three kills and the other got one. All I got was yelled at."

Nevertheless, it wasn't long before Matz put more missions under his belt and gained the experience and savvy he needed to survive. April 29, 1944, was a day that demanded it. As part of Task Force 58, the airmen of the *Yorktown* launched two days of strikes against the huge Japanese anchorage and airfield installations at Truk Atoll in the Caroline Islands group. Home to the Japanese Combined Fleet, Truk was very heavily defended and had long been considered a serious threat to American advances in the central Pacific. Already crippled by an earlier strike during February, this later attack was designed to deliver the final knockout blow.

The Japanese antiaircraft fire was murderous. "Truk was rough," Matz understated. Loaded with heavy 1,000-pound bombs, he and his flight leader were tasked with striking a shore installation. Under fire from shipboard guns in the harbor, as well as the antiaircraft guns ashore, Matz dropped his bomb and made repeated strafing passes. "My division leader couldn't get his bomb to come off," he remembered. "It was insane. We made three passes before he was able to drop it. On the third pass my engine started running rough and I had to switch over to my emergency fuel pump to keep it running."

All around Matz, aircraft fell to the Japanese defenses. "The Navy posted submarines at various points around Truk during the attack. The pilots had their positions and if they were in trouble they were supposed to ditch at a point where the submarines could pick them up. One submarine, the *Tang,* made history and the cover of *Life* magazine when it picked up 22 pilots and crewmen."

Doing his best to save the submarines some unnecessary work, Matz nursed his sick aircraft clear of the atoll's defenses and landed aboard the first aircraft carrier that could handle him. In this case it was the *Hornet.* "The crew on the *Hornet* worked on the engine, and I was able to get the plane back to the *Yorktown* the next day. When we got back to Hawaii, that particular aircraft was the only one that wouldn't start. They had to crane it off when they came into port."

The knockout blow at Truk was a success. Of the 104 Japanese aircraft known to be in the area before the strike, 93 were either shot down or destroyed on the ground, and numerous ships were sent to the bottom. Additionally, the remaining fuel, ammunition, and supply depots were ruined. From that point, Truk ceased to be a real threat to American movements in the Pacific.

Back in Pearl Harbor during May 1944, Matz watched in dismay as many of his squadron mates, combat tours complete, shipped back to the States. His own time with VF-5 had been only eleven weeks—one short of the twelve he needed for a complete tour. Although he had participated in nearly fifteen strikes against heavily defended targets such as Truk and Palau, as well as missions that covered MacArthur's invasion at Hollandia, regulations dictated his immediate return to combat. "There were several of us in the same situation," Matz remembered. "We wanted to get it over with, so we volunteered to join VF-1, the High Hatters, and go right back out on the *Yorktown*."

During the brief period before the *Yorktown* and the rest of Task Force 58 put back out to sea, the skipper of VF-1, Commander Bernard Strean, put the finishing touches on his squadron; he led the unit through a tranche of intense training to ensure that his men were prepared for the combat to come. It was during this time that an incident occurred which illustrates the sorts of things that happen when a military service—in this instance the aviation component of the Navy—grows from a small cadre of professionals to a gargantuan military branch composed of personnel only a couple of years removed from civilian life.

Matz related the story: "The squadron had some planes and pilots over at Barbers Point and they needed to get them back to the field at Kaneohe Bay. There was a dive bomber pilot there, Earl Graf, who was friends with Chuck Ambellen, one of the VF-1 pilots. Graf had had a lot to drink and for whatever reason he and Ambellen decided to fly back to Barbers Point in the same aircraft. What they did was, they took the parachute out and Graf sat on Ambellen's lap.

"Well, they made it over there okay, and Graf decided that flying fighters wasn't that big of a deal. Anyone could do it! Anyway, the skipper took the entire squadron up on a night flying mission—a total of 32 airplanes—and Graf put on a flight suit and a helmet, then signed for an aircraft as Chauncey Clogmeyer. He took off right behind the skipper and screwed up the whole formation. It was a mess.

"They put him up for a general court martial and he beat it. They fined him two hundred dollars and did some other stuff to him, but he went out on a combat tour just a few months later."

It was May 29, 1944, when the *Yorktown* sortied out of Pearl Harbor again to form with the rest of Task Force 58, led by Admiral Marc Mitscher, at Majuro. From Majuro the task force headed for the Marianas archipelago in the central Pacific on June 6. There, at bases on Guam, Tinian, and Saipan, the Japanese maintained enormous air, naval, and army forces. The destruction of those forces, and the seizure of the islands for use as bases from which to launch B-29 raids against Japan, was critical to America's strategic goals.

Desperate to pinpoint the location of the American task force, the

Japanese commanders dispatched patrol aircraft of all types. Matz was part of a four-plane division flying Combat Air Patrol over the fleet at mid-day on June 11, 1944. "We were vectored to an Emily flying boat," he remembered. Emily was the Allied codename for the Kawanishi H8K. "The Emily was down at around 10,000 or 12,000 feet, and we descended from our CAP [Combat Air Patrol] to about 15,000 feet and set up for overhead gunnery runs." Executing textbook procedures, the four Hellcats dived on the lumbering, four-engine flying boat. "I fired 750 rounds," Matz recalled, "and knocked out the left inboard engine and set it on fire." Virtually helpless against the American fighters, the hapless Japanese aircraft fell flaming into the water.

Later, Matz's gun camera film confirmed the mortal damage he inflicted on the Emily. "I shot the Emily down," he said evenly, "but credit was given to another pilot because he was killed on the initial strike against Guam that same day. He was also the first pilot the squadron lost."

That day marked the first of three days of air strikes against shipping and installations on the islands of Saipan, Tinian, Guam, Rota, and Pagan. The attacks were intended to soften the area prior to the invasion of Saipan by elements of the Marine Corps and the Army.

Matz remembered this as the most dangerous flying he did during the war. "A lot of people don't realize that after the first couple of days when we went out against a Japanese-held installation or island, that the enemy aircraft were pretty much decimated. From that point, the fighters flew fighter-bomber missions. We carried a 1,000-pound bomb or a 500-pound bomb, plus an external fuel tank on the belly. And of course we always carried 2,400 rounds of .50-caliber ammunition.

"Or we might fly on Combat Air Patrol. That was usually hours and hours of droning around chasing after nothing. It was very boring and the seat was very uncomfortable after several hours; it had a can or something in the life raft that would stick you in just the wrong place.

"During my combat career it seemed that the further north we went, the more intense the antiaircraft fire was. By the time we got to Guam and Saipan the antiaircraft fire was horrendous. On June 13, our division was strafing near the runway at Saipan. An ammunition dump exploded and one of our ensigns flew right through the explosion. There were coconuts, fuel drums, pallets, and palm trees passing him by on the way up.

He was very fortunate to make it back to the carrier. He had a badly missing engine, more than sixty holes in the aircraft, and a chunk of palm tree embedded inside one of his engine cylinders. They just pushed the airplane over the side.

"Small arms fire was devastating too," Matz recalled. "In the squadron I had been in before, VF-5, we had an unwritten rule that we didn't go down below about 2,000 feet because of the danger from small arms fire. In VF-1 I noticed that new replacement pilots were strafing much lower— sometimes just over the treetops. Well, it didn't take too long to learn how dangerous that was. Actually, as the time remaining in the combat zone started to near the end, it seemed that we bombed and strafed from higher and higher." Toward the end, few pilots went below 2,500 feet because everyone wanted to survive the tour.

By this point in the war Japan's leadership knew that victory was not a realistic goal but was nonetheless desperate to strike a devastating blow against the American naval forces. They hoped that a crippling attack on America's mightiest fleet might compel the United States to settle for a negotiated end to the conflict rather than Japan's unconditional surrender.

Accordingly, a clever and complex scheme—Operation A-Go—was drafted. With American forces poised to invade the Marianas, the Japanese, under Admiral Soemu Toyoda, planned to ambush Task Force 58 by shuttling air strikes between its remaining carriers and its bases on Guam and Tinian. Then, with the American fleet wounded and in disarray, the First Mobile Japanese Fleet, divided into two components, was to pounce and deliver the killing blows.

After searching in vain for days, the Japanese finally fixed the location of the American fleet in the Marianas. On June 19, 1944, the Japanese launched the air attacks they hoped would turn the tide of the war to their favor. On that same day Matz again was part of a four-plane division on Combat Air Patrol. Near noon the flight received a radar vector. "What often happened when we received vectors," Matz recalled, "was that we'd get mistakenly sent after clouds, or friendly aircraft or sometimes just nothing." Radar technology was new and neither the equipment nor the operators were perfect.

In this instance, the vector was a good one. Matz and the other three fliers caught sight of a formation of about one hundred Japanese aircraft.

The enemy planes, already under attack from other American fighters, were desperately trying to break through to the fleet. "It was like all hell broke loose," Matz said.

All hell did break loose when Matz and his squadron mates reached the fight. "I was ass-end Charlie—number four," he remembered. "We were in a right-hand turn—we had just shot down one plane—and as we turned I slid underneath and saw a Zero coming down directly at me. I pulled up and turned into him and squeezed the trigger and he just blew up. I normally flew with my canopy partially open and when I flew underneath the fireball I could feel the heat."

Matz spotted another three enemy aircraft below him—two of them were being chased by other Hellcats. He pulled his fighter down hard into a left-hand turn after the unmolested enemy aircraft and fired his six .50-caliber machine guns. The rounds found their mark and the Zero erupted into a flaming ball.

A few minutes later he was attacked by two Zeros and a Ki-61 Tony—a more modern fighter with an inline liquid-cooled engine. Matz was rescued when two other Hellcat pilots drove off the enemy Zeros while he continued to turn with the Ki-61. The Ki-61 dived head-on at Matz; Matz's gunfire struck the Japanese fighter in the engine and it fell burning out of control.

The fight, as nearly all aerial engagements do, spiraled downhill. At this point Matz was down to 6,000 feet. He spotted a Zero, made a slashing, high-side firing pass, and sent the enemy aircraft down in flames. The battle continued with the Japanese desperate to reach the American fleet, and the Hellcats just as desperate to stop them. By the time the fight was over, the fleet was safe, the sky was empty of Japanese aircraft, and Matz claimed four aerial victories.

But he was allowed only two. The other two were credited as probables. "They said that you had to see it hit the water to claim it as a kill," Matz remembered. "Hell, you couldn't wait to see it hit the water if you were at 20,000 feet, but you knew it went in. I was positive about those four. And I was careful when I made the claims because I was new and just an ensign with a tough skipper."

The Battle of the Philippine Sea is popularly remembered as the Great Marianas Turkey Shoot. It was the greatest and most lopsided aerial battle in history. Through the course of two other major aerial engagements that day, the Japanese lost nearly 300 aircraft against American losses of only 29. So severe was the loss of trained pilots that the Imperial Japanese Navy was never again able to mount a serious strike from its aircraft carriers.

It was late afternoon the following day, June 20, 1944, when American reconnaissance aircraft finally located the Japanese fleet. Weighing the risks of a night recovery—such operations were quite dangerous—Mitscher decided to launch a late afternoon strike against the retreating ships. The attack was successful, as the American flyers sent the carrier *Hiyo*, and several smaller ships, to the bottom. Additionally, three other carriers, as well as several other large combatant vessels, were heavily damaged. Those losses, combined with the loss of the carriers *Shokaku* and *Taiho* to U.S. submarines the previous day, guaranteed victory to the Americans.

However, the night recovery of the strike force was every bit the nightmare that had been feared. Having flown to beyond their maximum combat radius, the returning aircraft were desperately short of fuel. Darkness exacerbated the problem. Matz remembered the mayhem. "I was the number four aircraft scheduled to take off on the mission. I thank God that our particular mission was cancelled because I probably wouldn't have made it back.

"There were young kids out there, low on gas, in the dark, trying to land on anything. It was pretty scary. Our high scorer, [Marshall] Tomme, was killed when a kid from the *Hornet* took a cut when he was signaled to wave off. He landed right on top of Tomme, who had just landed and was taxiing forward." Aside from Tomme, several other sailors were killed in the resulting explosion and fire.

"That sort of thing wasn't uncommon during the war," Matz said. "A lot of good people were lost because things were hurried, or people were inadequately trained, or they were just in the wrong frame of mind."

The enemy, the darkness, and the confusion made this a costlier battle than the previous day's victory. It is estimated that twenty aircraft were lost to the Japanese defenses, while more than eighty fuel-starved aircraft ditched into the water. Fortunately, the majority of the crews who went down in the water were recovered.

A few days later, elements of the task force attacked airfields, barracks, and fuel dumps in the Volcano and Bonin Islands. These included strikes against the heavily defended and infamous islands of Iwo Jima, Chichi Jima, and Haha Jima on June 24, 1944. Matz was there as well. "We were the first squadron over Iwo Jima."

He remembered with frustration watching from altitude as a number of Zeros took off from one of the airfields while his division leader failed to engage them while they were still slow and vulnerable. "We could have strafed them head-on as they were taking off," he remembered. "I have no idea why we didn't. Instead we chased a vector that they were calling over Futami Cove. By that time the Zeros, who climbed faster than we did, were up at 30,000 feet. At the same time we were getting kind of strung out in a big turn. Then, down came about a half-dozen of them firing at us. We pushed over after them, and my flight leader claimed a probable. He never even came within a mile of them. Those were the sorts of things I got irked about."

For much of the rest of his second combat tour Matz bombed and strafed Japanese positions throughout the Marianas, Volcano, and Bonin islands. During this time he also took part in strikes against shipping and earned a second Distinguished Flying Cross—he received his first for his actions at the Marianas Turkey Shoot.

He remembered the fierce Japanese antiaircraft defenses on the small volcanic island of Chichi Jima; part of the Bonin Island group. The date was July 4, 1944: "Our target was the docks and the cargo ships that were tied up alongside. Up at the higher altitudes we could see the antiaircraft fire as it burst around us. But as we dived through about 4,000 feet, I could see the tracers coming from their guns. It looked just like a damned water hose—it was so constant and intense.

"My division leader, William Mosely, took a direct hit. His aircraft caught fire and was smoking badly but he managed to make a dead-stick landing in the water. I circled his aircraft but he never got out. I stayed out so long that they thought I was missing as well. Later I learned that he couldn't swim. That was my second of three missions that day. I ended up with 10.7 hours of flight time on that particular Fourth of July."

However, Japanese aircraft in that area during that time were few and Matz never had another opportunity to score an aerial victory. "It's just one of those things; it's time and place and a lot of luck too."

When the *Yorktown* finally pulled into Pearl Harbor again later in July, the Top Hatters of VF-1 teetered on exhaustion. They were no longer the robust, fresh group of flyers they had been just more than a month earlier. During that period the squadron lost 11 of 32 pilots—more than a third of their original number. "When we got back to Pearl Harbor," Matz said, "they decided that we had lost too many and they sent us back to the States."

After returning to the States, Matz married Maxine Wilson, his hometown sweetheart of six years. He then transitioned to the F4U Corsair. He was with VBF-100 in Hawaii training pilots for action in the Pacific when the war ended. Following the war he did aircraft test work, pioneered the introduction of Navy drones, and helped introduce the AIM-7 Sparrow radar-guided missile to the fleet. He retired in 1960 to Poway, California, where he prospered in the lumber and concrete business.

Walter Kaestner (standing, far left) and crew of the B-24 *Tough Titti*. Kaestner's navigator, John Crawford (standing, second from right), was particularly talented with a sextant. This was especially important over the poorly-charted Chinese geography. Ch'engkung, China, 1944. —*Walter Kaestner Collection*

CHAPTER 9

AMERICANS OVER CHINA

Of all the theaters of war, the Allied nations gave the China-Burma-India Theater, or CBI, the lowest priority. Daunting and immense in terms of its size and population, the region swallowed entire armies. Neither the United States nor Great Britain possessed the means or the will to commit vast quantities of men and equipment at the expense of their forces fighting in Europe or the Pacific. Likewise, the Soviet Union was too hard pressed on its own territory.

Politically, too, China was an incredible morass of competing egos, interests, and ideologies, difficult to describe, or even understand. Notwithstanding the tough and formidable Japanese military, this tangled political skein, combined with the sheer size and difficulty of the Chinese geography, made the command and control of military forces in the region an extremely formidable proposition.

Still though, the Allies recognized the importance of keeping China in the Allied sphere of influence. The fight in China required the Japanese to commit over a million troops—more than were deployed throughout the entire Pacific. Comparatively, the American and British reciprocal commitment of ground troops was small. To the Chinese was given the responsibility of providing the huge numbers of troops required for the war on the ground. The Americans chose to wage their fight in China from the sky. From there the United States could influence the war with an effect disproportionately larger than its investment in men and resources.

Walt Kaestner

THE SON OF GERMAN IMMIGRANTS, KAESTNER WAS BORN IN
Bloomington, Illinois, on July 5, 1918. Coming of age during the Great
Depression, Kaestner was fortunate to find work with his father who, as a
skilled carpenter, specialized in converting large estate houses into apart-
ments. "I got out of high school in 1936 and went to work for my dad
pushing around a wheelbarrow, and removing walls and that sort of thing.
I worked six days a week and made two bits [twenty-five cents] an hour,
which worked out to twelve bucks a week. Later, I worked as a superin-
tendent in charge of maintaining 119 apartment units. That was a chore.
In the winter the big coal furnaces had to be tended by hand—I got my
fill of that real quick."

Like many young men at the time, Kaestner knew that a better education was important to a successful career. He was particularly interested
in engine technology and engineering. So, between working plumbing
problems and feeding the big, coal-eating furnace-beasts of the apartment
buildings, Kaestner took correspondence courses, primarily in math.

As the 1930s gave way to the 1940s, world events compelled much of
the nation into the realization that war against the Axis was inevitable. To
meet the threat posed by Hitler and the increasingly brazen Empire of
Japan, America began to mobilize. Selective Service—the Draft—was in-
stituted and significant portions of the nation's manufacturing capacity
was modified to produce defense material. The military services, pitifully
small and grossly ill-equipped when compared to the armies across the
oceans, readied to train the eventual millions of men who would be mus-
tered into service.

It was not a smooth transition. Kaestner remembered, "I enlisted on
February 17, 1941, to become an aircraft mechanic. When I first showed
up, I was given an old World War I uniform—there weren't enough new
ones being produced yet. After basic training they sent me to Chanute
Field in Illinois but there were a lot of classes in front of me, so I had to
wait." While he waited for training as an aircraft mechanic, the Army
needed his help in the kitchen. Kaestner's career was detoured for a time
while he was trained in meal preparation. "They were feeding thousands
of men three meals a day, so I ended up as a butcher for a while."

America had the men to fight the war but it took time for the nation's leadership to figure out what to do with them all. Kaestner's case was representative: "I finally took a course in aircraft welding and they assigned me to a mobile aircraft repair unit. They kept us in a 4H Club barracks at the state fairgrounds in Springfield, Illinois. It was designed for kids. We had to pretty much get down on our knees in front of a line of tiny little sinks and mirrors just to shave."

Eventually, Kaestner was assigned to the first cadre of soldiers to open Keesler Field, in Biloxi, Mississippi. He took part in platting the base; "They'd drive a stake, or make an 'X' on the ground and send someone out about three hundred feet with another stake, and say 'Okay, this will be A Street,' and we'd move over about 75 feet or so, and do the same thing for B Street." Through a fluke in circumstances, in the confusion of the quickly emerging military airfield, Kaestner, the would-be aircraft mechanic, cum butcher and welder, was made a lifeguard. "We put over a thousand people through beginning swimming and lifesaving classes, but I was tired and bored. I wasn't getting anywhere and was still just a private, doing nothing, really."

At some point, during all the shifting about and menial job assignments, and the heightened frenzy of activity that followed the nation's entry into the war, Kaestner took the qualification test for flight training. During June 1942, just as his mobile aircraft repair unit was being embarked for service overseas, orders came that directed him to report to Montgomery, Alabama, for duty as an aviation cadet.

During 1942 the training and rigors associated with the aviation cadet program included not only extensive academic, military, and flying instruction, but also a great deal of hazing. At the time, it was believed that the stress caused by harassment helped prepare the prospective flyers for the vicissitudes of actual combat, and additionally helped to weed out those cadets of weaker character. "They made it pretty tough on a person," Kaestner recalled. Later in the war hazing was scaled back significantly. It was found that the harassment sometimes got out of hand, and that at best, its affect on training was neutral. Often it was counterproductive.

Aviation Cadets during World War II didn't stay in one place very long. "After ground school at Montgomery," Kaestner remembered, "I flew PT-19s in primary training at Jackson, Tennessee, then BT-13s in basic training at Walnut Ridge, Arkansas, and then AT-10s and AT-9s in advanced training at Stuttgart, Arkansas. They decided I wasn't cut out to fly fighters so they sent me to Smyrna, Tennessee, to fly B-24s."

After receiving about 120 hours of training on the big four-engine bombers at Smyrna, Kaestner was sent to Salt Lake City. There, pilots, copilots, gunners, bombardiers, radiomen, and navigators were all brought together to form crews for follow-on training. "My first copilot was a rounder. He showed up late, or drunk, or hung over, or not at all. A lot of times we missed training because of him. We finally got rid of him and the training went pretty well from that point."

Follow-on training at Casper, Wyoming, from November 1943 to February 1944, included navigation, night and day bombing, formation flying, air-to-ground and aerial gunnery. "For aerial gunnery we fired special frangible bullets at specially modified P-63s that were armor protected and wired so that lights on their propeller spinner illuminated when we hit them. We called them pinball machines because of that. On one sortie we somehow got a bullet up through the exhaust and into the engine and actually shot it down!"

Kaestner and his crew departed the States for the CBI on February 17, 1944, three years to the day after he enlisted. "We left from Topeka, Kansas. We were supposed to get immunizations and pick up new gear and an airplane but they didn't have enough airplanes, so we just got our shots and shipped out as replacements."

Upon arriving in India, Kaestner and his crew were transported to the American air base at Chabua, a terminus for the aerial resupply flights over the Himalayas—the Hump—into and out of China. From Chabua, on April 16, 1944, Kaestner was flown into Kunming where he was attached to the 375th squadron of the 308th Heavy Bomb Group of the Fourteenth Air Force. The Fourteenth was headed by Major General Claire Chennault of Flying Tiger fame.

It was the only USAAF air force sustained by airlift. After being moved from halfway around the globe, the men and material the Fourteenth needed to operate had to be flown over the Himalayans from India into China. The route was known as the Hump; it was a formidable barrier with peaks reaching to more than 15,000 feet. The route was also known as the Aluminum Trail because of the enormous number of wrecked airplanes that marked it. They were victims of the often abominable weather, and of the altitude and rugged terrain; there were few airstrips along the route for aircraft in extremis. It was exceedingly dangerous for novice pilots, which the majority of the USAAF's airmen were.

The route was organized and put into service by the United States Air Transport command after the Japanese captured the Burma Road during 1942. During July of that same year, the first month of operations, 82 tons of supplies were airlifted into China. By the time Kaestner arrived in theater nearly two years later, the effort had increased by orders of magnitude. More than 18,000 tons were airlifted during July 1944 alone. Nevertheless, it was still a difficult and dangerous mission.

And inefficient. Kaestner, like most of his squadron mates, pulled double-duty flying the B-24 in combat as well as on missions back and forth across the Hump ferrying supplies, fuel, men, and equipment. "We had to fly two Hump missions to ferry enough fuel and bombs to fly a single combat mission," Kaestner recounted. "We didn't have special tanker airplanes. We took off from China with about 1,000 gallons of fuel and burned most of that getting to India. Then we loaded almost 4,000 gallons of fuel and used 1,000 gallons to fly back to China. After offloading about 2,000 gallons, we'd go back to India and do it again." In effect, it cost 2,000 gallons of fuel to get 2,000 gallons from India into China. And this cost did not include the wear and tear on airframes and aircrew. Nor did it account for the losses of men and equipment. It was a very expensive way to run an air war.

And difficult. Because every drop of fuel, every bomb, and every spare part was precious, and because America's focus of effort was elsewhere, the Fourteenth Air Force did not have the men or aircraft to mount the huge raids that were typical of the air war in Europe. An attack on a target with more than twenty bombers was a big effort. Maintenance was difficult. The overworked crews were short of supplies and the B-24s, difficult to maintain in the best of conditions, often experienced failures. "Our ground crews were real experts, and did a fine job with what they had," Kaestner recalled. "They used their imagination and resourcefulness to do what was necessary to make an aircraft fly. In fact, they often used an aircraft graveyard to find the parts they needed."

A mission that highlighted these maintenance difficulties is recounted in Kaestner's diary entry for May 1, 1944. It was Kaestner's third combat mission—a nine-hour nighttime sortie: "May 1st, 1944: Left Chengkung at 1830 hours for Hainan Island . . . Target was three ships anchored outside of the inner bay . . . could not locate ships because of clouds . . . Dropped six 500-pound bombs on an airfield from 800 feet . . . Encountered machine gun fire and heavy flak . . . On way home lost number-two engine, number-three engine prop governor, flaps, radios, and compass . . . Was plenty scared . . . Lost superchargers and had electrical fire in bombbay . . . Reached home but couldn't find field below clouds . . . Luckily missed mountains in let down and landed at 0330. Said my prayers."

The B-24 was used in China rather than the B-17 because it had much greater range. The targets struck by the Fourteenth Air Force ranged from French Indo-China in the far south, to well out into the South China Sea and the island of Formosa, and far into north central China. The B-17 could not have reached all these targets.

A 1,500-mile mission Kaestner flew on May 5, 1944—only a few weeks after his arrival—illustrates the long reach of the B-24. "Many times we staged out of other bases so that we could reach farther out," he remembered. "For this mission we flew east to Liuchow and loaded the aircraft with 3,500 gallons of fuel and twenty 100-pound demolition bombs. It was to be a night mission. After takeoff we headed south over the Gulf of Tonkin and then over French Indochina, then back out over the water again near Saigon. From there we turned inland up the river into the city. We were the third ship over the target which was already burning brightly. Ack-ack, searchlights, pompoms, and machine gun fire came up at us— the fireworks were beautiful and there was plenty of it.

"We were at 5,000 feet and the light from the burning warehouses and the searchlights, and all of the antiaircraft fire was so bright that we could have read a newspaper by it. We took hits which put holes in our bomb bay doors and tail. After dropping our bombs we turned for home and landed five hours later. It turned out that only three of the seven ships that initially took off made it to the target. The rest turned back because of weather. Two ships from another squadron that hit the same target an hour later were lost. On that mission we were over Japanese-held territory for more than nine hours of the eleven-hour mission."

Japanese ground fire was not the only threat the Americans faced over China. Fighters—both day and night types—were a real danger. Kaestner recalled a mission to Yochow on July 25, 1944. "Our aircraft for this mission was *Tough Titti*. We were carrying twelve 250-pound demolition bombs. After takeoff we joined formation, and after clearing some weather we proceeded to Chichyang where we circled once at 19,500 feet and picked up eight P-40 fighter escorts before continuing.

"After finding Yochow we dropped our bombs—we hit railroads, barracks, warehouses, and factories. Yochow was one of the main Japanese logistics depots. Over the target light ack-ack bursts detonated close under us. But it was the heavy three-inch guns that had our range. One shell burst under us and lifted the tail about five feet. Then several others burst around us and soon they really cut loose. The sky was full of black patches of flak, but we still flew through it.

"As soon as the flak stopped," Kaestner remembered, "we got hit by forty or fifty fighters. We tightened the formation and the gunners started firing almost continuously." It was then that an enemy fighter somehow inserted itself into the middle of Kaestner's formation of seven B-24s.

"I don't know how that Japanese fighter got into our formation," Kaestner said. "There were seven of us, and he was right in the middle. The fronts of his wings were lit up with muzzle flashes, and he was really giving it to the lead bomber. I was flying formation but I could still see him—and that big red meatball insignia on his airplane. The pilot was wearing one of those little helmets with the fur around it. All I could think to do was shout, 'Don't shoot, you'll hit the other bombers!'"

Fearful of shooting each other, the gunners held their fire while the enemy aircraft attacked the lead bomber. Finally the Japanese fighter pulled up to leave the formation. "At least six gunners opened fire on him," Kaestner recounted. "We watched him go down in flames. At the same time we saw a P-40 go down smoking and crash into a lake. It turned out to be our only loss."

Soon after, Kaestner's own ship came under attack from a white-painted enemy fighter that was hit and knocked down by the waist and tail gunners. "All this time the P-40s were dogfighting—airplanes were all over the sky. It was just like what you see in the movies. They really did a swell job protecting us. Following the mission we heard Radio Tokyo report that thirty bombers and ten P-40s were shot down."

Early B-29 raids were flown from China during mid-1944, and Kaestner recalled that they were not popular at his base. "They landed once or twice at our base and took all the gas we had. They were huge. And of course because they were bombing Japan, they had first priority on everything."

Operating in poor conditions from primitive airfields with runways of hand-crushed stone, accidents were common. Kaestner recalled that July 18, 1944 was an especially poor day for safety. "I saw a B-24 land with the right landing gear unlocked. No one was hurt. Five minutes later I saw two P-51s crash into a ditch at the end of the runway on takeoff. No one was hurt. Ten minutes after that I saw a P-40 go wild on takeoff and run off the runway. Again no one was hurt. It must have been a lucky day."

Not always was everyone so fortunate. Kaestner recalled watching a fighter pilot showing off around the airfield. "I saw a P-40 pilot buzz the barracks and then the runway. He touched his prop on the runway and scraped his belly tank. He climbed up as high as he could until the propeller fell off, and then he ended up crash landing and tipping over. Four enlisted men raced out and reached the plane first. While three of them held up the wing, the other went into the burning plane and dragged him out. The crash broke both of his legs, one arm, and smashed his face, while the whole upper part of his body was burned black. He only lived six or eight hours."

And again, three weeks later, from Kaestner's diary: "Saw a P-40 pilot split-S out of a practice flight and dive into the ground at a very fast speed. He dove straight into the ground. The plane was almost buried. The engine was twelve feet under."

Nor were the bombers immune from accidents. Kaestner's diary described a mission which met with disaster before the last aircraft even became airborne: "We were to takeoff [sic] with twelve 250-pound bombs and 2,750 gallons of gas to bomb Pluchi Airdrome near Yochow. Three ships from the 374th squadron took off to the south at 2300. The third got off the ground okay, but for some unknown reason didn't climb quickly enough and hit the ground about a thousand feet from the end of the runway and exploded. No one got out. They reversed traffic and two of our ships got off okay. We saw the sixth bomber takeoff, but they didn't climb like they should have and they crashed and exploded. We were to be the seventh to take off. When we got into position Major Edney called us from the tower and told us to taxi back in. That made us rather happy after seeing what had happened to the two other aircraft just before us."

After climbing out of their bomber, Kaestner and his crew rushed into the night toward the towering blaze that marked the spot their squadron mates had crashed. "The Doc—Albert Mattson—was working on the four fellows pulled out of the crash and those that were thrown clear. They found the pilot on fire and dragged him out, but he was dead. All of this time bullets were exploding, as was the fuel. And of course everyone was worried about the bombs. The ground men that went into that wreck deserved the biggest honor there was for risking themselves. They saved three lives that night by going into the fire."

Accidents aside, the B-24s of the 308th Bomb Group were in China to carry the war to the Japanese, and they did so nearly daily. A mission that Kaestner remembered clearly took place on September 8, 1944. It was a daytime mission with Kaestner in the lead of a flight of three B-24s. The target was the Doc Tho railroad bridge near the town of Vinh in present day Vietnam. "We flew about ten miles out to sea and followed the coast until we came to our turn-in point. At this time the flight split up to attack individual targets. I turned inland until we picked up the railroad then followed it at a thousand feet until we got to the bridge. With the bridge in sight we dropped down to fifty feet and released our bombs. We were carrying five 1,000 pound bombs with delayed fuses. We stayed down low until we heard the bombs explode and felt the concussion." So low over the target, the aircraft was particularly vulnerable and sustained numerous hits from small arms and antiaircraft fire.

With the bridge destroyed, Kaestner climbed up to 3,000 feet and took pictures of it before heading home. The target area was a shambles—boats were capsized all up and down the river, with some having been blown a couple of hundred feet onto the shore. Still, the mission wasn't over. "On the way home we saw two trains and went down to strafe them. We blew one of the engines up and set an oil car on fire.

"On the way back after buzzing the trains, we passed over three airstrips and saw two fighters take off from one, and three from another. They climbed above us while we waited for them to attack, but they never did. They just followed us for about a half an hour before they turned back," Kaestner recalled. "In the meantime we lost two of our generators and were quickly losing gas from one of our tanks."

The crew salvaged what gas they could by transferring it to another tank. In the meantime, to make matters worse, the weather deteriorated badly. "When we finally got back to the field it was raining very hard. We made an instrument penetration and broke out at 400 feet. When we touched down we had a flat tire and the brakes were no good—we had to hold the aircraft straight with the throttles."

After climbing out of their airplane, Kaestner and his crew counted more than twenty bullet holes and one hit from a 37mm antiaircraft gun. The single hit from the antiaircraft gun had knocked out a generator junction box, perforated a fuel tank, and blown a tire.

Many of Kaestner's missions were marked by the same sort of action. On his very next sortie on September 17, 1944, his aircraft caught fire on takeoff when a fuel tank cap came off and spewed flaming gasoline back over the top of the wing. "We all expected the plane to explode any second. We made a close approach, landed and stopped very quickly. Three of my crew were out on the wing and had the fire out before the rest of us could even get out of the plane," Kaestner recounted. Wasting no time, they calculated that there was still enough fuel remaining to complete the mission. Within fifteen minutes Kaestner's crew installed a new fuel cap and got airborne again. After joining the formation they attacked the target at Changsha where they were hit by antiaircraft fire. On the way home, now in total darkness, they lost their number three engine and three hundred gallons of fuel. Thanks to an outstanding performance by his navigator, and his own fine flying through difficult icing conditions, Kaestner and his crew, separated from the rest of the formation, brought their crippled bird home twenty minutes before the rest of the bombers.

Kaestner recalled an unusual event that marked how desperate the Japanese were to hit the USAAF in China. "We were watching the base movie and it was just about dark when they announced that there was an air raid. Everyone rushed out of the theater to find a trench to hide in. And then, we saw an old transport coming over the airfield. In the door of this thing were two Japanese guys and they were dumping out boxes of little bombs. The bombs weighed just a few pounds apiece and had square fins and a little propeller to drive the fuze. The body was like a 37mm shell.

"They flew down the middle of the runway and dropped these things which made holes that could be easily filled in with a shovel. But they didn't all explode and some of the enlisted men collected them for souvenirs. A lot of them subsequently blew up and the men lost hands and fingers and eyes and such."

Difficulty in navigating, and the rudimentary weather reporting system, were hazards that continually plagued the American crews over China. "Our biggest problem was navigation," Kaestner said. "Miles between places didn't mean anything. You would cross rivers and look at the maps and things weren't where they were supposed to be. The maps were very poor. On night missions celestial navigation was very important. I was fortunate that I had a very good navigator in Harold Crawford. Many of our missions were flown at night and he was an expert with a sextant."

Kaestner's diary recounted the fate of a crew that fell victim to poor navigation: "August 11—John Apsega went as copilot with Bachelor to hit Changsha. On the way back they got lost. They flew around and got more lost. Called for bearings but was given reciprocal which took them farther away from home. Over Yunnanyi got more bearings and got further lost. Finally saw small village and circled and bailed out at 2340 because they were out of gas. John slept all night where he was and the next morning walked into the village. There he offered the Chinese 1,000 Chinese dollars for every American brought in. Before the day was up, all nine men were brought in. The ship which was lost was named *Innocence Abroad*."

Like airmen in all the other theaters, the men of the 308th Bomb Group named their aircraft and decorated them with colorful and sometimes garish artwork. Some of the names themselves were colorful: *Tough Titti*, *The Bitch's Sister*, and *Willie Maker*. Kaestner remembered aircraft assignments. "My assigned aircraft for a while was *Tough Titti*. And after that it was *Georgia Peach*. What that really meant was that it was our turn to take care of the airplane. We were responsible for cleaning the glass turrets, and sweeping out and cleaning the aircraft. Mostly though, we all pretty much flew everyone else's aircraft. Depending on the schedule we were assigned whatever airplane was in good shape and ready to fly. Also, we always had one crewman sleep in the airplane to keep an eye on the two Chinese guards posted at each airplane."

During the summer of 1944 the Axis armies were reeling from the Allied onslaught on almost every front. In Europe, the Nazis were being squeezed from the west, the east, and the south, while in the Pacific the Japanese were rapidly falling back before the combined advances of the American Navy, Marines, and Army.

However, the situation in China was vastly different. With an army that approached a million men, the Japanese launched an offensive during April 1944, codenamed Ichi-Go, that gobbled territory until the spring of 1945. One of the primary objectives of the push was to capture the airbases from which the Fourteenth Air Force was launching its devastating raids against Japanese shipping. In this, they were somewhat successful. In fact, during the whole of Kaestner's tour, the Allied forces in China were actually on the defensive.

Kaestner's diary cryptically recalled a mission to the airbase at Nanning. Used by Fourteenth Air Force fighters, the P-51s at the base had run out of fuel defending the city, and B-24s from the 375th Squadron were sent to deliver badly needed aviation gasoline and supplies to the beleaguered defenders: "November 17th—Flew *Georgia Peach* to Nanning with 3,700 gallons of gas. Gas fumes very bad after takeoff. Landed at Nanning's short grass strip. Unloaded gas directly from bomb-bays into wings of P-51s and spent an hour talking to P-51 fighter pilots. Ate dinner there. Japanese eight miles away. Took off with bomb bay loaded with 39 people and let Crawford fly the plane back. Weather good. Had pictures taken by newsreel cameramen. They said pictures would be shown back in the states as Evacuation of Nanning. Nanning was taken by the Japanese forty-eight hours later."

Kaestner remembered that "the Japanese were advancing all the time. They ran us out of base after base. The Chinese were just poor soldiers. They were poorly equipped and trained and had no sense of anything mechanical. . . ."

Still though, in large part thanks to the American air presence, the Japanese were slowed, stopped, and eventually turned back. That such a huge enemy force was so decidedly influenced by such a small number of men and aircraft over such an immense geographical area is remarkable. That success is directly attributable to the training, skill, and ingenuity of airmen like Kaestner and the ground support personnel who persevered despite harsh and primitive conditions. He recalled: "The Fourteenth Air Force had the best record in terms of the most damage done per aircraft, and the most shipping tonnage sunk. And we had to do it all by ourselves. Everything we used had to be flown in. There were no seaports, the Japanese had them all. And the Burma Road was closed, the Japanese had it too. We flew everything in over the Hump."

Kaestner left for the States in December 1944 after flying nearly sixty missions in only seven months. "They were ready to make me a captain if I wanted to stay a couple of more months, but I wasn't too sure I wanted to make the military a career. By that time I had about had my fill."

After the war, Walter Kaestner worked for the U.S. Post Office for a short time and also started a small construction concern. In 1955 after going to work for the Civil Aviation Authority—later to become the Federal Aviation Administration—Kaestner was appointed head of recruiting and training for air traffic controllers in Indianapolis, Indiana. In this position he made invaluable contributions to the profession until his retirement in 1977.

Kaestner's personal wartime decorations include the Distinguished Flying Cross and multiple Air Medals.

Jack Dentz (center) celebrating with two fellow pilots at Fritzlar, Germany. The date is May 9, 1945, the day after Germany's surrender. —*Howard Dentz Collection*

CHAPTER 10

CRUSHING THE REICH

When twenty-two-year-old Howard Dentz began flying combat out of England during April 1944, the United States was only just reaching its stride in terms of its output of aircraft and the men trained to fly and maintain them. During 1943 alone, the Army Air Forces trained and graduated more than 60,000 new pilots and received more than 85,000 new aircraft. Dentz, class of 43-G, was one of the new pilots

Germany's situation was quickly becoming desperate. It was under attack from all sides, and from two other major combatants—Great Britain and the Soviet Union. And it managed to produce only 25,000 aircraft and many fewer pilots during the same period. The eventual outcome of the war could not be in doubt.

Howard "Jack" Dentz

HOWARD DENTZ WAS BORN ON MARCH 11, 1922, IN NORTH Plainfield, New Jersey, and was fascinated by aviation from a very early age. "I know this seems unbelievable," he said. "People say you can't have recollections from so early in life, but I remember my parents visiting an airport, and an old Standard biplane blew dirt in my face when I was nine months old. I remember the noise of the engine, the wind, and the stinging in my face and such. Anyway, I grew up building model airplanes and hanging around the local airport, Hadley Field, and the Naval Air Station at Lakehurst where the great airships used to operate. We had to be forcibly restrained from going down there on our bikes on the day that the *Hindenburg* burned.

"I went to Bound Brook High School, an excellent school," Dentz recalled. "While I was there I started their first aviation club. We were fascinated with aeronautic design and tried our ideas out with airplane contests—building and flying experimental model planes. Interestingly enough, a lot of the kids who were members of that group ended up flying during World War II.

"While I was in high school I planned to be an aeronautical engineer, so I took a lot of math and engineering courses to prepare me for college. But it turned out that I couldn't afford to go to college so I got a job working for Gibbs and Cox in New York City; they were one of the foremost naval architecture concerns in the world at that time. So I kind of got sidetracked. I was eighteen or nineteen years old and worked as a draftsman in the hull design department. Within a year I was promoted to designing and installing ventilation systems on naval vessels. It was pretty advanced stuff for a nineteen-year-old kid."

America's entry into the war soon switched Dentz back onto the aviation track. "Right after Pearl Harbor the Navy still wanted two years of college for entry into flight training, but the Army dropped its requirement," he remembered. "I took a two-day entrance exam, kind of like a Scholastic Aptitude Test, with a portion that also covered motor coordination. At the time they qualified and selected you for service as a fighter pilot, a bomber pilot, or a transport pilot. It was a way of sorting us all out. If you qualified for all three then you got your choice. I did, and chose fighters."

Dentz signed up for duty with the Army Air Forces during March 1942. Nevertheless, the training infrastructure was still so overwhelmed that it wasn't until more than six months later, during October 1942, that he reported to Maxwell Field in Alabama for primary training. "At Maxwell," he recalled, "they had an impressive program based on the type of training given at West Point, except that it was concentrated into about two months. We got a heavy dose of close-order drill infantry training, too. We had to crawl through the mud with live ammunition being shot over us; training with rifles, pistols, machine guns, grenades, and that sort of thing.

"From Maxwell we shipped to Dorr Field in Arcadia, Florida. It was one of the many civilian schools under contract to the Army. Embry Riddle operated it under Army supervision. We did our first flying there in the Boeing PT-17 Kaydet. By that time the Army had more flying cadets than they could handle and was washing them out wholesale and sending them off to bomber command to train as gunners. All you had to do was scratch a wingtip and you were gone. Fail a check ride and you were automatically out—we lost half of our class to washouts. Then," he recalled, smiling, "what was left of the class came down with measles and that stopped us flat. But we finally got flying again on an accelerated basis and finished on schedule.

"From Arcadia I went to basic training at Bainbridge, Georgia, where I flew the BT-13, 'Vultee Vibrator.' After that, I went on to advanced training at Marianna, Florida, where I flew AT-6s and graduated in June 1943 with the Class of 43G."

The Army had narrowed its fighter inventory to a handful of types by the summer of 1943. The Bell P-39 Airacobra had not fared well in combat and the Army was distancing itself from that type and its improved but look-alike sibling, the P-63 Kingcobra. Likewise, the P-40, an early stalwart of the war, was being replaced by newer types. Production of the P-38 Lightning, which had proven to be an effective combat aircraft, was being stepped up to its maximum but it still was not available in the numbers required. The P-51 Mustang, which had showed promise early, had been mated with the Rolls-Royce Merlin engine which ultimately made it a world-beater. Nevertheless, that combination was new, and it was nearly half a year before production models saw combat.

The Republic P-47 Thunderbolt was the one fighter type which the Army could buy in quantity, and which had the attributes to not only survive but to win against the best that Japan and Germany could field. The largest, heaviest, most powerful single-engine fighter of the war, the Thunderbolt was rugged, fast, heavily armed, and had respectable range. The first prototype took to the air in May 1941 and the type entered production soon after. It first saw combat in Europe during March 1943. By war's end it had served in combat with more than 40 different fighter groups. No other American fighter was produced in such quantities; ultimately 15,660 examples were built before production was halted.

But it looked ungainly and much too big and heavy for a fighter. "I went to Richmond Army Air Base in Virginia to fly P-47s," Dentz remembered. "A lot of us there were disappointed. I know I was. I was young and inexperienced and wanted to fly the P-38—I thought that the Lightning was the plane to fly. If I couldn't fly that, I wanted to fly the P-51. But here I was, getting ready to fly the P-47. And the reason that I didn't want to fly it was that there was a story around that it would kill you in a dive. Like a lot of us new pilots I was scared to death of it."

Dentz's fears were not wholly unfounded. Like any new aircraft, the P-47 experienced its share of teething problems and a few were lost in highly publicized terminal dive accidents. It was a huge machine. Compared to the P-51D's fully loaded weight of 11,600 pounds, the P-47D grossed the scales at nearly 18,000 pounds. The Thunderbolt's huge R-2800, 18-cylinder, radial engine generated more than 2,500 horsepower—nearly double that of the Mustang's much smaller inline engine.

The P-47's combination of power, weight, and size made it prone to a problem that was just starting to manifest itself in the higher performance fighters of the day. Those fighters were starting to venture into uncharted aerodynamic territory. In a dive, the aircraft could quickly accelerate to velocities approaching the speed of sound. At that point the airframe experienced a phenomenon known as compressibility. In effect, a compressed shock wave of air rendered the aircraft's flight controls immovable and hence the aircraft became uncontrollable. Occasionally, unable to recover their aircraft from high-speed dives, Thunderbolt pilots hurtled to their deaths straight into the ground.

"Some of us, and I'm one of them, thought that a few of the guys had gone through the sound barrier," Dentz said. His contention is refuted by experts who claim that the aircraft of the time were inherently incapable of reaching such velocities. Still, the anecdotal evidence was compelling to Dentz. "There was a friend of mine, Scotty Glasgow," he remembered. "He was over the Blue Ridge mountains in a deliberate full-throttle terminal velocity dive from 40,000 feet. Evidently when he started to recover he got straight and level at about 2,500 feet and had started up but he was between two mountains and ran into a rock quarry. Eyewitnesses said that they heard a distinct explosion before they saw the airplane, then they saw the airplane pulling out and pulling huge streamers from wingroot to wingtip, and then saw it fly into the rock quarry. They saw the flash and then they heard a second explosion. Naturally we thought he had broken the sound barrier. Most engineers said it was impossible."

After completing his indoctrination training in the Thunderbolt, Dentz was kept on as a fighter instructor. It was during this stint, in January 1944, that he also very nearly lost his life in the big fighter. "I was flying an older aircraft, not knowing that it had been belly landed three different times. It was bent up, but had been patched and cleared for flight. Once I was airborne I had to crank all my trim tabs up against the stops just to get it to fly reasonably straight and level. I was still too inexperienced to know why all that trim was needed. Anyway, another fellow and I started dogfighting at 14,000 feet and I got on his tail right away.

"Where the airplane should have stalled at about 90 miles an hour, instead it stalled at a much higher airspeed and at 9,000 feet I tumbled into an inverted spin. It should have come right out but it didn't and I had to jump at 2,000 feet. I was going so fast, about 350 miles per hour, that three panels were ripped out of the parachute and the right riser was shredded. Later, two engineering officers came from Wright Field in Ohio and wanted to know exactly how the hell I had gotten out. They told me that no one had ever bailed out of a P-47 while in an inverted spin. I told them that it was real easy—that I just slid back the canopy with one hand, released my seat belt with the other, put my heels on the seat and jumped straight up and out! My guardian angel was with me that day."

Finally, during March 1944, Dentz was en route to England. "We went over on a banana boat, the SS *Brazil*. It had been converted to a troop ship. During peacetime it carried bananas and coffee and about fifty first-class passengers in staterooms. Well, they put five hundred pilots in the tiny staterooms on Navy pipe-racks, and seven thousand Negro troops from the Transportation Corps' Red Ball Express down below. Those poor troops were all sick and vomiting. We had the worst storm the ship's crew said they'd experienced in forty or fifty years. The waves broke over the ship. Knowing what little I did about naval architecture, I feared we would founder. But somehow we didn't. One nice thing was that the storm kept the German submarines away!"

After the crossing, Dentz disembarked in the Firth of Clyde, Scotland, and was sent by train to the airfield at Shrewsbury in England, near Wales. There he was put through a short refresher course and introduced to some of the tactics used over the Continent. That the United States could afford to do this rather than to send new pilots straight into combat was an indi-cator of how the air war was going.

Following refresher training, Dentz was assigned to the 386th Fighter Squadron of the 365th Fighter Group of the Ninth Air Force. The 365th had been flying combat only since February and Dentz was among the first replacement pilots. "The squadron was flying out of a place called Beaulieu, south of London, near Christchurch and the Isle of Wight—an easy landmark to come home to when the weather was nice," he recalled. "The Americans had rebuilt it. It had concrete runways but the quarters were Nissen huts with cots. For mattresses we had three British biscuit cushions stuffed with straw. It was awful, but much better than what we had later.

"Once again I was disappointed," Dentz recalled. "Not about the air-plane though. I had actually come to master and love it. But there were rumors that our mission was going to be changed from strategic escort of the bombers to the tactical role—ground attack. I figured that I'd see few German planes, and was never going to get to be an ace. I just knew that I was going to get my ass shot off by flak gunners while I was carrying bombs close to the ground."

Although the rumors eventually proved to be true, Dentz, along with the rest of the 365th, continued to fly bomber escort missions in support of the strategic air war against Germany's industrial strongholds. "I started flying combat missions during early April 1944. These were escort missions which we flew at anywhere from 25,000 to 40,000 feet in altitude while we S-turned over the bombers to keep enemy fighters away. Our range was determined by our fuel capacity. We'd burn anywhere from 110 to 120 gal-lons an hour in cruise, and up to 300 gallons an hour in War Emergency Power. In a pinch we could slow down and burn only 80 gallons an hour. We carried 306 gallons internally and then we could carry fuel externally in wing or belly tanks. The best arrangement," Dentz recalled, "was a single belly tank. It didn't have much drag and you could actually dogfight with it although you weren't supposed to."

Dentz's experiences on the bomber escort missions were opposite of what he expected. "The Luftwaffe generally stayed away from the bombers we escorted. At times, one P-47 group would escort them to the target area, another would protect them over the target area, and a third group would escort them home—all P-47s. The Germans stayed away from us; I think they respected the P-47. Also, they were not around in the numbers that they had been because a lot of them had been sent east to the Russian front. On thirty-four escort missions I never personally got engaged with German fighters. Rather, all of my fights with German aircraft came later after we switched over to the tactical air support role."

In preparation for the upcoming invasion of the Continent, the crews of the 365th were given a quick primer in ground attack tactics and techniques. "During training in the States we were forbidden to buzz and fly close to the ground. Now, all of a sudden, our mission was to fly at tree-top level and to strafe and bomb." Dentz recalled the preparations: "We were given about two weeks of training. We were taught how to skip bomb and dive bomb vertically, and at a 45 degree angle. We only had our gun-sight to aim with, so it was a lot like learning to pitch a baseball. But still, we were far more accurate than the twin-engine and heavy bombers. In the end, two weeks really wasn't enough time to figure out anything. But if nothing else, we learned to pull out of our dives early enough to avoid the fragmentation from our own bombs."

So then, for about a month prior to the invasion until the war ended, the 365th Fighter Group was thrown into the meat grinder that was ground attack. Unlike the pilots of the Eighth Air Force who could generally rotate back to the States after reaching various combat hour milestones, the pilots of the Ninth Air Force had no established rotation. Often they flew in excess of one hundred missions, or until they were shot down and captured, or killed.

Nevertheless, the P-47 was an excellent aircraft for this type of work, and with a little experience the pilots excelled at their new mission. "We had all sorts of armament," Dentz recalled. "We flew with bombs, rockets, and napalm. And of course we had our eight .50-caliber machine guns. We carried two or three 200-hundred gallon tanks of napalm. It was terrible but effective for knocking out columns of armor, particularly entrenched tanks. And actually, we could kill an Mk IV tank with our machine guns alone. We could fire and knock the bogey wheels off and de-track them. Or we could fire from behind and ricochet bullets up into the engine and spill fuel all over. Or we could knock them out with rockets.

"Or bombs," he remembered. "The 500-pound bombs with a delayed fuse were the weapons of choice. We'd fly real close and stick it into their sides. We could fly with three 500-hundred pound bombs. Or our maximum load was three 1,000 pound bombs, but we'd have to pull the tail fin off of the bomb on the belly so that it would clear the ground when we taxied."

In keeping with their new role, the squadrons of the Ninth Air Force moved from England to the Continent following the D-Day invasion so that they were close to the front lines where they could best ply their trade. "We were sort of a flying circus," Dentz recalled. "Through the whole war we flew out of eleven different air bases, and if the front moved twenty miles, then we moved. Three weeks after the invasion we were operating out of Advanced Landing Ground A-7 at Fontenay-sur-Mer which was next to little towns in Normandy called Azeville, and Sainte-Mère-Église. The engineers bulldozed out hedgerows to make a 6,000-foot strip, put a crown on it, and put down wire mesh. Then they staked it into the ground. It was terrible. The stakes came up and punctured our tires, or the wire piled up in front of our wheels and got tangled in our props and turned us over. It was a bunch of shit. That didn't last long. They started using steel mat material which was okay."

Dentz used the term "flying artillery" when he described how the P-47s were used to support the American ground troops. He described with horror the missions he flew in August 1944 during the destruction of the German forces trapped in the Falaise pocket. "It had been a very rainy season that turned dry. The Germans used a lot of horses to move their guns and supplies through the mud, which was terrible stuff. Otherwise their armor got stuck in it. So we had to go in and kill the horses and troops. They were in there so thick that they just couldn't hide. I guess we killed nearly everything. We went in like flying artillery and just destroyed it all. It was hideous. It was the only time I actually came home feeling sick. I killed over sixty horses on just one mission; they had been pulling 88mm guns."

The 365th Fighter Group was flying a mix of different models of the P-47D. Early on, the pilots were flying the Razorback version, so called because of its flush canopy and the upper fuselage which rose to a sharp hump or spine. The disadvantage of the design was the blind area behind the aircraft caused by the combination of the upper fuselage and flush canopy. Later versions of the P-47D remedied this shortcoming with a bubble canopy and reduced upper fuselage. This design afforded excellent visibility to the rear and no doubt saved many lives.

Another improvement that was arguably even more important was the replacement of the thin "needle-blade" Curtiss-built propeller with the Hamilton Standard "paddle-blade" propeller. While both designs had four blades, the paddle-blade propeller greatly enhanced the aircraft's climb rate and maneuverability. With it, the P-47 was able to turn with the German fighters on more equal terms.

All through August 1944, Dentz's squadron flew attack missions in support of the Allied drive out of northwest France. During the last week of the month, the Allied armies were poised to liberate Paris. "On August 25, we were scheduled to fly air support for the French Army," Dentz recalled, "but the missions were scrubbed because no one could find the French. They were scheduled to roll into Paris, but had stopped instead to party with liberated French villagers.

"The mission was changed and our group was ordered to strafe Chateaubernard, the airport at Cognac in southwest France. The Germans were using the airfield to relocate their troops and it was reported to be jammed with enemy transports." Missions against enemy airdromes were particularly dangerous as they were defended fiercely with all manner of antiaircraft guns. These ranged in size from the vaunted 88mm antiaircraft cannon, all the way down to light-caliber machine guns. Because the airfields were so heavily defended, and because the attacking aircraft made easy targets as they sped across the flat terrain, the loss rate on these missions was often quite high.

"Our ground crew rushed about to remove the three 500-pound bombs that were loaded on each aircraft. At the same time they scrambled for the glass tubing and rubber hoses they needed for the external fuel tanks. Each aircraft had nearly five hundred rounds of ammunition for each one of its eight guns. The ammunition was loaded so that two rounds of armor piercing bullets were followed by two rounds of ball, which were followed by one tracer round. The last two seconds of ammunition was all tracer to let you know you were about done.

"My flight leader, Captain George Porter, was leading the mission. I was his element leader. He was a West Pointer and always flew by the book.

And he always had his canopy open for takeoff. Well, his charts went flying out of the cockpit on this mission and he lost them. But he had the course and timing inked on his hand so he just headed out. At any rate, it was a beautifully clear day—it seemed we could see for a hundred miles.

"Now I had been flying escort and close air support missions for about five months and still had not seen an enemy aircraft close enough to tangle with. This time we were guessing that there would be heavy fighter cover over the airfield. I hoped so. I wanted to shoot down a couple of them. On a scale of one to ten, I guess I was about a twelve where self-confidence was concerned.

"About an hour after the takeoff, I looked ahead and down, and spotted the airport. Sure enough, it was crawling with enemy transports. They were all over the airfield. There were dozens of them on the runways and taxiways with their engines running. And there were more along the revetments where they were loading troops, and in the hangars.

"I got really excited. I looked up and checked all around. There wasn't a single enemy fighter anywhere in sight. We had caught them flat-footed! It was too tempting to wait for methodical 'by the book' George. I had to go! I could see a Ju-52, a three-motor transport turning onto the runway. I figured if I dove straight down I could hit him as he broke ground. That would make it an aerial victory!

"I racked my airplane over hard and flew directly over the end of the runway. From 16,000 feet I did a quick split-S and ended up aligned vertically with my gunsight bead and reticule right in the center of the Ju-52. I trimmed in a little down elevator and my Jug accelerated then settled down beautifully; it was a very steady gun platform. When I passed through 11,000 feet, I fired a short burst for effect and then had to wait several long seconds for the bullets to reach the ground.

"Our guns were mounted four in each wing. I had mine aligned to converge at 300 yards. When the bullets finally hit, they kicked up dirt on each side of the runway—perfectly bracketing the transport. All this time the transport was getting larger and larger in my gunsight. I fed in right rudder and a little bit of left aileron, estimating how much I needed so that my four left wing guns would hit the fuselage center. I fired a long burst then watched as the bullets hit all around the cabin, cockpit, and fuel tanks. The plane stopped rolling and burst instantly into flames.

"The Ju-52 was getting awfully big in my windscreen. I pulled hard on the stick and reached down with my left hand to roll in half of a turn of up elevator trim to help me recover from the dive. I was now dangerously close to the ground. The aircraft responded beautifully. Pulling about six Gs, I tensed my legs and diaphragm. My vision grayed out a little as I leveled out at 200 feet. I was set up perfectly for a strafing run across the field ahead of the flak.

"There in front of me was another Ju-52, all three engines running, sitting in front of a large metal hangar with planes inside. I could see crewmen scattering for shelter. I pushed the nose down a few degrees and fired again from about 500 yards. This time the transport blew up right in front of me. I could feel its blast as I cleared the explosion and flew over the hangar roof. I was amazed when I glanced down at my airspeed indicator—it showed me flying at more than 600 miles per hour! Looking back over my shoulder, I could see Porter and the rest stringing down, picking targets out all over the airfield.

"Well, all the way back to base I feared repercussions since I had broken formation to make the attack. I was still a second lieutenant and I should have waited for George to go. But I needn't have worried. George Porter was a fine gentleman, a great officer, and a terrific pilot. Not only did he never mention my impatience, but when he was promoted up to group headquarters he assigned me as leader of A Flight and promoted me to first lieutenant. I returned the favor by never mentioning how he came to lose his charts on takeoff.

"Interestingly, George's P-47 was hit by an 88 round on that mission. It hit right behind the cockpit, just a few inches from his head. Fortunately the shell didn't explode, but the hole in his razorback was very impressive."

The P-47s were quite often sent on armed reconnaissance missions without any ordnance other than their .50-caliber machine guns. On these missions they were free to engage any targets, air or ground, they encountered. It was while on one of these sorties that Dentz scored his first aerial victory. "We were patrolling around Aachen on September 18, 1944, when fighters were reported in the area; the visibility was poor with scattered cloud decks." Dentz was flying high cover for his flight leader but lost sight of him as he and his wingman passed under a bank of clouds. He dove down when frantic shouts came over the radio calling for someone to "break," or maneuver aggressively. "When I came down below the clouds I spotted my flight leader and his wingman in a shallow left turn. Behind the wingman—obviously unseen—was an FW-190. The German fired and hit the wingman right in his cockpit." The P-47 went down with its pilot dead at the controls.

The FW-190 pilot dove away as soon as he saw Dentz. "I pulled into a hard left turn and brought my nose in front of him until I had enough lead. I fired a short burst at 300 yards and hit him right in the cockpit. The pilot slumped over and I followed the aircraft down until it hit the ground and exploded."

Similarly, Dentz's second victory came on December 8, 1944, while on another armed-reconnaissance mission. "We got calls that there were fighters in the area but we couldn't see them. And then I looked over my shoulder and saw four Me-109s lined up perfectly behind us. I'd never even considered it before, but for some reason I just yanked the throttle back. The propeller blades went into fine pitch and the aircraft lost a bunch of speed while I was thrown up against my harness.

"All four of those 109s ended up right in front of me and rolled over into a dive. I shot the tail off of the lead aircraft and watched the pilot bail out. As I banked around, my number three man chased after the other three but they got away in the clouds. In the meantime I wanted to make sure that I got credit for the aircraft I shot down. I turned off my guns and flew right at the German pilot in his parachute and photographed him with my gun camera. I'm sure I scared the shit out of him!"

But not all of the pilots of the 365th were so chivalrous. "We were on a strafing mission when we spotted a lone Me-109. I could tell it was an older model because it still had braces under the horizontal stabilizers. The flight leader—a West Point graduate—led us down after it. The German pilot saw all of us coming and just bailed out. When he finally got on the ground our flight leader strafed and killed him. It made me sick. I never forgave him for that. It really went against what most of us believed in terms of acting honorably and such."

By the fall of 1944, the Germans were fielding advanced weapons, and the 365th Fighter Group was among the first to encounter them. Dentz recollected an encounter that occurred just after the unit hit railroad targets near Jülich. "I saw a smoke trail going straight up but had no idea what it was. I kept scanning the sky until I saw a small dot that quickly grew larger as it came down at us. It occurred to me that it was one of the rocket-propelled Me-163s—we had been briefed about them earlier."

Anxious to increase his speed, Dentz pushed his throttle forward and went into a dive while he watched the tiny little aircraft approach. "I turned into him and we passed each other head on. I went over the top of him about the same time he hit his rocket and climbed again. It was kind of crazy because I knew I was never going to hit him and I'm sure he knew he couldn't shoot me down. He just kept climbing away while I pulled up to watch him until I finally couldn't see him anymore.

"I had a similar experience with Me-262s," Dentz recalled. "They made a pass at us, but didn't fire and dove away. We had water injection which gave us almost 2500 horsepower, and we could go like a scalded cat. But they just sort of sniffed at us and decided to leave before we caught them short of fuel."

Dentz was quick to refute anyone who questioned the ability of the P-47 as a dogfighter. "Its greatest advantage was its ability to accelerate in a dive and to outturn any fighter at speed. It could outturn anything, friend or foe at high-speed, and with the paddle-bladed prop could otherwise slow-speed climb and turn with anything the Germans had except the jets and rockets. The Germans had a tactic where they would dive, make one firing pass and then keep diving away. They had gotten away with that for years. Well, with the P-47 we could dive faster and catch them. They began to lose a lot of pilots—and they couldn't replace them."

Dentz's contention is borne out by the records. To the P-47 goes the credit of breaking the Luftwaffe's back in Europe. It destroyed more German aircraft than any other American fighter. The later-arriving and highly regarded P-51 helped administer the coup de grace. And whereas other aircraft sometimes came apart under the rigors of combat, the Thunderbolt was arguably the sturdiest fighter ever built. "A P-51 lost his wing right in front of me," Dentz recalled. "We were both chasing the same Me-109. The 109 pulled it in real tight and when the P-51 tried to follow it, his wing flew off and he fireballed." Dentz fired and knocked pieces from the enemy fighter before it disappeared in a bank of nearby clouds.

"Our engineers estimated that one of our pilots pulled more than eleven Gs. And with no G-suit. He was horribly messed up and lost a piece of his colon. About four inches of it—it just turned inside out. He bled terribly but fortunately didn't faint and was able to get it back on the ground. He had had a 190 on his tail and needed a high-G turn to shake it."

Still though, the aircraft was not invulnerable and many were lost to enemy action. Dentz himself was very nearly downed by antiaircraft fire. "I caught a burst right in front of the airplane and it killed the engine. We were at about 20,000 feet over Cologne and I was leading my squadron that day. I started gliding but didn't have enough altitude to reach our own lines. I was over the heavy fighting that was taking place on the Cologne plain—I was scared shitless. Hitler had ordered that any pilots shot down were supposed to be killed immediately by German civilians. And they had started to do this.

"Finally, after gliding on a dead engine for nearly five minutes, I resigned myself to bailing out over the battlefield between Koln and Aachen, still over enemy held territory. But luck was with me. As I began to roll over to bail out, the engine caught and started up again." It was a very relieved Howard Dentz who returned to base that day.

Ground attack operations for the 365th Fighter Group reached a fever pitch during the Battle of the Bulge in late December, 1944. "As soon as the fog lifted after the first few days our squadron found one of their armored columns and napalmed them. From then on, every twenty minutes, we sent out a flight of four aircraft with bombs or napalm, to strafe other columns until we killed all we could find. Sometimes I don't think that enough credit is given to what the Ninth Air Force did to stop them."

Dentz did his share on December 18, 1944, while leading a four-ship of P-47s to Stavelot, Belgium, where the German Army was threatening to break through the American lines. Each aircraft carried three 500-pound bombs. "There were a number of fires from previous 365th attacks and the heat dissipated the fog so that there was some visibility. I found a ten-mile long column of tanks, armored vehicles, heavy guns and troops. I called for my flight to spread out in trail and aligned myself with the road and dove from two thousand feet on the lead tank in the column."

Dentz's bomb found its mark and the German tank exploded. He climbed, flew to the rear of the column and bombed the rearmost tank; the column was effectively trapped on the road. "I then called in my wingman, who attacked the center of the column, his bombs striking tanks and armored vehicles squarely. Then my element leader [number three aircraft of the flight] and his wingman attacked and soon the entire column was ablaze. After we expended our bombs we made repeated passes at high speed, strafing the remaining vehicles and along the wooded, pine tree-covered areas."

Ammunition spent, Dentz gathered his flight above the thick undercast and headed to the 365th's base at Chièvres. "I was very familiar with the field at Chièvres and its orientation to Mons, which was a city on a hill, its spires sticking up out of the fog cover. I called the field for a landing flare to mark the end of the runway and led the flight through the thick fog down to the runway. All of my planes landed safely and each of us had to be led off the runway to our revetments, as the fog was too thick to taxi alone. We had been airborne for two hours and nineteen minutes, and claimed forty tanks and armored vehicles destroyed and eighty damaged."

Dentz also remembered something from that period that isn't well known or even corroborated. "The Germans were flying some P-47s that had bellied in and that they managed to rebuild. These P-47s had black German crosses on the top of the wings and American markings on the bottom. They used them to strafe our troops which caused a lot of bad blood. Our troops thought we were doing it to them. They caused so much trouble that Eisenhower sent some of his staff out to make peace and he even visited some of the bases personally, including ours, to smooth things over. Finally one of the renegade P-47s got shot down with a German pilot in full uniform. The *Stars and Stripes* carried the story and from then on feelings improved between the G.I.s and us."

Dentz's last aerial victory came on December 31, 1944. "I was flying a razorback with a damned needle-nosed prop and my wingman was flying a paddle-blade prop with a bubble canopy. We were just stooging around near Trier, Germany, looking for trouble at about 16,000 feet. Then here came what must have been a brand new group of about fifty FW-190s. They flew in perfect formation about 6,000 feet over the top of us. I was scared. I had this needle-blade prop and couldn't climb or turn very well.

"The leader detached and started a maneuver I haven't seen before or since. It was sort of a powered tail slide, perfectly controlled. I was in a kind of a medium-bank turn to see what the heck he was going to do. Then I realized that he was going to try and come down right in the middle of our turn and pop his throttle and try to shoot us both down—me and my wingman.

"But he made a mistake," Dentz recounted. "He got into a position where I was able to rack it in, pull my nose up, and fire. I hit him right in the cockpit. He spun over the top and then went down and crashed and burned. The rest of the FW-190s just flew off."

As the tide of the Battle of the Bulge was reversed, and the Allies once again seized the initiative, the Luftwaffe launched an operation that proved to be a last-gasp effort. Believing that they could gain a valuable respite for their beleaguered armies by striking a decisive blow against Allied air bases, German Air Force commanders marshaled scarce aircraft, fuel, and armament for Operation *Bodenplatte* (Baseplate).

Launched early on January 1, 1945, hundreds of German aircraft struck Allied airfields throughout Europe with some success. Several hundred American and British fighters were destroyed or damaged, most on the ground. But those successes came at a dear cost. Nearly three hundred German aircraft were lost to various causes, and over two hundred German airmen, by this time irreplaceable, were lost. And while the Allies replaced their losses within a week or two, the Luftwaffe never recovered.

Dentz remembered that morning well. "We were in bed when the Germans came over and instantly recognized the sound of those big, wide propellers on their Me-109s. We all jumped out of bed and grabbed whatever weapons we had. Some guys had their side arms and a lot of us had souvenirs we had picked up or gotten by trade. Anyway, we all ran out into the snow in our underwear and started shooting at those guys as they tore up our airfield. It was quite a scene."

The German unit that hit the 365th was JG 53, which had earlier been based at Metz. More than three dozen P-47s were destroyed, including Dentz's aircraft. "Victor Morales was one of my crew chiefs," he recalled. "He was out working on my airplane when the Germans shot it up. It was full of gas and loaded with bombs and Morales still stayed with it and tried to beat the flames out with his hat. It didn't work out too well and he got burned a little bit but ended up okay."

The attack on Metz cost the Germans eight aircraft. Only one of the pilots, *Oberfeldwebel* Stefan Kohl, survived. "He was the stereotypical German fighter pilot," Dentz recalled. "He had a fur-lined uniform with beautiful boots and carried himself like he owned the place. His English was perfect. After they brought him over to our headquarters he pointed to our flight line, which was nothing more than dozens of smoking wrecks. He said, 'Say, what do you think about that?'

"Later," Dentz continued, "after all our aircraft were replaced we took him out to see them. We asked him what he thought about all those shiny new P-47s. He said, 'That is why you are beating us—you have so many aircraft and pilots and unlimited gasoline and supplies. If we shoot an aircraft down you can easily replace both the plane and the pilot.'"

———————

Within two weeks of Bodenplatte *all of the 365th Fighter Group's losses had been replaced. Dentz continued to fly combat missions until February 1945. During that month, as one of the few pilots in his squadron qualified to fill a task from higher headquarters, he lost a draw for a burned match, was promoted to captain, and attached to the First and Third U.S. Armies' 99th and 76th infantry divisions as a forward air controller. With these units he crossed the Rhine on the captured bridge at Remagen, swept through Germany, and with Patton's Third Army in late April, met the Russians at the Elbe. He finished the war with ninety-two combat missions, three confirmed aerial victories, a probable, two destroyed on the ground, the Distinguished Flying Cross, and the Air Medal with eighteen Oak Leaf Clusters. He survived five major campaigns.*

Following the war, Dentz had a full and varied career. Besides retiring with twenty years in the Air Force Reserve, he owned and operated a flying school and charter business in Nyack, New York; received a college degree from Rutgers University where he later developed and managed their first television commercial and educational programming; worked as an engineer for Republic Aviation; and traveled internationally as the chief of public relations for Hughes Ground Systems, California. He finally retired in 1986 after government posts including Assistant Commissioner of the Food and Drug Administration, an appointment he received during the Nixon Administration.

Willard Caddell relaxes beneath the wing of an F-5B—the photo reconnaissance variant of the P-38. —*Willard Caddell Collection*

CHAPTER 11
PHOTO RECONNAISSANCE

"A picture is worth a thousand words." It is perhaps worth more in wartime. Indeed, it might be argued that a picture is worth a thousand lives. It is doubtful that any nation relied more on aerial reconnaissance during the war than did the United States. And it is inarguable that this same reconnaissance was a significant contributor to the success of American forces in every theater of operations. The bravery and skill of the uniquely trained airmen who flew these machines, often unarmed and frequently under fire, was remarkable. They ranged over enemy territory and brought back the information so vital to the ground commanders.

Willard Caddell

WILLARD CADDELL WAS BORN IN CLEBURNE, TEXAS, ON DECEMber 29, 1923. "My dad worked for the Santa Fe Railroad," he recalled. "He died in 1939 and didn't have a thing in the world to leave us. He didn't leave us a lot of debt, but he didn't leave us anything to live on either.

"I walked the streets in town and went into every store, one after the other, looking for a job. Finally, a local department store hired me. For five dollars a week I worked before and after school and all day Saturday. I paid a nickel for Social Security, and kept a dollar for that week's lunch at school, and gave the rest to my mother."

After graduating high school in 1941, Caddell enrolled in a machinist's course at a local college. Recognizing the huge demand for skilled labor that the mobilization of a wartime industry would create, the government subsidized, and often paid outright, to train unskilled workers. Caddell finished the course but was unable to find a job in a defense plant because he was still only seventeen. Unable to find work that matched his newly acquired vocational training, his aspirations turned more and more toward flying. He had loved the idea since childhood.

"I dreamed airplanes every day and night since I was a kid, and I kept bugging my mother to let me join the Air Corps." During the spring of 1942 Caddell finally persuaded his mother to sign papers that permitted him to enter the Army as an aviation cadet. He breezed through the testing process; only two of the fifty local high school students who took the college equivalency exams passed them. Caddell was one of the two but at only 130 pounds he was too slender to pass the physical. A determined young man, and a fine eater, he took only a week to consume the seemingly numberless chocolate milks, bananas, and other goodies needed to gain the nine pounds required to meet muster.

"When they finally called me to get sworn in, I was higher than a kite with excitement. I went to Dallas, ready to start my military service. When I got there they herded us all into a room and swore us in. Then they told us to go home and wait until we were called up. I couldn't believe it. I thought we were going to start right then and I didn't have a way to get back home. I had no money—not even enough for a sandwich."

Dejected and tired, Caddell lugged his suitcase onto the highway and tried to hitch a ride home. "We didn't have any telephones back then," he recalled. Eventually he made his way twelve miles to Grand Prairie where he found family friends who arranged to get him home.

"I finally got called up in November 1942. I started out at Santa Ana airbase near Los Angeles. I was there for three months and that was the longest I was at any base during the entire war. I had 36 changes of station in 33 months!" Except for some early problems with airsickness, Caddell completed flight training with no serious problems. He graduated and received a commission at Williams Field, in Chandler, Arizona, during August 1943 as part of class 43H. Anxious to fly fighters, Caddell was excited when he received orders for P-38 training. Then, following indoctrination training in some of the early-model P-38s, he was posted to the 337th Fighter Interceptor Squadron at Payne Field, in Washington.

"While I was there, orders came down from the Third Air Force asking for forty volunteers who had at least forty hours in the P-38. Well, as it turned out, the first forty names on the alphabetically arranged roster ended up as 'volunteers.' My name, Caddell, guaranteed that I was on that list."

He and the others were sent to Oklahoma City, to train as photo reconnaissance pilots. Intelligence was an important part of any military operation and aerial photography was one of the primary sources. American forces were especially keen on gathering as much photo intelligence as was practicable prior to beginning any offensive. Accordingly, a great deal of emphasis was placed on developing the right mix of equipment and appropriately trained personnel.

The aircraft type to which Caddell was assigned was a modified version of the P-38—the F-5. "We joked about it," Caddell said. "Leave it to the Army to give its fighters designations that began with 'P', and its photo aircraft designations that began with 'F'."

The F-5 differed very little from the P-38. The most important distinction was that the F-5 was unarmed. Camera arrangements varied and could be specially tailored in the field but it was typical to have two K-17 cameras with six-inch focal length lenses mounted obliquely, and two more with fourteen-inch focal length lenses mounted vertically. Most of the cameras were installed in the nose so that there was no room for the normal complement of machine guns and cannon. There was also a feeling, perhaps justified, that the pilots would be more attuned to completing their missions and less apt to hunt up mischief if they had no guns.

Caddell boarded a ship at Newport News, Virginia for the port city of Oran, Algiers, during March 1944. "We went over on a fast troop transport and were unescorted. The ship had three five-inch guns. Their way of thinking was that if a submarine surfaced, he'd be outgunned, and if he didn't surface he'd be 'outrunned.'" The ship arrived unmolested in North Africa after a transit of nine days.

After spending two weeks in an open bivouac area at Oran doing mostly nothing, Caddell was loaded with others on a train bound for Tunisia. "We rode on an old French train. We spent three nights and two days in old forty-and-eight boxcars; they were built to carry forty men or eight horses and were rickety old things with a single set of wheels at each end and no springs. They almost beat us to death and we were crammed in so tight that there wasn't even room to lie down unless we flopped down on top of each other. And it got so cold at night."

Exhausted, Caddell eventually reached Tunisia, and from there was taken by C-47 to San Severo, Italy, where he was posted to the 3rd Photo Reconnaissance Group of the Twelfth Air Force. Of the two American Air Forces operating out of Italy, the Fifteenth operated heavy bombers in support of the strategic campaign. The Twelfth was tasked with providing tactical air support to the ground units mired in the gruesome wallow that was the Italian campaign.

Eager to exploit the German defeat in North Africa in May 1943, and hoping to bring about an early Italian capitulation, the Allies had hastily cobbled together an invasion of Sicily and the Italian peninsula; Sicily was secured by August 1943, and Italy was invaded a month later.

Nevertheless, the relatively quick success on Sicily was not repeated in Italy. Very rugged terrain ideal for defensive warfare was only one factor that worked against the Allied forces. The Germans were well led by Field Marshall Albert Kesselring, and despite overwhelming American and British air superiority, they built successive lines of fortifications from which they doggedly contested the Allied push up the peninsula. Also, the weather—often rainy and cold—made much of the terrain impassable for the Allies whose highly mechanized forces were dependent on trafficable topography. Finally, the Allied goals and objectives, as well as the leadership, were often confused and at odds with each other. This was somewhat understandable when it is realized that their forces were composed of fighting units from more than twenty different nations. Ultimately, what had been hoped to be a swift and conclusive campaign developed to be an exhaustive meat grinder. The Allies were forced to fight for every inch of terrain.

Caddell didn't know or care about much of this, but the difficulty and confusion seemed to work its way down to the lowest levels. Originally posted to the 12th Photo Reconnaissance Squadron, Caddell had been in theater only a short time when he was transferred to the 5th Combat Mapping Squadron. "I didn't realize until long after the war that I was in a different squadron than the one I thought I had been! That seems absolutely ridiculous, but we were simply intent on fighting the war and surviving. We had no careers in mind—just survival."

Caddell's confusion was no doubt due in part to the type of flying he did. Service in a photo reconnaissance squadron was different than flying in a fighter outfit. Because they generally flew alone—single aircraft missions—there wasn't the same demand for teamwork and close coordination that there was in the fighter squadrons. "Half the time," Caddell said, "and I mean fully half the time, I didn't even know who the squadron commanding officer was! I'd go get a brief, fly my mission alone and then land and go back to my hut."

Caddell remembered that being so close to the front lines, his unit was never visited by the USO or Red Cross, or other similar organizations. "The enlisted men got a ration of beer occasionally, and instead of bingeing on it, they stashed it until they were ready to drink it. There were no refrigerators, so they resorted to ingenious means to get it cold. Many times I came back from a mission to find a G.I. opening the small tail compartment where he had stowed a can of beer to cool it. Also, they learned that when the photo lab dissolved a batch of chemicals, the fluid became very cold and was perfect for cooling beer. They also put the beer in a bucket of 100-octane gasoline and blew a strong stream of compressed air over it. The evaporation cooled the beer very quickly."

When Caddell started flying out of Pomigliano, near Naples, south of the Anzio beachhead during April 1944, the Allies were preparing their fourth and final attempt to breach the famed Gustav Line near Cassino. After just one orientation flight, Caddell was put to work. "The missions I flew were high altitude sorties," he remembered. "Most of our targets were individual point targets rather than area mapping missions." His targets included troop concentrations, logistics lines, enemy fortifications, airfields, and rail routes.

"On my second mission," Caddell remembered, "I was tasked with mapping an area south of Rome. After the first track I turned around and got set up straight and level for the next one. I looked in the rearview mirror and saw—BOOM! BOOM! BOOM!—flak bursts right where I had finished my first track. Well, I lost interest in that area pretty quickly!

"My typical technique was to approach the target and turn in several different directions as I came in. Even though the Germans had excellent antiaircraft fire, they couldn't hit you if you changed direction or altitude often enough. The only way they could hit you was with a barrage. Normally they wouldn't waste that much ammunition just to hit a single aircraft.

"Then," he continued, "when the feeling hit me, I flopped out straight and level and started taking pictures." Although the pilot could take photographs manually, an intervalometer was generally used. It triggered the camera shutter automatically and ensured overlap between frames. This overlap provided the stereoptic effect desired for imagery interpretation. "We also provided imagery for bombing missions," Caddell recalled. "The coverage from our cameras gave three-dimensional imagery so that the bombardiers could practice their runs from the initial point to the target with the exact view they would have when they flew the real mission."

There were many dangers. "When we flew in support of the Anzio beachhead we landed with our film right there at Anzio, which was constantly under fire from the German artillery. They rushed us to safety in the town while they unloaded our cameras—the film went to the commanders right there in the field. Then, when the airplane was ready to go, they brought us back and we took off and went back to Pomigliano."

Poor maintenance of the aircraft was another danger. Hardships in procuring parts and in maintaining the engines in a field environment were constant. "The aircraft weren't very well maintained," Caddell said. "It's a wonder to me that the crew chiefs did as good a job as they did when you consider their training and the conditions. I was a dumb twenty-year-old kid at the time and didn't know enough to appreciate it." He remembered the V-1710 Allison in-line engine. "When it worked, it was a smooth, beautiful engine. But I didn't trust it. I never ran those engines at full power. When they went bad, they went bad all at once."

He recalled what happened when one of his tent mates lost an engine. "I was standing about two hundred yards from the approach end of the runway and he was coming in on one engine—I didn't know who it was at the time. He would have been in good shape but he thought that he was going to undershoot and he put power on the good engine and didn't put in any correction. The asymmetric power pulled him over in a roll and he went in about 45 degrees nose low right at the end of the runway.

"I took off running," Caddell continued. "His head wasn't showing because he'd been jammed down into the cockpit. Right away the flames started licking up. By the time I got over there it was on fire. He burned up in there. I feel sure that if the plane hadn't caught fire he would have survived because he didn't hit the ground that hard." Caddell recalled that by the time the flames were put out, the charred body had been burned back upright in the seat.

Caddell's Distinguished Flying Cross citation cited his bravery in pressing on with a crucial mission despite mechanical difficulties with his engines. It was on June 2, 1944, while covering numerous targets on the Bologna-Prato rail line that he experienced problems with his left engine. "It was crucial for us to stay exactly level when we were on our target runs. Anyway it wasn't very easy with the P-38 on just one engine, but I guess I was able to get them the photographs they needed."

Although the Allies enjoyed air superiority over the Italian peninsula, the unarmed F-5s of Caddell's squadron were occasionally harassed by German fighters. He recalled a close brush he had with an FW-190: "Before making a turn, I always dipped my wing and checked behind me. Well, I made a turn and looked out and there was an airplane. It was too far away for me to see what it was at the time, but it was alone and about two to three thousand feet below me—I was at about 30,000 feet or so."

After realizing that the other aircraft was a German FW-190, Caddell started a shallow climb and tried to get further above the climbing enemy fighter. "We were headed east and he was south of me and home was south. So, we were going to have to cross paths sooner or later. I kept edging closer to him—I didn't want him to have enough room to set up for a firing pass on me. Finally, he turned in and I turned in and we were set up for a head on pass. At least I was going to get it over with in a hurry, and I was pointed toward home! I lowered my nose and he rolled over on his back. It was a favorite tactic of theirs—they would fire, then split-S and then climb back up for another run.

"Well, I reached over and toggled my drop tanks off. That messed up his firing run and he pulled off to one side. By that time I was headed for home at high speed while he struggled to recover from a bad firing pass.

"I was in the process of congratulating myself when both of my engines quit simultaneously. I had forgotten that the engines were drawing fuel from the tanks I had just jettisoned! I dived for the tank selectors and changed them to 'Main Tank.' The engines, supplied with fuel again, and at full throttle with the props at low pitch, oversped so high and gave me such a boost in the tail that I actually sat there and laughed!"

With both engines on line and his aircraft screaming down at top speed from high altitude, Caddell outran the German aircraft and made it safely home.

———

Caddell's logbook shows that from April to November of 1944, he flew 57 combat missions while operating out of seven different air bases in Italy in support of the Allied push up the peninsula. The log does not include a period during which his squadron was deployed to Corsica in support of the American landings in southern France. That the imagery his unit provided was invaluable is indicated by its receipt of the Presidential Unit Commendation. His personal decorations included the Distinguished Flying Cross as well as multiple Air Medals.

Willard Caddell left the service at war's end and earned an engineering degree at Texas A&M. He worked as an aeronautical engineer for Chance Vought Aircraft and General Dynamics for 35 years.

CHAPTER **12**

ATTACK AND MEDIUM BOMBERS
OVER NORTHERN EUROPE

The Ninth Air Force, assigned the tactical role of supporting troops on the ground, was not equipped with the huge numbers of heavy bombers that the Eighth Air Force used to smash Germany's industrial complexes. Instead, fighters and medium bombers were better suited to its mission. The A-20, the A-26, and in larger numbers, the B-26, served with distinction over the battlefields of Western Europe.

Harry "Bob" Popeney

HARRY V. "BOB" POPENEY WAS BORN IN DETROIT, MICHIGAN ON JUNE 16, 1920. His father was an early pioneer of the automobile industry, having started with the Ford Company in 1905. Nevertheless, he disliked Mr. Ford and in 1911 he went to work for Dodge Brothers Motor Cars, eventually advancing to become that company's Secretary and Treasurer. "Later, my father became interested in aviation," Popeney recalled. "He invested in an airline that flew from Detroit to Cleveland. They had one Loening amphibian, and one Sikorsky amphibian.

"These airplanes had room for about four passengers inside and one pilot outside in an open cockpit. The terminal was only about a mile from where I lived, and when I was a kid I used to ride my bicycle down to the Detroit River by the Belle Isle Bridge and wait for the planes to come in from Cleveland. I was able to get rides in it because my dad was a stockholder.

"So that's how I got interested in aviation," Popeney said. "But I had my first airplane ride while we were on vacation in Pennsylvania in 1926.

There, a World War I pilot had an old Curtiss Jenny. He had enlarged the front cockpit so that two people could fit in it. And he put it on pontoons so that it was a seaplane. That ride was a real thrill for me," he remembered. "The next week though, the pilot crashed and killed everyone on board."

Notwithstanding his knowledge of that accident, Popeney's interest in aviation stayed with him. "When I was a junior at the University of Detroit, I went through the Civilian Pilot Training Program and got my license—#114536. Following that, I tried to sign up to fly with the Navy. I wanted to be a Navy pilot—ice cream, steaks, two clean sheets, coffee in the wardroom—that sort of thing.

"But they wouldn't have me. I was plagued with poor eyesight. So I tried the Army Air Corps. They turned me down as well." By this time, 1941, Popeney had moved to California and was working as a clerk for North American Aviation at the company's plant in Inglewood. "At that time the plant was producing B-25s and AT-6s. Also, the new Mustang was just starting to come off of the line. Later on in my career," he remembered, "I flew all of them.

"During this time I met an eye doctor at a cocktail party; Doctor K. D. Lacy changed my life. He worked with me three or four nights a week in his Beverly Hills office for a couple of hours at a time. Just with me. Well, it turned out that he had his work cut out for him. I was farsighted, 20/40 in one eye and 20/50 in the other. I had poor depth perception as well. Not only that, but I was partially colorblind."

Undaunted, kindly Doctor Lacy worked with Popeney for six months. Finally, after a great many eye exercises and some creative studying—chart memorizing—Popeney passed the Army's flight physical in September 1942. "I can still remember a line from one of those damned eye charts: T-P-E-O-L-F-D-Z!"

Backlogged under a crush of new pilots, the Army didn't start Popeney in flight training until February 1943. Except for earning more than his share of disciplinary demerits, Popeney's training was routine until midway through the basic flight training phase. "At Marana, Arizona, I got my nose broken in a water polo game. They took me to the hospital and the doctor sat me down in a kitchen chair and put a tray on my lap and started cutting cartilage out of my nose—no anesthetic, no nothing! Well, there was blood, and bits of bones and cartilage and flesh dropping into a tray. Hell, I fainted four times. By the time he finished, my uniform was soaking wet and my brown shoes were black because I had perspired so much."

While he recovered in the hospital, Popeney was volunteered by his instructor to take part in a new training syllabus that emphasized multi-engine instruction. "He said he did it because he knew how much I wanted to fly P-38s," Popeney recalled. "Well, I ended up in La Junta, Colorado, in advanced training flying B-25s. Just before graduation we were informed that we would be assigned to B-25s, B-26s, A-20s, or C-47s but not P-38s."

It was while stationed at La Junta that Popeney, not wanting his aerobatic skills to atrophy, and never one to believe that regulations applied in every instance—particularly to him—found himself in trouble. "I was flying with another aviation cadet over the Royal Gorge. This was an enormous chasm bisected by a suspension bridge. Well, I wanted to loop-the-loop around this bridge. This other cadet called me a son-of-a-bitch, and said that he was going to turn me in if I did. Well, I did and he did too!"

As he had done more than a few times before, Popeney worked off the disciplinary punishment and pressed on. Wintertime at La Junta was hard on flying. The weather was quite often poor and consequently whenever the weather was good the cadets transitioned to a twenty-four hour flying schedule. This was stressful and led to accidents. "After a sortie," Popeney remembered, "if there was enough fuel, we left the engines running and two new cadets got in while the other two got out. One night we had three cadets killed in two different incidents when they walked into whirling propellers. A couple of nights later two B-25s collided in mid-air and killed everyone on board. Anyway, we got a hell of a lot of night time."

Out of flight training, Popeney asked for and received orders to fly the A-20 Havoc. The Havoc, built by Douglas Aircraft as a private venture, was designed as a twin-engine, low-level, light attack bomber, and served in a number of different variants. Initial interest was shown by the French, who in 1938 placed an order for 105 early versions of the aircraft, designated DB-7s. Following the fall of France, deliveries followed to England, and large orders were placed by the Army. Ultimately, the A-20 became one of the most widely used attack bombers in the USAAF; 7,385 examples were produced.

Smaller than its cousins, the B-25 and the B-26, the A-20 was also faster. With a top speed of nearly 340 miles per hour, it was nearly as fast as any fighter in service during 1940. Also, unlike the two medium bombers, the Havoc was flown by a single pilot rather than a pilot and copilot. It was powered by the Wright R-2600 series of radial engines, each of 1,650 horsepower.

In most instances the pilot flew with two gunners. Heavily armed, the "G" model, which Popeney flew, carried four fixed .50-caliber machine guns in the nose and two fixed .50-caliber machine guns in the lower fuselage. These were fired forward by the pilot. Additionally, there was a dorsal turret with two .50-caliber machine guns and a ventral position with a single machine gun. Most models could carry up to 2,000 pounds of bombs while later variants carried up to 4,000 pounds. "I loved the A-20," Popeney said. "It flew just like a fighter. I used to do rolls and other aerobatics. It was a terrific, fun airplane to fly."

Popeney completed training in the A-20 during May 1944 at the Replacement Training Unit at Morris Field in Charlotte, North Carolina. "I was all finished with training and one of my instructors—I one of his favorites—asked me if I wanted to fly one of the new higher-powered A-20Hs. Well the damned thing just leapt off the ground! This was about dusk, and after an hour I decided to fly over to Queens College. I was dating a beautiful girl there and wanted to put on a show. Anyway, I hot-dogged it. I just tore the place up for ten minutes—everything you could do with the airplane except a loop. I wasn't too worried about getting caught. It was dark and I figured there was no way they could see the numbers on my plane.

"When I got back though, there was a staff car waiting with the colonel and his deputy, and my poor instructor. I felt bad that I had betrayed his trust. Of course I admitted what I had done right away, but still was curious about how they knew it was me. They called me a goddamn fool and pointed out that I had been the only aircraft from the base that was airborne.

"So, I was set up for a court-martial. That meant losing my wings and going into the infantry as a private. Anyway, my instructor must have worked his tail off because the next day he got me orders overseas. I left in a hurry before the court-martial convened without even saying good-bye to my girlfriend."

After a short layover in Savannah, Georgia, Popeney left for England flying one of six A-20Ks. The A-20K had a glass nose for carrying a bombardier. He was tasked to ferry the aircraft across the Atlantic and then report to an A-20 group for combat duty. At Goose Bay, in Labrador, his flight of three Havocs was joined by six B-26s. "The B-26 pilots thought they had a pretty hot airplane and told us so but we knew better. Out of Labrador, en route to Greenland, we gave them a fifteen minute head start. Well, it didn't take too long to catch them. As we caught up, we climbed above them, lowered our wheels, then dived down and passed them with our landing gear down; we utterly humiliated them. It wasn't a very bright idea though. We could have ruptured a hydraulic line. That would have been real trouble."

The route across the North Atlantic was a treacherous one. Miserable weather, long distances, and limited bases claimed large numbers of American aircraft. "Later in that flight," Popeney recalled, "we hit solid weather and became separated. My aircraft began to ice up and I tried to get above it but it was no use. I was burning fuel like it was going out of style and had already passed the point where I could make it back to Labrador. And there was no way I was going to make it to Greenland at the rate my engines were using fuel. So I dropped back down. When I finally broke out of the clouds, I was flying among, through, above, and below icebergs. Some of those bastards must have been three or four hundred feet high.

"I made Greenland okay. The airfield was Bluie West One. The runway was situated on a fifteen degree incline into a box canyon at the end of a fjord that was marked by a sunken German freighter. Other than two or three nurses who were reputed to be millionaires, there was nothing to do there other than fish. I fished."

The next leg of Popeney's journey to Iceland was uneventful until the very end. "We came in for landing and I was the last of the A-20s. The B-26s were still a bit behind us. A layer of scud clouds and fog rolled right over the airfield immediately after I landed. It was so thick that I couldn't even see my wingtips, and I had to stop at the end of the runway and call for a tug. In the meantime," he remembered, "the B-26s showed up and were hitting the panic button." Trapped by the weather, and without the fuel required to return to Greenland, there was nowhere for the B-26s to go.

"We never heard from them again."

After arriving in England in July 1944, Popeney was assigned to the 670th Squadron of the 416th Light Bombardment Group, one of three A-20 groups in the Ninth Air Force. "My best friend Tom Murphy and I were assigned together. We were based at Wethersfield, about thirty miles east of Cambridge."

Popeney was far from impressed by the training he received with the 416th. "We just bored holes in the sky. There was very little organized training." He remembered an accident on August 25, 1944, just west of the town of Stone. "We were flying at low level with a full bomb load, which we'd never done before. It was the flight leader, myself, and Norris Haney—an oil millionaire Indian from Oklahoma. Anyway, we were down on the deck and we pulled up to miss something and Haney didn't make it. He wasn't used to the heavy airplane and he mushed right into a telephone pole. It broke off his tail and he went in. We buried him in Cambridge."

Popeney started flying combat missions at the end of August 1944. His first missions were to targets in the vicinity of Rouen, in northern France, and Compiegne where the Germans signed armistice papers at the end of World War I, and where Hitler received the French surrender on June 21, 1940. "On one mission to Compiègne the flak was extremely heavy and our flight leader, who was a bit flak shy, turned us away a little too soon. But we had our bomb-bay doors open anyway," Popeney recalled, "so as we turned away we toggled the bombs out. Well, we accidentally hit a fuel dump and blew it all to hell. Instead of something else, that flight leader ended up coming back as a hero.

"This was also about the same time that the Krauts were sending over the V-1s and V-2s. The V-1 sounded like a diesel truck in the distance. Wethersfield was almost in a direct line between the launching sites and London and at night we heard them and hoped that they'd keep going and hit someone else. One night one of them hit a hardstand where three aircraft were parked. The concussion blew us right out of our beds."

Popeney noted that another enemy they fought was the weather. "It was notoriously bad in Britain. Most of the time we took off and flew through the overcast singly, and then joined up once we got on top of the clouds. But, some idiot got the harebrained idea that we should penetrate the overcast in formation, six ships at a time. Sometimes this didn't work because you couldn't even see your own wingtips. We had a procedure worked out in case we lost sight of the other aircraft in the formation. But it didn't work because people didn't follow it to the letter. Everyone usually ended up in someone else's propwash. We lost people because of this, and it was so unnecessary.

"One of the guys in my hut got disoriented doing this and went into a spin. He bailed out but his two gunners went down with the airplane. A day later he just disappeared. They got rid of him in a hurry."

Through August and September 1944, the 416th flew missions in support of ground operations in northern France. "Most of our missions were flown between 7,000 and 11,000 thousand feet, in a very tight formation," Popeney remembered. "The lead aircraft had a glass nose and carried a bombardier-navigator. The rest of us dropped our bombs when he did but it wasn't very accurate. Oh, they'd claim all sorts of destruction, but really it was pretty abysmal. I felt that we were wasting ourselves—that we should have gone down to low altitude where we would have been much more accurate and effective—as General Kenney proved in the South Pacific."

Popeney remembered that some of their most devastating work was done after they hit their primary target. "On the way back to base we sometimes loosened up the formation and looked for targets of opportunity—trains, trucks, troops, tanks, whatever. Our firepower was devastating. When we'd find a target we'd get in an echelon formation and dive down singly and tear the hell out of it. This was never something that we were taught or anything we practiced, however. We did this on our own initiative.

"Also during this time we were hit by the new German jet fighters, the Me-262s. Now most books say that they didn't come into play until much later, but that simply isn't true. On one mission two of them made a single pass through our formation without doing any damage. We also got hit by the little rocket ships, the Me-163s. For the most part though, the fighters left us alone. For one thing, we were about as fast as their propeller-driven fighters, and for another they were probably more interested in the big bombers—we were just small potatoes to them."

Like most of the pilots who flew over Europe, Popeney remembered the German antiaircraft fire as being the biggest threat. "The flak was awesome—very heavy. And it was quite accurate because we didn't fly as high as the heavy bombers. I was on missions where there were over a hundred 88mm guns putting up a salvo at one time. That made your back-end pucker up! It got so thick that the whole damned place was covered with orange bursts and black puffs. Afterwards we wondered how we made it through. Most of our losses were to flak."

It was in September 1944 that the 416th Bomb Group moved onto the Continent. Not as long legged as the heavy bombers, the A-20s needed to be closer to the action. "We moved to Melun, about thirty miles southeast of Paris," Popeney recalled. While the unit was there, an incident occurred that bothered him a great deal. "We had a flight leader who was having an affair with one of the Red Cross girls on our station. You know, they'd dispense coffee and doughnuts and that sort of thing; actually some of them dispensed more than that. Anyway, this flight leader was on a mission and one of his gunners was badly shot up. Instead of landing at any one of probably a dozen emergency fields between the target and our base, this bastard flew all the way back so he could be with his Red Cross girl. By the time they finally got that poor gunner out of the airplane he had bled to death. From that point on, I despised that pilot."

Only thirty miles away, newly-liberated Paris was a huge temptation for Popeney and three of his squadron mates. "Here we were, thirty miles from Paris, and we couldn't even get a two-day pass. Well, every major or lieutenant colonel that had a squadron also had a jeep. Four of us got together and stole the CO's jeep and went into Paris. Of course there weren't any keys for a jeep, just a switch. Being very clever fellows, we figured that after we parked it we'd take the rotor off the engine so that nobody else could steal it.

"So after we got into Paris we pulled the rotor and went into a bar and had just a wonderful time; we really lived it up. When we came back out the jeep was gone. Someone had stolen it. So we checked out a few of the other bars around there until we found another jeep. Well, that dumb bastard had done the same thing we had—he had taken the rotor off. So we stuck our rotor on his jeep and drove back to our base. We left the jeep at the CO's tent and by noon the next day it was already painted with our squadron numbers on it."

Meanwhile, missions continued into the fall. "The flak was very intense," he recalled of a mission he flew to Bitburg, Germany, on September

29, 1944. "I happened to look down at [Arthur] Nordstrom, who was flying in the slot—the number four position. Just at that instant he took a hit right behind the wingroot and broke in half. The metal of the fuselage was curled the same way a firecracker does to a tin can.

"I could see the inside of the airplane—and I could see Nordstrom's eyes. He looked confused. I presume it was because he couldn't feel the stick or the rudder. He had no controls. And then immediately he flipped up and went tumbling down. All of this happened in just a split-second. I told my gunner to follow it down and watch for parachutes. We never heard from Nordstrom again."

By early fall of 1944, heavily engaged and on the offensive in Europe, the USAAF was ready to field its latest attack aircraft. "On September 30," Popeney recalled, "we were sitting around outside our tents when we saw these strange airplanes overhead. They were twin-engine and silver where our A-20s were painted olive-drab. They circled the field and landed, and it turned out that they were Douglas A-26 Invaders. I was terribly disappointed. I loved the A-20, and the A-26 was just too damned big for my liking. At any rate, we were to be the first unit to field the A-26 in combat."

The A-26, like the A-20, was built by Douglas. Although it wasn't as compact and nimble as the A-20, it was a bit faster, could carry more armament, and had a greater range. A more modern design, the aircraft, like the A-20, was flown by a single pilot, and carried only one gunner who operated the two, twin .50-caliber turrets by remote control.

"We went to ground school and checked out in them right there on the base at the same time that we flew A-20 missions," Popeney remembered. "I was checked out on October 12, 1944. On October 15 they woke us for a pre-dawn takeoff and sent six of us individually on a training mission. The airbase was socked in and we took off on instruments with five hours of fuel on board. The forecast was for it to burn off in an hour or two. Unfortunately the weather over all of northern Europe deteriorated into a total overcast. I was on solid instruments for over four hours. There were no breaks in the clouds and I was unable to make radio contact with anyone. I had no idea whether I was over land, sea, or Germany.

"Finally I heard a C-47 pilot on the radio heading to England after being unable to land at Paris. I called him for a heading to England. Fearing

I might be a Kraut, he asked me who Babe Ruth and Lana Turner were. Finally convinced, he gave me a steer and I let down, breaking out at about 500 feet over the English Channel near Dover with less than thirty minutes of fuel remaining. I landed at Cranford."

When the weather cleared four days later, Popeney returned to Melun amid a chorus of cheers and a big bear hug from the group deputy commander. "The command in England had never contacted my squadron, and I had been given up as lost. Two other aircraft from the mission crashed and one crew was killed. The downside of my triumphant return is that they had already divvied up my personal gear. It took me a while to get it all back.

"Of course, once we were checked out in the A-26 we had to give up our A-20s." Popeney and the other pilots in the unit flew their A-20s to Blackpool on the western coast of Scotland. Once they landed they were stopped on the runway and told to get their gear and get out of their aircraft with the engines still running. At that point a mechanic pushed the throttles forward and the aircraft dribbled off the end of the runway, over the cliffs and into the sea. "That's how we got rid of our A-20s," Popeney recalled. "It broke my heart."

The 416th flew their first A-26 mission on November 19, 1944. Popeney remembered it as an inauspicious start. "The target was a supply depot at Hagenau, Germany. There was some weather so we had to fly on instruments in and out of cloud layers. For some reason," he recalled, "the whole damn sky was yellow—it was probably smog. It finally got so bad that we couldn't stay together anymore. When I got on top of it all hell broke loose. There must have been a battery of twenty 88mm guns firing at me.

"I started dodging and headed toward the deck. On the way down, knowing I was over Germany, I armed and dropped the bombs. In the meantime my gunner, who had been test firing the guns, shot the control cables out of the rudder; the automatic stop had failed. He was shaken up and asked if he should bail out."

Popeney kept his gunner aboard and broke out of the clouds just above the ground. "I got down on the deck and the troops on the ground—our own troops—started shooting at us. They had no idea what an A-26 was. There was antiaircraft and small arms fire everywhere! Anyway, I got back and landed with no rudder. It turned out that nobody made it to the target on that mission."

The machinations of military justice might have been slow, but they were dogged. Popeney's display of aerial wizardry over Queens College earlier that year came back to haunt him. "I had just been made a flight leader when my CO called me into his office and threw a letter at me and chewed me out. The letter was from the commanding general of the Third Air Force. Since they never had the chance to court martial me, they ended up docking my pay for $75 a month for six months."

Like the rest of the Ninth Air Force, the pilots of the 416th found themselves fully employed—weather permitting—during the Battle of the Bulge. "We bombed and strafed the field headquarters of Von Rundstedt at Zülpich, in Germany on December 24, 1944," Popeney remembered. "It was very heavily defended with antiaircraft guns. I also remember on this same mission that I could see a couple of groups of B-26 Marauders ahead of us in the distance—72 airplanes. They came under attack by a pair of Me-262s. Those two jets shot down a lot of B-26s. That jet was so superior to anything that we had."

All through the Battle of the Bulge the pressure on American troops was unrelenting. The Ninth Air Force was one of the key instruments used to relieve that pressure. "I lost my best friend, Tom Murphy, on January 1, 1945," Popeney recalled. "While I was off on a laundry detail the operations officer asked for six volunteers for a low-level mission." They were to make a coordinated attack with P-47s against troop concentrations at Mont Le Ban, in Belgium.

"Murph volunteered," Popeney said. "During the attack, he took a hit in the cockpit. He opened the bomb-bay and screamed for his gunner, Larry O'Connell to get out. O'Connell wanted to climb up into the cockpit to help him but Murphy was cursing at him to get out—he was blind and couldn't see to fly. He managed to pull up and O'Connell bailed out at a pretty low altitude, then Murph just flipped over and split-S'd into the ground.

"O'Connell was taken prisoner. We got to talk to him after the war. Murph never got any posthumous decoration. Only the Purple Heart."

As with the introduction of any new airplane, there were problems with the A-26. Some of those problems cost lives. "The A-26 had a Davis wing," Popeney said. "With the A-20 and its thick wing, we hadn't had much of a problem with clear icing, but the Davis wing was very thin and quite susceptible to icing." This susceptibility caused a tragic accident at Melun on January 2, 1945. "It was zero-zero weather," Popeney recalled, "and I was in my tent as the guys taxied out for a mission. They had to stay within about twenty feet of each other to keep from losing sight in the fog. At the end of the runway, instead of launching the mission with a flare, they had to break radio silence. No one would have seen a flare.

"Well the first guy took off, and ten or twelve seconds later, the second guy, and so on. Then, we started hearing all these damned explosions. We thought it was the Krauts bombing us—typical nuisance raids. But instead, the explosions were from our aircraft crashing. The guys were getting to the end of the runway with full flying speed, but when they pulled back on the stick nothing happened. Ice was building up on their wings as they rolled down the runway." Three aircraft were involved in the crashes and one crew was killed. One pilot and gunner only barely escaped from the wreckage of their aircraft before its bombs exploded.

"After that we had a briefing. They told us that we'd never fly in that sort of weather again." Nevertheless, less than two weeks later, on January 14, another aircraft crashed on takeoff. The crew was killed. "Then I took off," Popeney recollected. "As I lifted my wheels I saw the tail of the crashed airplane and felt a bump. Those of us who got airborne went ahead and flew the mission while the rest aborted." As it developed, one of the main landing gear tires on Popeney's aircraft was blown when it struck the wreckage of the crashed aircraft.

Popeney recalled a particularly frustrating and dangerous mission that he flew on January 23, 1945. "One of the operations boys came by my tent and said that they needed six volunteers. There were several hundred enemy tanks and trucks trapped near Luxembourg and we were supposed to bomb and strafe them. It was a 'hurry-up' mission personally called for by General Samuel Anderson of Ninth Bomber Command. We were in such a hurry that the flight leader was the only one who got briefed. The rest of us didn't even know where we were going—just somewhere near Luxembourg." In fact, the German vehicles were holed up at Arzberg, less than ten miles east of Luxembourg.

"The weather was atrocious," Popeney recalled, "but we knew that when we volunteered. The ceiling was so low that we were flying around obstacles instead of over them—slag [coal mining detritus] piles and low hills. When we got to the initial point we met with a P-51 that was supposed to lead us to the German vehicles. Well, the whole goddamn sky lit up with antiaircraft fire and small arms, but it was snowing and the visibility from the snow and flak was so poor that we couldn't see a thing to fire at. The P-51 went straight up into the clouds and deserted us. He'd had enough. We'd only gone a minute further when the flight leader took a hit in the nose.

"The flight leader called me and said that his bombardier-navigator had just had his foot shot off. He told me to take over because he was going to turn back and try and crash-land next to a tent with a red cross on it that he had seen earlier."

The stricken flight leader put his aircraft down on a hillside while Popeney, hardly prepared to do so, took command of the mission. "I didn't know where the hell we were or where the target was or anything. The 88s and machine gun tracers were so thick you could walk on them. Anyway," he recalled, "I circled this mess, but I couldn't find anything—not one tank, or gun, or truck. Nothing. The visibility was horrible and everything was covered with snow and perhaps white camouflaged tarps.

"Everyone knows you never go back over a target a second time at low level. It's a sure way to get shot down. But I went back in. Two of my four wingmen deserted me; they just peeled off and left. Still, I couldn't find anything and we were getting our asses shot off. I went back a third time. And a fourth. Nothing."

Finally, unable to find a target he could positively identify in the swirling maelstrom of snow and smoke and fire, and unwilling to just dump his bombs in the general area because of the risk of hitting American troops, Popeney headed for home. "We got within ten minutes of base and they told me to divert the flight to Ninth Air Force Headquarters at Reims. After we got to Reims, we froze our asses off in the back of a truck on the twenty mile trip to General Anderson's headquarters." Popeney remembered the General as "a short, trim, nice-looking officer. He gave us three bottles of Johnny Walker Black and told us not to be so drunk that we couldn't talk at a debriefing at 0900 the next morning.

"At the debrief the next morning the general asked me what I had seen and wanted to know why we hadn't bombed and strafed. I told them everything, and that I had been worried about hitting our own troops and that we hadn't seen any enemy trucks or tanks. This went on, back and forth for about five minutes. Finally, he summarily dismissed me.

"It turned out that the flight leader was awarded the Distinguished Service Cross for saving his bombardier-navigator's life. The two wingmen who deserted me became separated and got lost in the weather. One of them was shot down by antiaircraft fire but managed to go down in friendly territory and survived. The other crash-landed and survived as well. Two days later the *Stars and Stripes* newspaper wrote up the mission and described what a great job we did and how much equipment we had destroyed and so on.

"And nobody had fired a goddamn shot."

On February 6, 1945, the 416th moved to Laon, near Reims, France. "We had too many pilots by that time and they asked for volunteers to go fight with the infantry for a while. Not as commanders or anything—just as basic riflemen. They wanted to help build understanding between us and the ground people." Popeney took the opportunity and was assigned to the 84th Infantry Division of the Ninth Army. At the time, American forces were preparing to cross the Ruhr River. After a brief with the division commanding general, Popeney was driven to the front by the general's driver who also doubled as his interpreter. "This soldier spoke with a very guttural German accent," Popeney recalled. "He had dark, curly hair, and very thick glasses. He was a pretty nice fellow by the name of Henry Kissinger!"

The time on the ground was an educational experience for Popeney. "Of course I was a pilot rather than a soldier. I didn't know what I was doing, or even when to hit the deck. They had to teach me everything. I learned to tell the difference between the German machine guns and ours though. Ours went 'pop-pop-pop,' while theirs went 'grrrrrrr,' twice as fast as ours.

"We got holed up in a cemetery once and the Krauts hit us with trench mortars. They were blowing the old, dead bodies out of the ground. The stench was something else."

Unlike the air war, the war on the ground brought death close and from all quarters. "I remember this one dead German lieutenant," Popeney said. "He was a nice-looking young man. I can't recall where his wound was, but he was deader than a mackerel. I relieved him of his sidearm—a Walther P-38. Another time our machine gunners were hit by a mortar. I came up and one of the men had his legs blown up over his shoulders. There was a letter from home laying close by. It was heartbreaking, and tears rolled down my cheeks.

"There was also a lot of dead livestock—horses and cows. They'd swell up to three times their normal size during the day. Guys would take their burp guns and blow holes in their sides and they would explode."

Popeney remembered the preparations for the crossing of the Roer near Jülich on the night of February 23. "The night before, the artillery put up a huge barrage to protect the engineers who were assembling the pontoon bridges. The artillery and the tracers were so bright you could have read a newspaper. They got a couple of bridges up, but before we could even use them two Me-262s dropped out of the clouds—the ceiling wasn't over a thousand feet—and knocked them out. At night! It was magnificent flying and unlike anything I'd ever seen.

"But anyway we got more bridges up and made the crossing. The casualties weren't too heavy and came mostly from sniper fire and machine guns." By this time in the war it was obvious even to the Germans that an Allied victory was inevitable. "We took a lot of prisoners," Popeney recalled. They were fairly docile—not supermen by any means. They seemed happy that the war was over for them."

By March, Popeney was back with the 416th. "Being with the infantry saved my life; while I was gone a new guy tried to land with one of his engines shot out. He missed the runway and started to go around but was below critical flying speed. He flipped over and split-S'd right into my shack. Of the four of us, I was gone, John Cook was killed, Teddy Merritt was in the hospital for over a year with terrible leg and back injuries, and Jay Warren was airborne on the same mission.

"Well the airplane was nothing but a crumpled-up ball. It took two hours to extricate the badly injured pilot from the wreckage. They couldn't find the gunner for quite a while. Finally they found him where he had been thrown by the crash—unconscious, sitting up against a tree without a scratch on him!"

Popeney continued to fly missions until the end of the war. Rather than getting easier, as the Germans were pushed further and further into their homeland, the missions instead grew more dangerous. "As they withdrew," Popeney recalled, "they took their flak guns with them. So they had less area to defend with more guns than ever. It was murderous at times."

Popeney recalled a mission on March 18, 1945, that illustrated his point. "The target was the communication center at Worms, in Germany. I was assigned to escort two groups of eighteen aircraft each along the railroad from Bingen, Germany into Worms. The route was heavily defended by flak cars." Popeney was tasked with dispensing bundles of chaff. Chaff was made up of tiny slivers of metal-coated material designed to cloud the enemy antiaircraft artillery radar with false targets.

"I flew about a mile in front of the first group," Popeney remembered. "They were hit hard and the second group, instead of staying with the first, was about five minutes behind. I swung back to pick them up so that they would have at least some protection. It was a disaster. One aircraft received a direct hit and exploded in flames. Another was hit in the right wing and hit the ground on fire. Two others were hit by flak and went down. There were no survivors. We called it Black Sunday

"My last mission," Popeney remembered, "was on May 3, 1945. It was to Stod, in Czechoslovakia—a long-range mission across the Alps. The weather was terrible the entire time. The group leader was a squadron commander from another squadron who kept trying to get on top of the clouds. We got pretty well scattered as he tried to take us up to 18,000 feet.

"The problem was that the A-26 had a practical service ceiling of only about 14,000 feet. We didn't have oxygen and the cockpit wasn't pressurized. We had these Mickey Mouse two-stage superchargers, and at that altitude we were straining like hell, pushing everything forward, flopping around, damn near stall speed. But we followed our leader.

"I saw three different guys spin into the undercast. They all recovered and survived but it was just stupid. The war was over—who the hell wants to be the last guy killed? And like that?"

―――――――――

Popeney finished the war with 45 missions, was awarded the Distinguished Flying Cross, nine Air Medals, and five battle stars. He remained in the active reserve, flying P-51s and P-80/T-33s, retiring in 1973 as a colonel.

CHAPTER 13

LOW LEVEL FURY

Medium bombers from the USAAF's Fifth Air Force took the war to Japanese forces in New Guinea, Indonesia, the Solomons, the Philippines and other island groups throughout the South Pacific. The crews typically flew at very low altitudes and attacked with little warning. Their strikes were deadly. Faster and more versatile than the bigger and heavier B-17s and B-24s, the B-25 Mitchell was an especially effective attack aircraft. Shipping, harbors and airfields in particular were critical to the Japanese war effort, and as such received special attention from the Fifth's B-25 units. Indeed, the contributions that the North American Aviation-built bomber made in paving MacArthur's return to and through the Philippines cannot be overstated.

Roman Ohnemus

ROMAN H. OHNEMUS WAS BORN IN CARLSBAD, NEW MEXICO, on March 9, 1922. During 1930 his family moved to Los Angeles, California, where he grew up and graduated from high school in 1941. "I was driving to work at a Standard Oil station in my 1935 Ford Coupe—it had whitewall tires—when I heard that Pearl Harbor was bombed. I didn't know exactly where Pearl Harbor was but I thought that it must be pretty serious. Then, as the day wore on I realized it meant going to war.

"So the next day," Ohnemus continued, "I quit my job and went down to the recruiting station at 5th and Main. I passed the physical with flying colors and they told me to bring a bag the next day along with a permission slip from my mother and they'd ship me out. Well, on my way to get my mother to sign the permission slip, my girlfriend—we had been planning on getting married—suggested that we get married and just wait until I got drafted. We had already bought some furniture so that we could set up house. So right then, we decided to go to Las Vegas to get married. It turned out that I needed to get my mother's permission for that too!"

After marrying and going back to his job, Ohnemus was intrigued by an aviation cadet who came through the service station. "I asked a lot of questions and he told me all about the program. By that time you didn't need any college. All you had to do was pass an equivalency exam. Well, I didn't think I was quite ready for that, so I took a preparatory course at John H. Francis Polytechnic High School for five nights a week over the next three months."

Ohnemus finally took the exam during the summer of 1942 at the Red Car Line terminal in Los Angeles. "After the test we took a break for lunch and came back to see how we did. If they called your name, it meant that you had failed and were supposed to leave. They went through the list alphabetically. I thought that I had done horribly and it wasn't until they were up to the Rs or Ss that I realized that I passed."

Nevertheless, it seemed that even in wartime a young man couldn't do anything without his mother's consent. "Because I was under 21, I needed my mother's permission," Ohnemus recalled. "My sister talked her into it, and on September 16, 1942, I was sworn in."

Ohnemus was finally called for training during February 1943. He recalled an incident that occurred while he was flying PT-22s out of Hemet, California. "After I soloed, I went up alone again to get some flying time. I figured that I would go up and do some spins, so I climbed up to about 3,000 feet. I got up there and put the airplane into a spin. After two turns I tried to kick the rudder to get out of it but it was jammed. The thing kept spinning tighter and tighter so I decided to bail out.

"I unbuckled my seat belt and climbed out over the side of the cockpit and had one leg on the wing and one on the seat." However, just before clearing the aircraft Ohnemus checked the altimeter one more time. As he did so he saw that the rod, which locked the rudders into place on the ground, had slipped and caused the rudder pedals to jam. "So I climbed back in, put the seatbelt back on, reached down and pulled the rod out. Then I recovered the aircraft from the spin.

"It wasn't any special act of bravery—I just didn't want to get washed out!"

He clearly recalled another incident from his early training. "I was on a hop with an instructor and he told me that he was going to show me some inverted flying. Just as he rolled over I looked down and saw that my seatbelt wasn't fastened. I grabbed the instrument panels and jammed my knees up against the primer pump and held on for dear life. I didn't say a thing because I didn't want to get washed out. I thought he'd never roll that thing back upright!"

Anxious to have a shot at flying the big, four-engine B-17, Ohnemus volunteered for multi-engine training out of Marana Army Air Base, Arizona, and by October 1943, found himself en route by rail to La Junta, Colorado. He remembered that the lightly supervised aviation cadets took advantage of every opportunity to live it up along the way. "Everyone had a big time—drinking a lot and so on. By the time the train reached La Junta, via El Paso and Albuquerque, quite a few cadets were missing."

The flying weather at La Junta was atrocious. "Because we had gotten behind in our flying—we were in B-25s at this time—we started flying six hours on, then six hours off, around the clock," Ohnemus recalled. "We got so tired that in the morning we'd just fall into formation and go to breakfast in our undershorts and overcoats!" Ohnemus completed the required number of hours and on January 7, 1944, received his wings and a commission as a second lieutenant.

Instead of an assignment to B-17s, Ohnemus received orders to Columbia, South Carolina, for further training in B-25s. Designed in 1938 and first flown in 1940, the B-25 Mitchell was more widely used by the Allies than any other medium bomber and nearly 11,000 were built. Rugged, easy to fly, and with a respectable range, payload, and defensive armament, the B-25 was popular with its pilots. "I really liked the B-25," Ohnemus remembered. "It was very reliable but noisy. A lot of pilots lost a good bit hearing because of it."

Before he finished his tactical training at Columbia, Ohnemus was assigned a permanent crew, and finally, during May 1944, he departed for Hunter Field in Savannah, Georgia. There he picked up a new aircraft and orders for overseas. "We were there for only a day before we left." Uncharacteristically, his aircraft was plagued by problems most of the way to the South Pacific. He had engine problems in Phoenix and fuel tank problems at Fairfield-Suisun Army Air Base. It was there in northern California that he also started having people problems. "We were delayed several days while they prepared our aircraft for the twelve-hour flight to Hawaii. They had to take off all the guns and armor and such to make the airplane lighter. While that was going on we were restricted to base. Well, my navigator sneaked off the base to be with his wife at a local motel. I watched him crawl on his hands and knees through the weeds and barbed wire, then dust himself off and hitch a ride into town."

When Ohnemus got a call at one o'clock in the morning to take off for Hawaii, his navigator was nowhere to be found. Finally, the military police found him and dumped him at the flight line. With his crew whole again, Ohnemus took off for the Territory of Hawaii. Along the way, Ohnemus sacked the Air Transport Command pilot who was assigned as his copilot for the trip. "After a few hours I needed a rest, so I handed him the controls then went back to take a nap. A few minutes later I decided to check on him and he was off course by twenty degrees and off altitude by three thousand feet!" After failing to maintain course a second time, Ohnemus sent the other pilot to the rear of the aircraft and flew the rest of the leg himself. Twelve hours and twenty minutes later, he landed the B-25 in Hawaii with only fifteen minutes of fuel remaining.

"When we finally got to Hickam," Ohnemus remembered, "James Pauley and W. J. Hunkin were headed over to Will Rogers Field to have some equipment reinstalled in their aircraft. We were all friends from training. Anyway, they decided to fly up to Waikiki Beach on the way to give it a buzz job like it had never seen before. Well, it was real hazy when they took off and they ran into each other head-on while they were trying to join up. They killed ten or fifteen civilians and burned down eleven houses."

Ohnemus's passage from Hawaii, through various South Pacific islands, Australia—where he had to give up his airplane—and finally to Port Moresby, New Guinea, was marked by enough mechanical problems, savage storms, and other incidents to fill an entire book. And he had yet to fly his first combat mission. "When we got to Port Moresby for two weeks of combat training," he recalled, "we were met by a first lieutenant who told us to forget everything we had learned. We were going to be taught the way it was done in combat. On my first flight I climbed into the airplane and about half of the gauges in the instrument panel were gone—

no airspeed indicator, no altimeter, and a couple of others were gone as well. When I pointed this out to my instructor he looked at me like I was slime and asked me if I had a problem flying without the instruments!"

From Port Moresby, Ohnemus was sent to the 501st Bomb Squadron of the 345th Bomb Group at Nadzab, New Guinea. Famous as the Air Apaches, the 345th was hated by the Japanese. Since June of 1943, the unit had wreaked havoc on various Japanese strongholds throughout the South Pacific. Attacking from low altitude with devastating firepower, the group earned particular enmity from the beleaguered Japanese defenders. "Tokyo Rose called us bastards," he remembered. "They made no secret that if we were ever captured that we would be executed."

Soon after Ohnemus arrived at Nadzab, the 345th was redeployed to Mokmer Airdrome on the island of Biak, north of Dutch New Guinea. Newly retaken by the Army from the Japanese during May and June 1944, the island was closer to targets in Indonesia and the Philippines. "We ended up moving the squadron in our own airplanes," Ohnemus said. "I flew an airplane that was packed full—dishes and whatever—tent poles sticking out the back. We were so poorly loaded that I had to fly in an angle of bank just to hold a steady course!

"I flew my first mission on July 27th, 1944," he remembered. "We hit Galela Airdrome, on the northern tip of Halmahera Island. It was one of the biggest Japanese airfields since Rabaul. My radioman, Weinstein, asked me if he could strafe the target with the waist guns. I told him to go ahead but to ensure that he saved some ammunition in case we got hit by fighters. Well, we came down the runway strafing and dropping our bombs. We hit a few planes and some bulldozers, and people running all over the run-way, and then strafed a ship anchored off of the beach.

"Well, when I got back I was thinking that combat wasn't so bad when I noticed a string of holes across my rudder. Jeez, I thought, we were hit on our first mission! Then I noticed that the metal around the holes was flared outward. I asked Weinstein if he had shot up the rudder and he con-fessed. So we credited him with a probable and put stops in the gun mounts after that."

The mode of attack that the 345th used maximized their armament, gave the best accuracy, and provided the best protection from enemy fight-ers. Generally deploying in three-ship elements, the pilots flew low, sometimes less than fifty feet, and as fast as the aircraft would go. The low altitude ensured better accuracy, as well as preventing enemy fighters from attacking from below. Additionally, the .50-caliber machine guns were much more effective near the ground than from higher altitude.

"We carried all sorts of bombs," Ohnemus recalled. "We carried 100- and 500-pound bombs. Sometimes 1,000-pounders. All in the bomb-bay. And lots of parafrags—parachute fragmentation bombs. They were great for lightly armored targets. For machine guns we had four, five or six .50-caliber guns in the nose depending on the aircraft model, two more on each side just below the cockpit pointing forward, one at each waist position, two in the top turret, and two in the tail. We had plenty of guns.

"On my second mission [July 30, 1944] I flew with John Nolan who had been there for a while and had about thirty missions; it was supposed to be a check flight for me. We were going after some shipping at Sele Strait, near Sorong, in the Halmaheras. He came in low over the water strafing and he skipped a 100-pound bomb into the side of a ship. I waited and waited for him to pull up until I couldn't wait any longer. I grabbed the wheel and we went right over the top of the ship, barely missing it. I thought to myself that I was going to get chewed out for grabbing the controls from the pilot. Instead, he looked at me, slapped me on the back and said, 'Thanks Ohnemus, I wasn't going to pull up!' He had been totally fixated on the target. Well, we made another run on another ship and the same thing happened.

"It turned out," Ohnemus continued, "that Nolan was suffering from combat fatigue. Later, on August 15, he was run into by another plane that had been hit while attacking some shipping at Halmahera. The other airplane crashed and killed everyone on board. About six feet of Nolan's wing was knocked off causing his aircraft to invert. He and his copilot, Ed Bena, got it upright while they went down a long ridge upside down and clipping trees. The other part of the wing was bent down and acted like a flap. How they did it I don't know, but they managed to get it level and climbed to 5,000 feet and flew 500 miles back to Noemfoor where they ditched short of the runway. They sent Nolan home after that."

Through the summer and early fall of 1944, Ohnemus gained experience and notched up missions. Targets included Japanese bases in New Guinea, the Halmaheras, Indonesia, and the Philippines. "Most of our missions lasted about eight hours, although my longest was eleven. To hit targets in the Philippines we flew up to Morotai and loaded up with more fuel before we pressed on. Unfortunately, guys who lost an engine usually didn't make it back from those long missions. The workload on the good engine was such that it normally overheated and failed."

One distinction that Ohnemus claimed was that of being the first pilot to bring a B-25 into the Philippines. The flight took place on October 28, 1944, immediately following the invasion at Leyte. His was the first of many courier flights the unit flew between Biak and the airfield at Tacloban. "Actually we flew two airplanes in," Ohnemus recalled. "The other was flown by Captain J. J. Jones. He had an appointment with MacArthur to get information about his father, Major General Albert Jones, who had been captured at Corregidor and was being held as a POW on Formosa.

"When I came in to land on that first mission," he recalled, "I saw what must have been fifty or sixty Navy aircraft sitting wrecked in the water. I thought that the war must have really been going badly. It turned out that they were from the *Princeton* and other Navy ships that had been damaged or sunk. When they landed at Tacloban they were pushed into the water to make room for Army aircraft."

Ohnemus remembered an attack during this time when the 345th hit Alicante Airdrome, on Negros Island in the Philippines. The date was November 3, 1944. "We were tasked with knocking out the *kamikazes* that were hitting the invasion fleet in Leyte Gulf. I was in the front three-ship element of the lead squadron. Usually we tried to hide our approach by coming in from behind hills, and through ravines and so forth. But this time we had to come in from over the water and the Japanese could see us coming. We saw the dust from their fighters as they took off, and people scrambling around as we started our run."

Under attack from twenty or more Japanese fighters, the B-25s pressed their strike through a deadly curtain of antiaircraft fire. "We flew over the runway, strafing and dropping our bombs. Then, Bill Leggett on the right side of my element got hit in the right engine and caught fire. Still though, he dropped his bombs and strafed. As we came off he was burning and trailing a lot of flames. Finally, out past the target, his right wing burned off and he flipped over and went into the water.

"I had played cards with Leggett the night before," Ohnemus recalled.

"And that morning, before we took off, I had lent my hack watch to his navigator, James Chance. He had lost his. And then they were all gone."

Soon, elements of the 345th were en route to the Philippines to support the ground campaign. It was to be a tough and costly fight. On November 12, the troop transports *Waite* and *Nelson,* loaded with 345th ground personnel were hit by *kamikazes.* More than a hundred men were killed.

Once established however, the Air Apaches wasted no time in renewing the fight. The mission Ohnemus recalled as perhaps his most memorable occurred on December 28, 1944, when the 345th was flying out of the airfield at Dulag on Tacloban. The target was Clark Field. "The Japanese were flying out of Clark and harassing the fleet. So, we in turn launched bombing and strafing attacks against Clark about every fifteen minutes. This particular mission was a night mission. We had twelve airplanes and were going to take off in a raging storm. We tried to get headquarters to cancel it, but they told us to go ahead and take off because the weather was good over Clark.

"So the leader took off, and then I took off. Well, it turned out that my radios went bad right after I got airborne and that the lead aircraft had engine problems and turned back. Not only that, but they cancelled the mission. With my radios out," Ohnemus recounted, "I didn't know any of this.

"I headed up alone across Luzon and came north of Clark and then went down. I had a new copilot—he was an eager little guy. Headquarters had been right; it was a crystal-clear, moonlit night over Clark. Anyway, we zipped over the airfield at about fifty feet. At night. I couldn't see the target I was looking for and was getting ready to come over the field again when my turret gunner called and said that the Japanese had just turned on the runway lights. I said 'What!?!,' and he said, 'They just turned on the runway lights.'

"I turned back," Ohnemus continued, "and saw two Japanese bombers in the traffic pattern. I figured this was quite an opportunity, so I pulled up behind the second one and indicated that I was going to land; I turned my lights on just like theirs. So we flew around the pattern, and as soon as the second one landed, I opened up the bomb-bay doors.

"I had parafrag bombs and came down the runway streaming those bombs across the two bombers." With chaos unfolding on the runway be-hind him, Ohnemus poured the coals to his own aircraft, closed his bomb-bay doors and made his getaway. "My turret gunner told me there were fighters overhead the bombers so I was anxious to get out of there.

"I came out between Bataan and Corregidor," Ohnemus remembered. "Off the coast of Bataan I saw the silhouette of a big ship and thought that maybe I'd go down and strafe it. But I remembered that the Japanese moved our POWs by ship so I decided to leave it alone.

"So we were heading back and it was still a really bright night. I asked my copilot if he wanted to hit our secondary target. It was a Japanese army barracks compound. Anyway, we went down there and I started flying a race-track pattern. I flew that pattern and we shot up the barracks until all of our ammo was gone. Then the tail gunner called up and said that the flak was getting close, so we headed back.

"By this time," Ohnemus remembered, "I was able to get the radios working. As we got to the inlet between Samar and Leyte, I saw that the weather was going to be very bad back at Tacloban—landing there at the Dulag airfield was too dangerous at night in the weather because of a hill at the end of the runway. Anyway, the code word for weather was 'Savan-nah.' Savannah One was good weather, and Savannah Five meant it couldn't get any worse," he explained. "They were calling it Savannah Five.

"This was the only time during the war that my hands got sweaty. I let down to 100 feet to try and get under it, then went up to 6,000 feet to try and get over it." Unable to find the airfield at Dulag and low on fuel, Ohnemus decided to order everyone to bail out, but changed his mind at the last minute when he spotted a hole in the clouds over Leyte Gulf. Dropping down to mast-top height, he navigated through the ships on station in the gulf until he found the airfield at Tacloban. Finally, after making four passes at the runway in the middle of a raging tropical storm, he set the aircraft down. After a mission of eight hours and ten minutes, his fuel gauges read below empty.

But the night wasn't yet over. "On the ride back from the airfield," Ohnemus recalled, "our jeep overturned into a swamp!"

Quartered at Tacloban, but flying out of the nearby airfield at Dulag, the 345th was constantly in the air. Destroying the enemy's ability to launch *kamikaze* missions against the American fleet was a high priority.

"On December 31, 1944, we hit three or four different airdromes, one right after another. Then we came back, refueled and rearmed and took off again to hit five or six more on Negros Island. We were carrying 100-pound bombs and flying in elements of four. As we came over an airfield, one aircraft from each element bombed and strafed.

"Well, over the second airfield I did something that I shouldn't have done. I didn't see much going on so I figured I'd go up to about 200 feet and see what I could see. I got up there and all of a sudden the whole aircraft shuddered. Immediately I grabbed the throttles because I thought that the engines had been hit. But they were okay, so I called back to Weinstein and asked if everything was alright. He said 'Yeaahh . . . oh my God, there's a hole big enough to drive a truck through!'" A 37mm shell had come through the back hatch and blown a big hole in the fuselage. Of course, the shrapnel from the explosion had also put hundreds of smaller holes all through the airplane.

"Anyway," Ohnemus continued, "the airplane was flying kind of wobbly but I went ahead and kept hitting the targets. I had to do a lot of over controlling because some of my elevator cables had been messed up. I was one of the element leaders and my wingmen were having a hard time maintaining formation on me so on the way back I sent them on ahead. When I got over the field," he remembered, "I made sure that everyone else got on the ground before I tried to land. When I finally came in to land, my controls jammed about a hundred feet off of the ground. I had the copilot try to help me but we couldn't get them free. I called the crew and told them to hang on, and fortunately I was able to rudder stall the aircraft onto the runway. We bounced real hard and then I was able to get it under control and park it.

"After taking a look at it I thought I'd better go tell the commanding officer that I needed a new airplane. However, as it turned out they eventually replaced the entire fuselage from behind the wings. Then, in April, it was shot down over Formosa."

Like nearly every combat aviator, Ohnemus lost comrades to the enemy. "At Tacloban I had a friend, Howard Peck. He had gone through the preparatory course at John H. Francis Polytechnic High School with me in early 1942, and then through preflight at Santa Ana, and primary training at Hemet. He washed out at Hemet and was sent to navigator school. We met again at Columbia and then joined the 345th at the same time and ended up in the same tent together. Anyway, his airplane was shot down outside of Manila near one of the Japanese headquarters. Everyone survived the crash but the Japanese executed them all. They hated us."

On January 7, 1945, just prior to the American landings at Lingayen Gulf, an attack was launched against Clark Field. The showcase American airbase in the Western Pacific prior to the war, Clark was captured by the Japanese at the end of 1941 and put to use as their primary airbase in the Philippines. Importantly, units at the airfield were staging *kamikaze* attacks against the American fleet.

"This mission was supposed to be the knockout blow against Clark," Ohnemus remembered. "It was a mix of 120 B-25s and A-20s. But after takeoff I had a fire in my right engine. Tower told me to wait while the rest of the planes took off. I told them that they could do what they wanted with those other planes, but I was going to land! Anyway, I landed and jumped in a spare plane and took off again."

The Japanese were keen to protect Clark. In addition to conventional antiaircraft defenses, their desperation led them to experiment with unorthodox equipment and tactics. Ohnemus remembered how it was as the bombers, after navigating through treacherous, cloud-veiled mountain passes, executed their attack. "The Japanese tried all kinds of crazy things. They had fighters trying to drop phosphorous bombs on us during this mission. On previous missions they put land mines and dynamite in the tree tops. When an airplane flew close overhead, they detonated the charges. It worked too," he remembered. "They got a couple of planes that way."

But on this mission, the American flyers were forced to deal with confusion that was self-generated. "The B-25s were supposed to come in first from one direction followed by the A-20s from another direction a few minutes later. Well, everyone got there at the same time. We were all dodging each other—flying at fifty feet and below—and strafing and dropping parafrags. We were flying so low," he pointed out, "that we were blowing camouflaged netting right off of the enemy fighters." Moreover, the danger of running into the parafrag bombs from preceding aircraft made formation keeping and targeting a nightmare.

"I lost another friend from my class on this mission," Ohnemus remembered. "Arthur Browngardt, Jr. He was hit by antiaircraft fire and crashed into a church. I had a buddy from grammar school who also flew on that mission. And he did it with dysentery. He later told me that he knew what it was like to have the 'you know what' scared out of him! The plane I was flying—*Cactus Kitten*—ended up with a couple of holes in it, too, and lost the hydraulic system. We had to use the manual emergency system to lower the gear and flaps."

Indeed, the entire month of January proved to be a tough one for the 345th. The month's operations cost the bomb group sixty-one crewmen killed and sixteen aircraft lost. "By the time I flew my last mission, we had moved up to San Marcelino on the Bataan Peninsula near Subic Bay," Ohnemus said. "We had gotten up there on February 12, 1945, and my commanding officer, Major Jones, told me that I had completed all of my combat missions and was free to go home. But he offered me a promotion to captain if I stayed overseas for a month longer. I told him that I'd think about it.

"In the meantime," Ohnemus continued, "on this same day, the Fifth Air Force and the Thirteenth Air Force were putting together a huge raid against the remnants of the Japanese fleet. It was a flotilla of two battleships, two heavy cruisers, and three destroyers. Our job was to go in at low level and scatter the destroyers. At the same time submarines were supposed to torpedo the larger ships, while B-24s bombed from high altitude.

"Now, I had agreed to go, but was starting to wish that I hadn't. The intelligence briefers were telling us that WHEN we got shot down, not IF, but WHEN, that submarines would be waiting at points X, Y, and Z. . . . Well, I couldn't get my airplane started. Finally, my line chief, Master Sergeant Passodel—he was one of the best—hand-cranked the engines and I got airborne about twenty minutes after everyone else. It was overcast," Ohnemus remembered, "and I decided to go under the weather. As it turned out, the rest of the aircraft had gone out over the top.

"There was a Navy PB4Y radar airplane that was shadowing the Japanese ships, and we homed in on him. There was a low ceiling at about a thousand feet and it was very stormy and windswept with rain squalls and such. Well, I found what was left of the Japanese Navy. I just circled them for a while, and every time I got in too close they started shooting at me.

"At the same time the guys up above me were talking; there was a lot of chatter. Finally, they decided that the weather was too bad and that they weren't going to be able to get down below the ceiling. So they left. I went ahead and circled while I weighed my options.

"Ultimately, I decided that my best option was to turn around and head for home. The crew was real happy about that. When I got back I found out that headquarters was mad as hell that the attack hadn't been made. They laid out plans for another attack the next day, and my CO asked me if I'd go out again. I told him that I'd prefer to go home as a live first lieutenant rather than a dead captain."

―――――――

The next attack was foiled by weather as well. By the end of the war, thirteen of the sixteen other pilots who joined the 345th at the same time as Ohnemus were dead.

Ohnemus stayed in the reserves and was recalled for duty during the Korean War. After Korea, he received a degree in Meteorology through the Bootstrap Program, and thereafter mixed his flying with duties as a staff meteorologist. His tours included Project Resupply in the Arctic, service in Europe, a tour in Japan where he used to taunt the Soviet early warning radars at Vladivostok in a T-33, an assignment as the Staff Weather Officer for Air Force One during the Johnson administration, and a stint as the Staff Weather Officer at Edwards Air Force Base where he worked with the XB-70 and X-15 programs.

Ray Crandall and Richard Deitchman enjoying a lighter moment on the Landing Signal Officer's platform aboard the USS *Manila Bay*, 1944. —*Richard Deitchman Collection*

CHAPTER **14**

SECOND BATTLE OF
THE PHILIPPINE SEA

If there had been any lingering doubts about the outcome of the Pacific War during late 1944, the Second Battle of the Philippine Sea, also known as the Battle of Leyte Gulf, should have dispelled it for good. It took place in late October and was the result of an elaborate Japanese plan to lure the large aircraft carriers of Halsey's Third Fleet out of the way while the Japanese Combined Fleet executed a pincer movement and smashed the landing forces at Leyte Gulf.

It came very close to succeeding. However the Japanese commanders were plagued by miscommunication, self-doubt, and bad luck. And of course, they were opposed by well-trained and overwhelming American forces that—once they recovered from their initial surprise—performed admirably. From that point, the Imperial Japanese Navy never again sortied a naval fleet strong enough to threaten American forces.

Ray Crandall &
Richard Deitchman

RAY CRANDALL WAS BORN ON JANUARY 8, 1923, IN SALT LAKE CITY, Utah, and moved with his family to Glendale, California, when he was still an infant. Growing up in the small community, he was more of an athlete than a scholar. "I went to high school to play basketball. And lunch; I was pretty good at lunch." Crandall had just finished high school when the Japanese attacked Pearl Harbor on December 7, 1941. "I didn't even know where or what Pearl Harbor was, but I thought that the war was terrific. I wouldn't have to stay in Glendale all of my life. Right away I tried to join the paratroopers but they wouldn't let me in. I was only seventeen, and my mom wouldn't sign the papers. She told me that the war would be over before I got my first uniform fitted."

But Mother Crandall's prediction wasn't borne out. Crandall was pumping gas for Standard Oil when he read that the Navy was accepting high school graduates for flight training if they could pass an equivalency test. "A Navy ensign came through the gas station one day in a convertible. He had his uniform on with those aviator's wings; God they were beautiful. And he had a gorgeous girl. And there I was all covered with grease and oil, telling him that I was going in for an interview for the NAVCAD program to be an aviator just like him!

"Anyway, everybody in Glendale kept coming up to me and telling me that I wouldn't be able to pass that damned test—no way! But I surprised everyone, including myself, by passing the test and being selected by the Navy for flight training."

Crandall went into the service in 1942 as part of the Navy's V-5 aviator training program. It was designed to get young men thoroughly trained and into combat as quickly as possible. "People don't understand the magnitude of what happened, what was accomplished during the war," said Crandall. "They took thousands of young men like me, eighteen years old and straight out of the vineyards or whatever, and in a short time turned them into trained aviators who could fight effectively together and win." He was correct. During the war the United States Navy alone trained almost 60,000 pilots.

The academics were difficult for Crandall and he struggled with navigation and trigonometry and other technical subjects. "I had a hard time in the classroom, but what saved me was that I had good monkey skills. It turned out that I could fly. It came so naturally that I couldn't believe that other people thought it was difficult. So my flying talent was my strong suit. That and my friend are what got me through the war."

There have been many brotherhoods forged in the crucible of conflict. None, as far as Crandall was concerned, compared remotely with the bond that developed between him and Richard Paul Deitchman. Crandall nicknamed Deitchman as "The Frame" because his medical records described him as "overweight due to muscular development; heavy frame." Deitchman, who Crandall met during preflight training, was the steady, even influence that tamed Crandall's sometimes misguided precociousness. "He was tall and good-looking, a great wrestler from Kansas," Crandall recalled.

Where Crandall was rash, Deitchman was thoughtful. Crandall complied with military strictures only as much as required to get by. On the other hand, Deitchman went so far as to roll and organize his underwear. Crandall was always in trouble. Deitchman was mature and encouraging, and accompanied Crandall as he walked off his demerits. And, unusual for the time, the Navy never broke them apart. They were roommates from flight training, through combat, and all the way to the end of the war.

"Anyway, when we finally graduated and got our wings in August 1943 in Corpus Christi, I was designated naval aviator number 301526 and The Frame was 301527—I outranked him. I had numbers on him! When the admiral gave me my wings he said, 'I understand you made it through training with more demerits than any Navy cadet in history.' I said that, yes, it was true. The admiral kind of sighed and said, 'Well, we *do* need pilots.'"

Following their graduation, the pair received orders to train in torpedo bombers, specifically the TBM Avenger. An ungainly looking aircraft informally dubbed the Turkey, the Avenger was a Grumman design (the aircraft carried a TB*F* designation when manufactured by Grumman) that was largely produced under license by General Motors. Although it wasn't attractive or fast, it was a rugged and honest aircraft with a good payload and good range. It was a capable and utilitarian machine and with its three-man crew it served in a variety of roles. It was the Navy's most important torpedo bomber from mid-1942 onwards.

"I was so mad I quit," Crandall said. "At the time you could do it. I told them that I was a fighter pilot and I had joined to become a fighter pilot, and that if they didn't want to let me be a fighter pilot, then the Army Air Forces would."

Deitchman remembered that time well. "Oh yes, we all wanted to fly fighters. That was everyone's dream. But torpedo pilots were what they needed." Fortunately, Deitchman was able to work his calming magic on the fiery young Crandall. Crandall decided to stay in the Navy and a few weeks later the pair began to enjoy and savor life as "real naval aviators."

Following torpedo bomber training, which included aircraft carrier landings aboard the paddle-wheeled flat-top *Wolverine* on Lake Michigan, as well as night flying over the deserts in the Southwest and torpedo training on both coasts, the young flyers were assigned to VC-80, at Sand Point, Washington. VC-80 was a composite squadron consisting of a mix of approximately twelve TBM Avenger torpedo bombers and sixteen FM-2 Wildcat fighters. Deitchman's brother, a full lieutenant and a fighter pilot, convinced a young clerk to get them all assigned together.

The squadron conducted more advanced training until the early summer of 1944. At that time the unit was ordered to San Diego, California, for embarkation to the war zone. Flying and training aside, Crandall recalled the sort of thing that made a real impression on a young fighting man. "During the few weeks before we shipped out from San Diego there was no room at the government quarters at the naval air station. So, incredibly, they put us up in the world famous Hotel Del Coronado. My God, I never felt so manly. It was really something to swagger through the lobby in my sweaty flying clothes with my parachute slung over my shoulder. Now that's what being a real naval aviator was all about!"

Crandall recalled his time at the Hotel Del Coronado with great fondness. Aside from flying, volleyball on the beach, drinking, and enjoying the world's finest weather, there were girls. "Every weekend they hosted Sunday afternoon tea dances. Girls from all over the area dressed to the nines and came in by Greyhound bus. It was Shangri-La!"

Finally, the summer of 1944 found Crandall and Deitchman and the rest of VC-80 truly at war aboard the escort carrier *Manila Bay* (CVE-61) in the Pacific. "Those escort carriers," Crandall remembered, only half-jokingly, "were designed to take two torpedoes: One in the side and one over the top as the ship sank. They were small and slow. They could only make about fifteen knots so they had no options in terms of engaging or disengaging during a battle. It was a lot like being in a prison, except a prison can't be sunk."

After flying a few minor air strikes against bypassed Japanese garrisons in the Marianas, the *Manila Bay* arrived in the Philippines for the invasion at Leyte Gulf. Crandall flew his third sortie of the day during the late afternoon of October 20, 1944. With him was his crew of two—the radioman and gunner—plus an Army liaison pilot. They spotted naval gunfire for the battleships, cruisers, and destroyers that were bombarding

The TBM Avenger was informally known as the Turkey. Here, a TBM launches from an escort carrier. Note the ship's antiaircraft guns. —*USN*

The FW-190 was the second-most produced German fighter, after the Me-109. Some contend it was the better of the two aircraft. Jack Dentz's second aerial victory was over an FW-190. —*San Diego Aerospace Museum Collection*

Jack Dentz's 365th Fighter Group operated in miserable weather during the winter of 1944–1945. Note the Maxon machine gun mount. —*USAAF*

A P-47 of Dentz's 365th Fighter Group on the beach at Aubin-Sur-Mer on D-Day. —*USAAF*

Jack Dentz in the cockpit of his P-47. —*Howard Dentz Collection*

Harold "Bob" Popeney (left) with his gunner Henry Candler, in front of an A-26 Invader, Laon, France, March 1945. —*H.V. Popeney Collection*

Harold "Bob" Popeney (left) with his crew in front of an A-20G Havoc at
Wethersfield, England, August, 1944. The A-20—fast and fairly maneuverable—
was well-liked by its crews. —*H.V. Popeney Collection*

A-20s of Popeney's 416th Light Bombardment Group. —*USAAF*

Note the invasion stripes of the A-20s of the 416th Light Bombardment Group. —*USAAF*

Roman Ohnemus (center) enjoys off-duty time with tent mates, Earl Wilkinson (left) and Howard Peck (right). Earl Wilkinson was later shot down and survived. Peck was also shot down near Manila. Although he survived the crash, the Japanese immediately murdered him. —*Roman Ohnemus Collection*

A B-25 of the 345th is hit over a refinery on Formosa. —*USAAF*

A kamikaze flier at the end of his life. —*USN*

Above: The massive firepower of the 345th's B-25s required equally massive maintenance.

Right: Alvin Anderson in front of P-61 *Fearless Fosdick* on September 27, 1944 at Coulommiers, France. —*USAAF*

The P-61 was reasonably fast and very maneuverable. It was also easy to fly and well-liked by its pilots. —*Alvin Anderson Collection*

Emilius Ciampa in the cockpit of an F4F Wildcat, El Toro California, 1944. —*Emilius Ciampa Collection*

A P-39 at Guadalcanal during late 1942. Julius Jacobson flew the P-39 and the nearly identical P-400 in bombing and strafing attacks against the Japanese. —*USAAF*

A pair of SDB Dauntless dive bombers, the type flown by both Jesse Barker and Emilius Ciampa. —*USN*

Maintenance conditions were primitive at Guadalcanal. Here, an Army crew works on a P-39 during late 1942. —*USAAF*

339th Fighter Squadron fighter pilots. Fred Purnell, Julius Jacobson, John Mitchel and Besby Holmes enjoying a leave in Australia. Mitchel, Jacobson and Holmes flew on the mission during which Japanese Admiral Isoroku Yamamoto was shot down and killed. —*Julius Jacobson Collection*

Belgium
With all my Love —
Robert

Robert Macdonald was born in Coblenz, Germany. During the Normandy breakout his gunfire caught a French butcher standing in a cluster of German troops. The memory stayed with him all his life. —*Robert Macdonald Family*

Above: The P-51 was the premier American escort fighter during World War II.
—*USAAF*

Top, opposite page: April 18, 1943, Guadalcanal. Major General Nathan Twining debriefs John Mitchel, leader of the mission that downed Japanese Admiral Isoroku Yamamoto—the architect of the sneak attack on Pearl Harbor. Julius "Jack" Jacobson was Mitchel's wingman on this historic mission. —*USAAF*

Bottom, opposite page: Maintenance conditions in North Africa were difficult for the mechanics of Jack Walker's 82nd Fighter Group. —*USAAF*

George Kesselring went from sharecropping atop this tractor in 1942 to bombing Nazi Germany at the controls of a B-17 in 1944. —*George Kesselring Collection*

Cadet George Kesselring. This photograph belies the tender ages of Kesselring and the majority of his peers. —*George Kesselring Collection*

A German FW-190 pilot prepares to bail out from his stricken aircraft. —*USAAF*

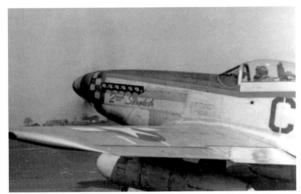

Left: A late-war photograph of Herman Schonenberg's P-51D, *Second Stretch*, at Wormingford, England. —*USAAF*

Below: Herman Schonenberg, at right, with two comrades from the 338th Fighter Squadron of the 55th Fighter Group. Schonenberg was credited with knocking down two FW-190s during his combat tour from August 1944 to April 1945. —*USAAF*

A B-17G of Kesselring's 91st Bomb Group. The B-17G was the most-produced model and was distinguished by the chin-mounted turret which was equipped with two .50-caliber machine guns. —USAAF

Bombs fall toward Bremen from a B-17 of George Kesselring's 91st Bomb Group. —USAAF

Japanese positions. The Army pilot was aboard to assist in the spotting and to also reconnoiter suitable landing sites for follow-on independent operations in his L-5 observation aircraft. "It was incredible," Crandall said. "As far as you could see in any direction there were ships—hundreds of them."

Following Crandall's spotting mission, the shipboard tactical controller directed him to take a look at a specific grass landing strip before returning to the *Manila Bay*. He also advised Crandall to lower his landing gear so as to appear nonthreatening to the fleet.

"And then the bastards shot me down," Crandall said. "They nailed me. I had turned down the line of landing craft and *LST-733* started firing at me and then the destroyer *Talbot* fired 2,470 rounds at me. They were firing 20mm and 40mm cannon. It stopped my aircraft dead in the air."

Miraculously Crandall and his crew weren't badly injured. "We hit the water and tumbled a couple of times. When we crawled out to get in the raft they were *still* shooting us." The gunfire eventually ceased and he and his crew were picked up. "They put us on the USS *Appalachian* where MacArthur was and apologized to us. An old buddy of mine met me and gave me a shot of scotch." He smiled as he remembered, "I threw it up all over his stateroom. That incident—getting shot down and almost killed—took a lot of the tiger blood out of me. I was never really the same after that."

A few days later he was transported back to the *Manila Bay* via PT boat. "That night we had a big party. We mixed a bunch of gin with apple juice and whatever. We had a hell of a time." Crandall's timing was unfortunate. The next morning, October 25, 1944, marked a watershed day in the Pacific war. It was also the same day that Crandall spent with one of the worst hangovers of his life.

The *Manila Bay* was part of Rear Admiral Clifton Sprague's group of eighteen unarmored escort carriers, and other vessels, which were on station off the island of Samar to support the landings at Leyte Gulf. These small carriers were part of the much larger Third Fleet commanded by Admiral William Halsey. Sprague's escort carriers were unexpectedly caught up in an elaborate Japanese plan that was to be the Imperial Navy's last effort to regain the initiative in the Pacific.

"So the next morning The Frame woke me up and said that the Japanese fleet was twelve miles away and that I'm going in with the first torpedo. I told him to stop screwing around and leave me alone or I was going to get out of the sack and kick his ass. He told me that he wasn't kidding, that I was supposed to lead and that he was going to be number two. Well, I sat up in my bed and told him again to leave me alone, that I was a wounded goddamn hero, and that my head hurt, and that I was tired and wanted to go back to sleep."

Finally Deitchman grabbed Crandall, dragged him outside to the gangway and literally pointed to the Japanese fleet. "They were so close that I thought the bastards were going to try and board us!" The Japanese ships were part of a strike force commanded by Vice Admiral Takeo Kurita. Attacked and damaged by U.S. forces for two days beginning on October 23, Kurita's force nevertheless passed through San Bernardino Strait essentially intact. And now they were attacking Sprague's escort carrier group near Samar at dawn on October 25.

"Well, this was what it was all about," Crandall said. "It was Crunch Time. This was where we were going to start earning our flight pay." Indeed, it was the acid test for the training that Crandall and Deitchman, and thousands of other men like them received when they came out of their schools, and fields, and factories only a couple of years earlier.

"I was terrified," Crandall said. "The Japanese were right in the middle of us. There were four battleships, eight cruisers, and sixteen destroyers, and they were shooting the hell out of everything. We went down to the ready room. There was no need for a brief; hell, the Japanese were almost in the damned landing pattern. Anyway, the skipper of the ship came down to the ready room and said 'Gentlemen, this is the chance of a lifetime.' I couldn't hear him very well so I turned to The Frame and asked what he had said. He just looked at me and said, 'The captain said that you've got a good chance of dying today.' When he finished talking, the skipper came to the back of the ready room and shook all of our hands. I didn't like that part one bit.

"This was not going to be a very good day," Crandall continued. "There was nothing organized about it. Frame and I were up on the deck checking the ordnance loads, and the Japanese were shooting at us, and because of that there was saltwater spray down on the hangar deck where the crews were trying to load the torpedoes."

The condition and storage of the "fish" was suspect. "These torpedoes—there were only six of them on the entire ship—had been lying around on the hangar deck for five months. We had always kind of snickered whenever we'd seen them before. We *knew* that we'd never be using those things because we were going to be bombers. Now, sure enough, the ordnance chief was looking at his manual which was soaked from the saltwater spray from the overhead sprinklers, and at the same time he was directing the loading of the torpedoes."

To their credit, the chiefs, mechanics, plane captains, and armorers persevered through the chaos and soon had the TBMs ready to launch. Crandall remembered: "Then, there I was sitting on the catapult and the Japanese were still shooting at us. I was thinking to myself that this wasn't how it was when I was a real naval aviator back at the Hotel Del Coronado enjoying those tea dances."

Finally, Crandall and the rest of the crews from the *Manila Bay* were launched. They readied to make their first attack in what had developed to be the largest sea battle in history. "The Frame and I got airborne with a couple of others. Somehow, in the turn to start our runs against the Japanese, Frame almost got run into by another plane and turned one way, while the other three of us turned the other way to set up for our torpedo runs."

Releasing a torpedo against alerted enemy warships was among the most dangerous missions of World War II. The torpedo aircraft pilot had to fly a slow, predictable flight path low to the water that made him an easy target for the ship's gunners. Additionally, the pilot had to accurately predict the target ship's path and estimate the lead required to ensure a successful intercept solution between the ship and his torpedo. Of course, all of these calculations could be ruined if the ship maneuvered after the torpedo had been launched. And while simply flying the aircraft into the appropriate parameters was difficult enough, the task was made more formidable and terrifying by curtains of gunfire from the defending ships.

Crandall recalled his torpedo run: "They fired their main batteries—their big guns—at us, which kicked up huge sprays of water that we had to fly through. Then, all of the smaller guns just filled the sky. Each ship had a different color of gunfire too. It was designed to help them adjust their fire. We flew through bright, colorful, phosphorescing explosions. It was damned scary.

"We were running against four battleships, eight cruisers, and sixteen destroyers all in an area about the size of San Diego Harbor. But the ships could really maneuver so we had to put a lot of torpedoes out there."

Crandall made an interesting observation about dropping torpedoes into a fleet of warships. "Now, anyone who says he can tell you what his torpedo did in the middle of all the other torpedoes . . . well, how would he know? It's just not possible. He can't hang around to watch it. Not if he's been where I've been. Anyway, we three made our run and shared credit for a torpedo hit on a cruiser. Frame, though, he made a run all by himself and blew the stern off of another cruiser. For that he got the Silver Star."

Deitchman—The Frame—recounted what happened to him after he got airborne from the *Manila Bay*. "After we took off, there were so many targets that I got confused in the turn and ended up pointed the wrong way. Well, right in front of me was a *Tone* class cruiser." The torpedo attack problem that he faced was one he had practiced many times in the waters off of San Diego. "I dropped the torpedo and really dove for the deck, jinking and weaving. The gunfire was really heavy. My gunner shouted up at me, 'You hit it! You hit it!'" But Deitchman was so preoccupied with evading the enemy fire that he didn't even look back. "They were really firing at us but I kept jinking and in fact was the first one back to the ship."

The heavy cruiser that Deitchman had blasted was the *Chikuma*. The blow he struck very nearly blew the stern from the great ship. It was finished off and sunk later that same day.

By now, Sprague's fleet of small escort carriers was running for its survival. The confusion was so great that Crandall, along with many others, recovered aboard the wrong ship. His new home was the USS *Ommaney Bay*, another small escort carrier. "They took me up to the bridge for a briefing. They wanted to know what I thought." Crandall was brutally honest with the ship's captain. "I told them that what I thought was that every ship we owned was going to be on the bottom by noon."

Still shaken from his earlier mission, Crandall watched as the ship's crew dragged another torpedo to his airplane. "I asked them what the hell they were doing and they said that they were going to send me out again. I got upset and said bullshit to that. Not with a torpedo. I told them that when everyone else in the Navy had done it once, then I would go a second time, and that I wanted a load of bombs, not a torpedo."

Crandall soon recovered his composure, collected his crew and manned his plane. He admired his two crewmen. They were still bruised and shaken from being shot down by the *Talbot* a few days earlier. Nevertheless, they had crawled out of sickbay to fly with Crandall on the first mission that morning and were willingly going into harm's way with him again.

Airborne once more, Crandall turned out of the traffic pattern, picked out an enemy ship, braved the deadly barrage of gunfire, and launched his torpedo. "I have no idea where that torpedo went," he said. "I know that it fell out of the airplane and the odds are pretty good that it landed in the water. But beyond that I don't have a clue where it went."

Returning to the fleet for the second time, Crandall found and recovered aboard his own ship, the *Manila Bay*. "There was a huge mix-up on all the surviving ships. There were guys from all different ships in our ready room. Some of them were off of the ones that had been sunk and many of them wore borrowed flight gear. It was chaos."

One of the misplaced pilots was Commander Richard Fowler who was later awarded the Navy Cross for his actions during the battle. Crandall and Deitchman quickly attached themselves to this senior aviator and prepared to go on their third strike of the day. By now the ammunition stores of all the ships were very nearly depleted. The torpedoes were almost gone and the aircraft were loaded with semi-armor piercing and general purpose bombs.

"So finally we got airborne with a bunch of guys this time instead of just a handful," Crandall recalled. "For some dumbass reason the Japanese had turned around and were running north. We were really ready to hurt them this time." Again, the value of their training was proven. Young men—Crandall was only twenty—who had never even met each other, went to work to chew the Japanese fleet to pieces. "That was the beauty of the whole thing to me. All the training in codes and signals and other crap that I thought was useless at the time because it didn't have anything to do with flying an airplane, finally paid off. Our only brief was for the aircraft with bombs to join forward, and those with torpedoes to join aft. We were standardized and trained so well that we made it happen when it really mattered.

"After we all got joined, the air director called on the radio and directed the group to attack. Fowler answered back that he'd attack at his own discretion. In other words, he'd attack when he was good and ready. Meanwhile guys were pointing out ships that were dead in the water or rolled over. Fowler told everyone to shut up. He said that we would attack the ones that were moving and save the cripples for the next day. And the entire time I was thinking to myself that I wanted to go home. I wanted to go back to the Hotel Del Coronado and play volleyball."

Fowler led his ad hoc strike against the now-fleeing Japanese fleet. Crandall followed him, this time with bombs, against an enemy cruiser. The attack left the enemy reeling in disarray. It was Crandall's final mission of the day. Inexplicably, the Japanese commander ordered a retreat and the escort carriers were safe. Nevertheless, the cost had been high. The enemy warships, together with attacks by *kamikazes*, destroyed two escort carriers, two destroyers and a destroyer escort. Four other escort carriers were damaged. Exhausted and spent, the combatants separated from each other.

Since that time, Admiral Halsey, commander of the Third Fleet, has been criticized for leaving Sprague's escort carrier group open to attack while he chased north after a decoy of large Japanese aircraft carriers which, because of their previous losses, were mostly without aircraft. Halsey's defenders have pointed out that he did not know the whereabouts of Kurita's striking force.

That point is disputed. Jesse Barker, introduced earlier as a dive bomber pilot during the Guadalcanal campaign, was vehement when he pointed out that the command of the Third Fleet knew exactly where Kurita was. At that time he was an F6F-5N Hellcat night fighter pilot assigned to VF(N)-41 aboard the *Independence*.

"I was launched at about 1800, on October 24. I found those Japanese ships at about 2000 and sat over them for an hour-and-a-half while I radioed their position. At about 2130 they went into a line-astern formation and by the time I left, the first few ships were entering the narrow strait between the island of Masbate and Luzon, with San Bernardino Strait pretty much dead ahead of the course they were on.

"When I got back aboard the *Independence* I was debriefed by the ship's operations officer in the presence of the ship's commanding officer. I know that the position reports I made were sent to the admiral on his flagship. But someone had already made the decision to haul ass and head north after the Japanese carriers. They covered up the fact that we found the

Japanese and knew where they were. They simply covered it up."

Although Crandall and Deitchman survived the battle, they were separated. For Deitchman, the battle was only the beginning of a weeks-long odyssey. The next day, October 26, he was sent west with a fighter pilot and his radioman aboard an Avenger to recover some aircraft that had diverted into Tacloban Airfield, now firmly in American hands. On landing, they were forced to take cover as the field was walloped by a typhoon which drenched the newly captured airfield. "Following that," Deitchman recalled, "the Japanese attacked and we ran for the trenches but they were filled with water. In the end we just stood outside and watched."

Finally on October 30, 1944, with the storm over and the airfield cleared of the enemy, Deitchman was airborne and leading two FM-2 fighters back to the escort carriers. But their ship was gone. Unbeknownst to them, the *Manila Bay* and the rest of the carriers making up the Seventh Fleet had retired to the Admiralty Islands. "I was looking around, and finally glanced up and spotted four Hellcats diving on us. Fortunately, at the last minute, they recognized us for what we were and didn't fire." Eventually Deitchman located the light carrier *Belleau Wood*, which was part of Halsey's Third Fleet, and led the flight aboard.

"It was just the four of us," Deitchman explained, "the two fighter pilots, my radioman and me. The two fighter pilots went with the ship's fighter crews and my radioman went down to the enlisted aircrew ready room, and I went with one of the ship's torpedo pilots." After lunch the other torpedo pilot gave Deitchman a tour of the ship. "We stopped by the enlisted aircrew ready room and I checked on my radioman, Joe Posateri. I told him that as soon as I knew what was going on I'd come and get him."

The *Belleau Wood* was attacked by *kamikazes* a short time later and took two hits. One of them struck the enlisted aircrew ready room and killed more than one hundred men, Joe Posateri among them. "Along with losing Joe," Deitchman remembered, "our airplanes got creamed and everything else did as well." The ship limped back to the anchorage at Ulithi Atoll, burying the dead in the sea along the way. From there Deitchman disembarked along with the two fighter pilots and embarked on a quest for the *Manila Bay.*

"From Ulithi we got on a Martin PBM flying boat and then boarded an LST at Kossol Passage. All we had was our flight suits." By this time they had picked up an Australian officer and a couple of other flyers. "The Australian told me that if we didn't find the *Manila Bay* that he'd take me to Australia and show me around. What I found remarkable is that although we were still in the war zone, there was food and supplies aplenty. We never missed a meal and we always found a place to sleep."

Eventually, the grubby pack of vagabonds found themselves on the still-contested island of Peleliu. Deitchman recalled one of his more incongruous memories of the war, "There was this Marine Corps Corsair pilot at the airfield, and he was dressed in full winter flying gear—heavy coat, trousers, gloves and so on. Anyway, he went over to his airplane which had two big, square boxes mounted on the bomb racks. He took off and climbed to 40,000 feet and stayed there for a bit before landing. As it turned out, those boxes were full of ice cream. And with the Japanese just a mile or so away!"

Finally, scruffy and covered with Guam Blisters—an uncomfortable tropical skin malady—and daubed with tincture of violet to prevent infection—Deitchman and his itinerant band of tattered aircrew boarded a C-46 for the Admiralties. In the meantime, Crandall had claimed squatter's rights to a Quonset hut on Manus Island, part of the Admiralties, where the fleet had anchored to recover. "I was pretty much doing what I wanted to do," he remembered. "I'd wake up and steal a jeep, then go down to one of the supply ships. I'd tell them that I was Lieutenant So-and-So from Such-and-Such a ship. Hell, they didn't know which ships had been sunk up north. I'd pick up a dozen or so cases of beer and go hide it or trade it for something else.

"We held parties at a shack called Duffy's Tavern. They were wild. By God, I was invincible. I could match my 'crunch-time' against anyone in the bar. I had been shot down, I'd been in a battle, I was newly promoted . . . I was bulletproof."

On one day during this time Crandall was in his Quonset hut brooding over the apparent loss of his friend. He was stunned when Deitchman, blistered, ragged and unshaven, appeared in the doorway. Crandall leapt to his feet, tears in his eyes and grabbed his violet-tinted comrade in a heartfelt bear-hug. "Look everyone," he shouted, "here's my . . . my great purple friend!"

Reunited, the two men continued their war against Japan, still as part of VC-80 aboard the *Manila Bay*. "We flew a lot of ground support missions as part of different landings all over the Philippines," Crandall recalled. "We hit targets on Cebu, Mindoro, Leyte, and Lingayen Gulf. Mostly we carried bombs and rockets. When we spotted a convoy we used our bombs first to destroy the front and the rear, and then followed up with our rockets. A lot of the times the Japanese scattered into the jungle which made it nearly impossible to find and bomb them. We also ran strikes on airfields and did some photo reconnaissance work.

"Another of the missions we were assigned was deep sector search," Crandall recalled. "The admirals were very keen on knowing where the Japanese fleet was—what was left of it, anyway. We normally launched with a fighter on our wing for protection. We flew on a certain heading, for instance, 330 degrees, to a predetermined distance. Then we turned about ninety degrees and flew on that new heading for a while before we turned back toward the ship. The pattern was shaped something like a slice of pie. Sometimes we peeked around the islands but most of the time it was an open-ocean search. We'd fly at anywhere from 500 feet to 5,000 feet. And it was boring. And hot. My nose would burn under that terrible sun. And many times we had to pick our way around some really awful thunderstorms. It really stressed my navigation skills—it made me wish I had paid more attention in class!

"Usually the ship wasn't where it was supposed to be when we got back. And of course we were always low on gas. So then, instead of searching for the Japanese, we'd have to set up a square search pattern to look for our own ship. It was very stressful. I was usually so scared that I couldn't look down to see my plotting board because my Adams apple was stuck so high up in my throat. If we were lucky we ran across the ship's track, or wake. It was kind of a slick, or smooth place in the water where the ship had passed. Then, all we had to do was decide which way to turn to follow it."

Much as it had struck the *Belleau Wood*, tragedy in the form of *kamikazes* finally caught up with the *Manila Bay*. The ship was hit on January 5, 1945, prior to the landings at Lingayen Gulf, on the Island of Luzon, in the Philippines. "We were scheduled for a launch when word was sent that there was an attack inbound," Crandall remembered. "They cancelled the launch and everybody scattered. I manned one of the .50-caliber machine guns. I shot at an airplane that was coming in low—right on the deck. And he shot right back."

The ship was struck by two aircraft. "There were bodies everywhere. It was a bloody mess. I climbed up a ladder on the prow and took a look. There were holes in the flight deck and everything was covered in Foamite to extinguish the fires. Then I went down to the Combat Information Center to help pull up bodies."

Everyone, regardless of rank, or rate, or specialty, fought to save the stricken ship. In serious danger of capsizing, and without communication, the ship was very nearly lost. Crandall credited the ship's captain, Fitzhugh Lee, a direct descendant of Robert E. Lee, with saving the *Manila Bay*. "He had been hit and injured by an aircraft tow bar which was blown loose during the blast. He got me to start up a TBM and with its radios we established communications with the rest of the fleet."

Crandall, who was decorated for saving lives during the disaster, remembered Lee's even temperament and his concern for the men. "Once the situation was in hand, his cabin boy came on deck and asked him if he'd like to eat something. Lee made certain that the men had all been given an opportunity to eat first, then, with the ship listing and people fighting fires all around him, said that he would 'have a cup of tea.'

"I was sitting in the middle of all that mess and Fitzhugh Lee asked me if I was a very good swimmer," Crandall said. "I told him that I was the best damned swimmer in the fleet—because I really thought that I was. He said 'Good. I'm not, so I want you in my life raft.' In reality, he was already making sure that we'd be ready to continue flight operations the next day."

Lee was an outstanding commanding officer, and the following day the *Manila Bay* was indeed launching missions. Within a few days Deitchman launched on what was to be his final combat mission; a poignant example of the waste that is war. "We had taken a *kamikaze* hit a few days before," he remembered, "and even though there was a big hump in the flight deck, we were still launching strikes."

The target for the predawn launch was near the mountain stronghold of Baguio on northern Luzon Island. It was a four-plane mission and Deitchman was flying the number-three position. As the planes went through their post-start checks, the leader of the flight experienced mechanical problems, shut down the engine, and exited his aircraft. "He got out of his plane and walked right into number-two's turning propeller." It was dark and Deitchman was unable to see. He was confused as he watched the plane captains shut down the number two aircraft. "All of a sudden I was leading number-four on a mission I didn't know much about."

Over Baguio, Deitchman dropped a plane-load of four 500-pound general purpose bombs and made his way out of the target area. "I'm not sure what happened to number-four. I don't know if he got hit or spun in, or what."

Now flying the only aircraft remaining out of what had been a flight of four, Deitchman headed for the coast. Along the way his aircraft started smoking. "I landed at Lingayen along the coast to have the aircraft checked." Once on the ground, a crew of mechanics swarmed Deitchman's aircraft but was unable to find anything wrong. Somewhat reassured, Deitchman got airborne again and headed out to sea.

"Ten miles from the carrier, it quit." As he quickly radioed distress calls, Deitchman put his aircraft into the ocean, and with the help of his gunner, "Book" Booker, extracted the radioman, Bernie Dabbert, who suffered a broken leg. "We waited an hour-and-a-half in a raft with the sharks starting to circle before we got picked up by a destroyer."

Crandall and Deitchman were in the process of transitioning to F6F-5N Hellcat night fighters when the war ended. Subsequently the great team was split when both men returned to their hometowns. They were called back to service as reservists during the Korean War, with Crandall back in combat flying F9F Panthers.

Crandall eventually left the Navy and joined Lockheed for a career as a test pilot. At Lockheed, he became very close to the famous aircraft designer Kelly Johnson, and played a major role in the testing and development of the F-104. Deitchman went on to complete his twenty years with the Navy Reserve as a fighter pilot, retiring as a commander. At the same time, he enjoyed a very successful career in the mail-order industry.

Howard Wilson was shot down over Yugoslavia on
August 26, 1944, and did a stint with Tito's
partisans before returning to Allied hands.
—*Howard O. Wilson Collection*

CHAPTER **15**

DOWNED IN YUGOSLAVIA

The Fifteenth Air Force started operating out of bases in southern Italy during November 1943. The Fifteenth was intended as a strategic adjunct to the better-known Eighth Air Force, which had been flying combat missions out of bases in England since August 1942. If the weather was poor in England on any given day, the odds were good that strategic missions could still be flown out of Italy.

Using both air forces, the USAAF maintained constant pressure on the European Axis powers. Indeed, the Fifteenth Air Force sent its bombers and fighters as far afield as Germany and France. Yugoslavia and Hungary were hit as well. Of chief strategic importance were the Fifteenth Air Force raids on the oil refining facilities at Ploesti, in Romania. The success of those missions played havoc with Germany's ability to keep its army and air force fueled.

Howard O. Wilson

BORN IN CHICAGO, ILLINOIS, ON MARCH 15, 1917, AT THE HEIGHT OF World War I, Wilson was nearly twenty-five years old when he enlisted in the Army Air Forces during February 1942. It was only two months after the Japanese attack on Pearl Harbor and he was a junior executive in a Los Angeles office of the Standard Oil Company. "My boss was ready to choke me when I told him what I did," Wilson said. "At the time I was fairly well insulated from the draft. I had a wife and a young son and my job was essential to the war effort.

"But I couldn't stand the looks that I imagined were being shot my way when I was on the streets of downtown Los Angeles. I was a healthy young man in suede shoes and a natty business suit." Indeed, his family and job did insulate him from the business of battle, but he felt guilty. "I didn't believe I was doing my part toward winning the war."

Wilson continued at his job with Standard Oil until he was called to flight training during August 1942. Following the completion of multi-engine training, he graduated and was commissioned a second lieutenant during February 1944. "It was a close thing. I was only a couple of weeks from my twenty-seventh birthday and they would have washed me out for being too old if I hadn't graduated in time."

Wilson was assigned to Kirtland Army Airfield, New Mexico, for additional training as a B-24 pilot. "Kirtland was the wrong place to train B-24 pilots," he said. "It's too high and it's too hot. And in the old war-weary airplanes they gave us to fly on low octane gas, it was dangerous. I'm not sure how we did it without killing more people."

Regardless, Wilson managed. Within a couple months he finished training at Kirtland as well as a follow-on assignment at March Field in Riverside, California. At that point he was assigned a permanent crew and a new, Ford-built, B-24J. "Oh, we loved that airplane. It was a beautiful, shiny, aluminum-finished beauty that was fresh out of the Ford factory at Willow Run, Michigan." Treating their newly-manufactured airplane like a precious newborn, Wilson and his crew took great pains to ensure that it looked and operated perfectly. "We swept it out and wiped it down after every flight. It didn't have a mechanical gripe on it. It was perfect."

Wilson and his crew finally left the United States for Europe during early August 1944. "We stopped over at Gander Field in Newfoundland before we left to cross the Atlantic. I must have spent twenty hours in the Link instrument trainer they had there practicing the instrument approach for Lajes Field in the Azores."

It turned out to be time well spent. After leaving Gander late at night, Wilson's crew arrived over Lajes at dawn the following day. Their navigation had been perfect but the field was socked in with fog. Wilson flew the instrument approach faultlessly and caught sight of the runway at the last moment. "We touched down, and for a moment I thought that I had forgotten to lower the landing gear. It was the first time I had ever landed on a metal-planked runway and the noise was horrendous!"

Lajes was crammed with transiting aircraft and the ground crews hurriedly refueled Wilson's aircraft and rushed him and his crew on their way. "We had flown the entire night already, and then they made us take off and fly to Marrakech, in Morocco. We got there okay, but it was quite a shock in terms of climate—going from Newfoundland one day and arriving in Africa the next."

They arrived in Italy a few days later with their new airplane still unblemished and untried in combat. At Gioia, Wilson's crew was dealt their first bloody nose of the war. "A major came out to the flight line. He looked at the airplane and counted that it had the right number of wings, the right number of engines, and the right number of wheels. Then he took it from me. All I got was a receipt for one, brand new B-24J." Half a world away from home and without an aircraft, Wilson and his crew were trucked to Fifteenth Air Force Headquarters at Bari.

Soon after, Wilson and his crew were sent to the 461st Bomb Group at Torretta and billeted in wooden-floored tents. "It was always muddy there," he recalled. "It didn't matter what season it was." A few days later Wilson flew his first combat mission, an indoctrination ride with another crew to the Italian seaport city of Genoa. He remembered that it was, "pretty much a milk run. Not much happened."

That wasn't the case on his second mission, another indoctrination flight, on August 22, 1944. "I was just sitting there with my arms folded," Wilson said. "We hit a petroleum storage site in Vienna, Austria. All along the way we were shadowed by Me-110s which were tracking our airspeed and altitude, and radioing the information back to the flak batteries. Every so often the Mustangs dove down and chased them off but a few minutes later a new one would show up.

"We were close to the target area when six enemy aircraft dived down on us and attacked a box of bombers in front of us. They were moving so fast that it was difficult to believe. They shot down every bomber in that box and guys were shouting into the radio and intercom, 'Jesus Christ, what was that?'"

Wilson remembered that the German aircraft were Me-262 jet fighters. The Me-262 had a top speed of well more than one hundred miles per hour faster than the best Allied piston-powered aircraft. Protecting the bombers against it was very difficult. "The intelligence officers really gave us a hard time when we got back," Wilson said. "They showed me flash cards and I picked out the Me-262. They told me 'Lieutenant, you couldn't have seen these aircraft because they don't exist!' Actually, 'Axis Sally' made quite a production out of the occasion that night by naming the squadron and the individuals that were lost."

The new German jets were not a threat to Wilson and his crew on August 26. "It was our first mission together as a crew. By God, we felt like we were going to go out and win the war together." The mission was the ninetieth of the war for the 461st Bomb Group. The target was the Romanian airdrome at Otopeni, located between the capital of Bucharest and the oil refining facilities at Ploesti.

Wilson recalled the aircraft they were assigned: "We were the newest crew in the group, so you can imagine what we got. That airplane was a bucket of junk. It was an old 'J' model that was already shot. It wouldn't even fly straight!" He illustrated the point with his hands. "It was bent or something. To keep it in formation I had to fly it sideways, or in a slip. The engines were junk as well, and it leaked fuel all over the inside."

Salvoes of 88mm flak exploded among the bombers as they arrived over the target. "We were coming in at 24,000 feet when we got hit," Wilson recounted. "And I mean hit—right in the number three engine. It almost tore the engine off the wing. It started to burn, but fortunately nothing burns very well at 24,000 feet. We pulled the fire extinguisher and miraculously, especially for that particular airplane, it worked."

Wilson and his crew struggled to stay with the group's formation. "After we got hit we fell out of our own box of bombers and tagged along as number seven with the box behind us. We lost a lot of fuel and were running all-out with the other three engines to stay in position." The crew had been briefed many times about the dangers of falling out of the protective screen of the other bombers. To do so was an invitation to enemy fighters; a solitary bomber was easy prey. "We held with the rest of the formation for about forty-five minutes until we were well clear of the target area. Finally, we realized that if we kept running the engines at full speed to stay with the formation we wouldn't have enough fuel to get back. So we eased out of the formation and set a course straight for home."

Regardless, it wasn't long before the crew calculated that they still didn't have enough fuel to make it back to Italy. "We thought about trying to make it to Vis, an island off the Yugoslav coast with an airfield maintained to recover aircraft in extremis. But we calculated that we couldn't make it there either. About this time one of the crewmen called out that there were fighters coming down at us from behind. They turned out to be friendly— they were Mustangs. They escorted us for a while, but then left. They were probably low on fuel too.

"Finally near the coast in southern Yugoslavia, the number-one engine quit. We were on two engines, numbers two and four," Wilson said. "Heavy bombers don't fly well on two engines. On two engines the B-24 was more of a powered glider than an airplane."

The stricken bomber made it to the southern coast of Yugoslavia, near the town of Cetinje, in Montenegro. "We had lost a lot of altitude by that point and were looking for a place to put it down," Wilson said. "But really, there was no place to crash-land on the hillsides, so I gave the order to abandon ship and put out a mayday call.

"Finally, after the last man in my crew bailed out," he remembered, "I pushed forward on the control column so that the aircraft wouldn't stall, then stepped back and jumped out the bomb bay. I watched the tail of the aircraft go by and figured that I had fallen far enough and pulled the rip-cord." Wilson was reassured by the jerk of the parachute deploying and blossoming above him. He quickly turned his attention to the crewless bomber plunging toward the hills. "That B-24 nosed over and went straight in. It didn't burn much but I was headed right for it and realized that if I didn't do something I was going to land in the wreckage." Wilson wrestled with his parachute risers and tried to steer away from the debris that had been his bomber.

"Whenever I pulled on the risers the parachute started to come down much faster, so I just stopped that nonsense and let it go. I got lucky and landed clear of the wreckage and onto a rocky hillside. I must have been knocked out when I hit the ground because when I regained consciousness the wind was dragging me along the hill. I stood up and started to walk down the chute to get the air out of it and when I got to the middle there was a peasant woman rolling up my chute from the other side! I don't know if she was collecting material for a new wardrobe or what. We stood there shouting at each other and I couldn't understand a word she said but we finally decided that we were probably friends. I unbuckled my harness and gave her the parachute."

At that point the woman's teen-aged son came scrambling across the rock-strewn hills shouting at Wilson. German troops were in the area and headed toward the crash site. The boy grabbed Wilson and the two of them dashed headlong into the brush. "After about two or three miles of running at full speed he brought me to an overhanging bank in a dry creek bed," Wilson recalled. "He motioned for me to crawl in and go to sleep, and that he would come back for me. It was a perfect place to hide, all covered with roots. Anyway I crawled back in there and went right to sleep. I must have been in shock."

The next day Wilson found himself as the honored guest of a band of Marshal Tito's partisans who were allied with the Soviets against the Germans. "I was kind of like their prize or their trophy," Wilson remembered. "Second Lieutenant Howard O. Wilson, their ranking American officer!" Wilson spent the next thirty days with the partisans as they carted him from one end of the district to another. "I was a recruiting tool. They showed me off like a great hero. If the mighty Americans had joined their cause then everyone else should too.

"Anyway they put me in charge of their band for an attack on what they described as a German outpost. I told them that I didn't want any part of it. I didn't know the first thing about guerrilla warfare and I refused to go. Well, their leader got very serious and said that I couldn't refuse to go, that I was being paid to kill Germans and that tonight I was their leader."

By dawn Wilson and his band of guerrillas encircled a stone farmhouse. With his .45-caliber pistol, the only weapon he had, he fired a shot into the side of the house to signal the start of the attack. "Everyone started shooting and throwing grenades," he remembered. "After about the third grenade someone inside the house put out a white flag and we stopped shooting." Out of the besieged house came a half-dozen Chetniks. The Chetniks were a guerilla force that was aligned with the Germans. They were rivals of Tito's partisans for control of Yugoslavia.

"During every briefing we got," Wilson said, "we were told not to talk politics if we got shot down over Yugoslavia. Those people took their politics very seriously. As it turned out though, those Chetniks were relatives of those same partisans of Tito's! They all seemed to be named Martinovich. Tito's partisans took their Chetnik kin prisoner and brought them back to their encampment. There was a big celebration—dancing, and jumping, and running around and all that sort of thing. They even killed a goat and made a big stew.

"Then," he remembered, "they took them out and made them dig their own graves. And they shot them. They were severe people."

During his time with the partisans, Wilson was befriended by a lovely, young woman. "Oh, I had a bad case for her. I was told by their leader though, that they treasured their women. And if they ever felt that I didn't treasure their women as well, then I wouldn't be around any longer." Wilson recalled that simply treasuring her wasn't easy. "She made it pretty hard on me. She thought I was wonderful and that I was going to take her back to the States and buy her a cow. She was quite a gal; she was fluent in French, Russian, and English and she carried a little machine pistol that she handled well enough to hit a bird at 25 yards."

The young woman came to Wilson with news that she only reluctantly shared. "There was a British army outpost operating surreptitiously out of the town of Gacko, about sixty miles to the northwest. They were aware of me and would be able to get me back to Italy if I could make contact with them. But she didn't want me to go."

Still, Wilson was anxious to get back to his unit. "When I left I gave her my fur-lined jacket, and my .45-caliber pistol. It was really something when a man cared enough for a woman to give her his gun! I really wanted to go back there someday and bring her a cow."

By that time Wilson had been reunited with four members of his crew. Remarkably, as he discovered later, all ten of his original crew plus a photographer who had been along just for the one mission, had survived and evaded capture. The copilot, who had been a substitute for Wilson's original copilot, suffered a broken leg and was turned over to the Germans for medical care.

Wilson and his four crew members left the partisans and walked along a railroad during the nights and slept during the days. "It was beautiful, September weather. We stopped along the way and picked fruit and bathed in the streams and slept in the sun. It was really nice." Happily they had no encounters with the enemy during their trek to the British outpost.

Three-and-a-half days later Wilson and his crew found the British. "We showed up at a military outpost right in the middle of tea. The Brits just looked at us like we had ruined their day. I was starving and started eating all their crumpets and whatever, and their commanding officer reminded me that they were only having tea and that dinner would be served later!"

Wilson stayed with the British several more days until the moon was out of phase. At that point the British felt it was safe to call in a C-47 from Bari, Italy. "These C-47s brought in supplies for the partisans and took out wounded fighters, and VIPs, and whatever pilots and airmen happened to be wandering around." The cargo aircraft landed in an open area that was cleared of brush and illuminated by six large bonfires. "We left at four in the morning with thirty-seven people on a twenty-one passenger aircraft. We were terribly overloaded. Once we got airborne I congratulated the pilot on making a wonderful takeoff and he just looked at me and cringed because we almost didn't make it."

Ironically, Wilson injured his hand on a truck bed immediately upon landing back in Italy. The hand quickly became infected and this, combined with his malnutrition, led to a two-month hospitalization. After returning to flight status he was assigned to the Staff of Major General James H. Bevans, the Commanding General of the Mediterranean Allied Air Forces, and promoted to first lieutenant.

Interestingly, the mission on which he had been shot down on August 26, 1944, missed the intended target utterly. The airdrome escaped virtually unscathed, however German warehouses, barracks, and fuel and ammunition sites were so heavily damaged that the mission played a significant role in the German decision to give up the Romanian capital of Bucharest.

CHAPTER 16
BREAKOUT ACROSS EUROPE

The aerial campaign that helped the Allied armies break out of the Normandy hedgerow country was performed at tremendous cost. From D-Day on June 6, 1944, until the end of August, nearly a half-million sorties were flown by the United States and Britain. More than 4,100 aircraft were lost. German antiaircraft fire caused most of those losses, as the Luftwaffe was only a shadow of its former self; it was utterly incapable of fielding and sustaining a credible defense of the German armies in France and the Low Countries.

Still, the Allied air forces supporting the ground campaign continued to sustain heavy losses through the end of the war. It was the Ninth Air Force and its British counterpart, 2nd Tactical Air Force, which bore the brunt of the losses as their primary missions—low level ground attack and battlefield reconnaissance—required that they fly in the heart of the German antiaircraft defenses.

Robert Macdonald

ROBERT MACDONALD'S FATHER WAS A TECHNICAL SERGEANT IN the U.S. Army during World War I. He was afterward posted to Coblenz, Germany, as part of the Army of Occupation. While there, he met and married the daughter of the older couple in whose home he was billeted. The newlyweds had a son, Robert Macdonald, in 1921.

"I had a difficult time after we got back to the States," said Macdonald. "The nation had just finished a bloody war with the Kaiser's armies. Of course, since I spoke nothing but German, I was 'The Hun' at school and I came home crying every day because the other kids picked on me.

"My father was a career Army man—he did thirty years—but after traveling all over the place, we finally settled in San Diego where I finished high school at St. Augustine." Like most men who served in World War II, Macdonald came of age during the Great Depression of the 1930s, and was acutely aware of the value of a job and of the power of the dollar. Both were scarce during that difficult time. "I was in my last year of high school when all of my buddies joined the National Guard. It seemed like a decent way to make a buck—we got one dollar per drill—so I joined too."

But the nation was preparing for war and it wasn't long before Uncle Sam demanded that Macdonald and many thousands like him fulfill their National Guard obligations. At the start of his second year in college, just before the attack on Pearl Harbor, he was shipped to Hawaii as part of the 251st Coast Artillery (Antiaircraft) Regiment. After the attack, his unit sat poised for a rumored Japanese invasion of the Hawaiian Islands that never came. Finally the 251st was shipped to the Fiji Islands to protect the 70th Fighter Squadron, a P-39 unit.

There was no action on Fiji and Macdonald grew bored as his unit languished on the small island. "I thought we were just kind of sitting there, waiting the war out. The next thing I know, the USS *Saratoga* came in. She'd been hit by a Japanese torpedo. Well, one of her crew chiefs came by our tents looking for booze. I gave him some Australian and New Zealand beer in exchange for a ride in a Navy airplane."

That airplane was a Grumman TBF Avenger torpedo bomber. "It was a night flight, and it was beautiful, especially the big blue exhaust flames that the engine produced. It was my first ride in an airplane, and it made me wonder what had happened with my application for flight training; I had submitted it several months earlier."

The nation needed young men to man the nearly three hundred thousand aircraft it would produce during the war. MacDonald was one of them. He was ordered from the Pacific to flight training during the summer of 1942 and graduated with Class 44A in January 1944. Fighter training followed.

"We were the first class that went through the brand new P-51 fighter training group at St. Petersburg, Florida. They gave us ten hours of training in the P-40, which I loved, and then it was on to the P-51, which I loved even more," Macdonald said.

The training was fast and furious as the need for pilots in Europe was desperate. Following hospitalization for an eardrum that was blown during a high-speed dive, Macdonald boarded the *Queen Mary* for England as a replacement pilot. He arrived at A-15 at Maupertuis, near Cherbourg, France, during early July 1944, only a month after D-Day. He was assigned to the 363rd Fighter Group, part of the Ninth Air Force, flying P-51 Mustangs.

Macdonald loved the Mustang. Like millions of young men during that time and since, he was enamored with the way the aircraft looked and performed. The Mustang was handsome and muscular and nothing in the skies over Europe at that time could outperform it. It was fast, maneuverable, well-armed and it could range farther than any other fighter in the theater. "I wouldn't have traded it for any airplane in the world," Macdonald remembered.

"So, I had just gotten there with two other new guys and the squadron commander told us to forget everything that we learned in training. He said that the only thing we had to remember was to see the enemy aircraft first and to make sure we had plenty of altitude. He told us not to worry about deflection shooting. Instead, we were just supposed to get behind the enemy aircraft and when our prop was about ready to chop his tail off, then that was the time to pull the trigger. That was the brief for my first combat mission; there was nothing more."

As it developed, the abbreviated dogfighting advice of Macdonald's squadron commander was wasted breath. Macdonald spent his first mission glued to his commander's wing, shooting up trains and flak towers. "All of a sudden he gave a couple of signals and down we went. Then he started shooting. I didn't even know what he was shooting at, but I shot too." As it turned out, the squadron chewed up a cluster of flak towers preparatory to shooting up an airfield. Up until that point, Macdonald had never heard of such a thing. Once the dangerous flak towers were neutralized, the fighters shot a train into pieces. This sortie was typical of those Macdonald flew during this period as the Allied armies fought to break out of Normandy.

The combat mission Macdonald remembered most came early in his wartime career. "I had been in combat for a little while by that time and was starting to get used to things. Again, I was flying on the squadron commander's wing and we had spotted a German convoy. Most of it was hidden in a forest, but the lead section of vehicles stretched into the center of a village. That old squadron commander [Macdonald's commander was twenty-six] had us well out of the way checking things out. Finally he dove down and I was in with him on his left wing as he lined up on the head of the column which was stopped in front of what looked like a grocery store or a bakery."

The line of German command cars and lorries, and the clusters of gray-clad troops halted in the center of the small French hamlet, grew larger in Macdonald's windscreen as the American fighters continued their dive. "We leveled off right down on the deck going straight at them and I was pointed right at some German officers but they were talking to a man with a white apron. He looked like a butcher, or a grocery clerk. And I thought to myself—and I'll always remember it—get out of the way, get out of the way, get out of the way!"

Macdonald's mental urging was not enough, and the butcher, along with the German officers, was cut down by the fire of his .50-caliber machine guns. "I never thought twice about strafing convoys, vehicles, airfields, marshalling yards, tanks and anything else that moved; they were just targets. They were things that we were supposed to destroy. But that guy in the butcher's apron . . . that always bothered me."

During September 1944, following the breakout from Normandy by the Allied armies, the 363rd Fighter Group was redesignated as the 363rd Tactical Reconnaissance Group. The advancing armies were desperate for intelligence on the disposition of the German units ahead of them, and the reconsititution of the 363rd as a photo reconnaissance unit was intended to address that need. The unit was reequipped with the F-6—the photo reconnaissance variant of the P-51. Unlike the F-5, the photo reconnaissance version of the P-38, the F-6 retained its armament.

At the same time, many of the 363rd's pilots were recruited by other Ninth Air Force fighter groups to fly the P-47 Thunderbolt. The P-47, although awkward in appearance when compared to the P-51, was a superior aircraft for ground attack.

"I was given a choice," Macdonald said, "I could keep flying the ground attack missions I had been flying, except in the P-47 instead of the P-51. That would have required me to transfer to a different unit. Or I could fly tactical reconnaissance in the Mustang and stay with the 363rd." Still under the spell of the Mustang, Macdonald chose to practice his trade as a tactical reconnaissance pilot.

"I didn't know anything about reconnaissance," he said. "And I really wasn't that good at navigating. For the first few missions, I just followed the flight leader around." However, Macdonald soon took a liking to the new type of work. All the flights were conducted as two-ship missions for which the pilots were given a route or target to visually reconnoiter or photograph. Interestingly, the pilots used prewar road maps that were overlaid with a military grid. Macdonald recalled that they were incredibly accurate. "The landscape in Europe had been the same for centuries. I could look down at a road map and it would show an odd shaped field just off of the road and sure enough, it would look exactly the same from the air."

Although the F-6 was armed for self-defense, the 363rd's pilots occasionally stretched their tethers and did a bit of offensive freelancing when opportunities presented themselves. This type of small element action was officially discouraged as it jeopardized the more important reconnaissance mission and subsequently the commanders' picture of the enemy situation. Still, discouraging the young pilots was difficult. "We never really saw our leadership," Macdonald remembered. "We flew around in pairs and we were all young and anxious to do our part. We shot up anything that looked like it needed it."

The photo reconnaissance work, almost all of it at low level, was dangerous. "We flew everywhere from right down on the deck up to a maximum height of about 4,000 feet, and at about 300 to 350 miles per hour. One set of cameras was set to photograph down at a 45 degree angle and the other was set to shoot vertically below us. But most of the time we did simple visual reconnaissance rather than photographic missions.

"The biggest danger was ground fire. The big stuff—such as the 88mm guns—usually missed us low and behind. If they didn't get you with the first salvo then they would never catch up because we were always jinking. When we jinked and flew low we were really difficult to hit. But it was a dangerous type of flying; on one mission we flew so low that I came back with pine cones in my gun ports."

The smaller caliber antiaircraft fire was much more effective. "The 20mm cannons used to tear us up," Macdonald remembered. The 20mm cannon, because of its smaller size and weight was more mobile and easier to aim. It was also produced and deployed in much greater numbers. These factors, combined with its very high rate of fire, made it particularly deadly to the low-flying reconnaissance types. "In fact, the first time I got shot up was somewhat ironic. I got hit by 20mm cannon fire over my own hometown, Coblenz, Germany."

Macdonald recalled one of the instances when he was caught by anti-aircraft fire. "I got hit and started to get out. The engine had stopped and I had already jettisoned the canopy, but the aircraft was going too fast; I was scared. I got halfway out but my headset was still connected to the aircraft and the slipstream was too strong. Anyway, it was like a big hand pushed me back in. At the same time, the engine caught, the aircraft started flying again and I got back home." This was just one of three instances when he coaxed aircraft back to base that were so badly damaged they were ultimately stripped for parts and then written off.

Macdonald remembered what they were briefed to do if they were shot down. "They gave us an option. It was up to us whether or not we wanted to carry our .45-caliber pistols. Some of the pilots saw no use carrying the heavy weapon into the cockpit, as it was more likely to antagonize enemy troops than to intimidate or defeat them. We were also told that it was much preferable to be captured by the Luftwaffe rather than the German army." Their counterparts in the German air force were much more likely than the enemy army troops to treat them fairly. Either service though, was more preferable than falling into the hands of war-weary, vigilante civilian mobs that occasionally killed Allied airmen outright.

Macdonald's unit hop-scotched across the continent on captured German airfields as the Wehrmacht was beaten back into Germany. "Of the ten different airfields we operated from, only two of them had concrete runways—Cherbourg and Venlo, in Holland. The rest were just wire mesh covered with tar paper." He remembered being impressed with the engineering details on some of the German fighter types that were disabled before being abandoned in the face of the Allied advance. "Some of the seats on their fighters were tilted back, rather than straight up. It enabled them to withstand higher G-forces."

Although his unit was constantly on the move, Macdonald remembered that the often spartan conditions had very little effect on the group's ability to carry out its missions. "Out of 81 combat missions, I aborted only once. The aircraft had low oil pressure. My crew chief was so disappointed that he cried; it was a matter of pride." He recalled a lighter side of the crewmen who maintained his aircraft: "They were a superb bunch. I never even did a walk-around on my aircraft before I went flying. I just climbed in and took off. The only thing I ever had to worry about was whether or not they had gotten drunk the night before and had used up all of the aircraft's oxygen to sober up." He had an arrangement with his mechanics that was typical in his unit. "We used to get liquor rations that were supposed to be allotted out in individual shots after each mission. We never did that. We just took the whole bottle—the pilots kept the scotch and the crew chiefs got the gin."

Macdonald's reconnaissance squadron, the 161st, was one of three that made up the 363rd Tactical Reconnaissance Group. Like the other two squadrons, the 160th and the 162nd, the 161st saw little air-to-air action. "I had one buddy who had two kills. He shot down a little high-winged German utility aircraft, and a British Tiffy; a Typhoon. Nothing happened to him after he shot down the Typhoon. It was just laughed off—everyone was too busy."

Occasionally though, he or his wingman did catch sight of enemy fighters. "Most of the time, they just scooted off. I'm not sure if we were just small potatoes, or if they were under orders not to engage fighters, or if they felt that the Mustang was too superior to their own aircraft." Macdonald wasn't particularly frustrated at the lack of opportunities to fight enemy aircraft. "It didn't bother me—that was a good way to get killed." Indeed, Macdonald and his fellow pilots gave their German counterparts plenty of respect. "We had been taught, and believed, that they were a ferocious bunch."

Macdonald recollected an event that occurred toward the end of the war as the Allies were breaching the Rhine defenses and striking toward the heart of Germany itself. "At the time I was thinking I might have made it through the damned war. During this time, and on this sortie, the Germans started shooting crazy-looking antiaircraft fire. It wasn't the standard heavy flak, it was different. Silver spires shot up and there were red flashing things. I'm not sure if it was supposed to shoot us down or scare us or both."

As it turned out his wingman was lost in heavy fog and was never heard from again, perhaps a victim of antiaircraft fire. Macdonald was alone. After reconnoitering his objective he started back toward the American lines and spotted a German command car racing down the autobahn. So late in the war, with Allied air superiority unchallenged, a command car on the open road during daylight was very unusual. "I thought to myself that this was probably someone important," he remembered. "The autobahn went right down the center of a big, long clearing. I dove right down on the deck and strafed it, and watched it roll over."

As Macdonald climbed toward safety his aircraft was bracketed by heavy antiaircraft fire. "Every time I started to lift up, it was in front of me. I was going to get hosed and I knew it." Ahead of him was a village, and the instant was fast approaching when he would have to lift up into the enemy cannon barrage or collide with a row of buildings directly in his flight path. "There were brick buildings in the village that were two or three stories high. When the time came when I was going to have to lift up or crash into them, I let go with a long burst." Torn with panic, Macdonald fired his .50-caliber machine guns directly into the buildings as he pulled up and over the village.

"I always wondered who was in those buildings. It's probable that there was no one in there but some poor civilians. I had absolutely no reason to fire my guns. I just did it out of absolute fright," he recalled. "Later, I felt bad. I shouldn't have done it. And through some small miracle I didn't even get hit—not a scratch."

After the war Macdonald returned to the States to wait for his discharge from active service. In the meantime he "gave blindfold checks in the P-51 to Brazilians and Chinese and whoever. And I went to the swimming pool a lot." He was called into service again during the Korean War and served as an intelligence officer on both the peninsula, and in Japan. He eventually retired as the Chief of the San Diego County Parole Department.

Robert Macdonald's personal decorations from World War II included the Distinguished Flying Cross and the Air Medal with multiple Oak Leaf Clusters

CHAPTER 17
NIGHT ARMED RECONNAISSANCE

Prior to Pearl Harbor, American aviation experts watched with interest and concern the night war being waged in the skies over Britain and Germany. The science of aerial night fighting was in its infancy, but technology was quickly being developed which would make it deadly. However, without a purpose-built system, the United States was in danger of being left behind in the race to dominate the night skies. Following the nation's entry into the war, a large-scale effort was begun to develop a dedicated night-fighting aircraft and to train the pilots and crews necessary to operate it.

Alvin E. "Bud" Anderson

BUD ANDERSON WAS BORN IN WARREN, PENNSYLVANIA, ON MAY 26, 1918. The son of an oil driller, he and his family traveled the country as the oil industry exploded to meet the demands of industry and the nation's growing numbers of fuel-hungry automobiles. His father had started in the oil fields of Pennsylvania at the age of thirteen. Before he was fifty he retired and the Anderson family ended up in Broken Arrow, Oklahoma, where the elder Anderson invested quite heavily in an oil lease. "I don't know how many wells he drilled," Anderson remembered, "but it was enough to go broke."

Eventually the family settled back in Pennsylvania where Anderson finished high school and went to work for an uncle in the baking business. "My goal was to go to the Fleischmann School of Baking in Chicago and learn to be a baker," Anderson recalled. In the end though, he left the baking business and found employment working in a service station. "From 1937 to 1940, I worked seventy-two hours a week, for fifteen dollars a week."

A tireless worker, Anderson was hired for a position of increased responsibility by Standard Oil, then again by the Atlantic Refining Company. Things looked promising for Anderson; he was smart, well-liked, and motivated. "But then I got drafted in March 1942. They sent me to Fort Knox, Kentucky, where I made corporal. I ended up staying there as a tank driving instructor. Then, one of my buddies from boot camp by the name of Vicinski wrote me. He had gotten called to go to the aviation cadets and wanted me to do the same thing. He told me to get the hell out of Fort Knox. He said the aviator's life was the way to go—clean sheets and good pay and everything.

"I hadn't ever had any interest in aviation because I thought that it was something that I'd never have an opportunity to do. It seemed so far out of reach. But old Vicinski, he wrote back again and said, 'Listen; if a dumb Pollock like me can pass the aviation cadet test, then a smart Swede like you might stand a chance. Go take it!'

"So I did. And I passed it. The next thing I knew I was in training at Santa Ana, California, in October 1942. God bless Vicinski. I never saw or heard from him again."

Anderson's training was fast and furious. At various bases throughout the Southwest he flew PT-17s, BT-13s, AT-9s, RP-322s (an early P-38 derivative), and AT-6s. "I was in pilot class 43G, and finally graduated from Williams Field, Arizona, on July 28, 1943."

It was typical during pilot training for the cadet classes to be briefed by pilots with experience flying different aircraft. It gave the students an idea of the capabilities and missions of the different types, and also information as to which aircraft they might want to fly—needs of the Army Air Forces permitting. "They had this guy come talk to us about night fighters. For some reason, that sort of appealed to me so I put in for night fighters. I'm not sure why; I guess I was always kind of a night person. But at the time I didn't know very much about the airplanes at all. I was just finishing primary flight training."

The United States had gotten a slow start in the night fighting arena. While the English and Germans were stalking each other through the night skies since before America entered the war, the USAAF was still short of experience in 1943. And it lacked the special equipment that was demanded by such operations. Still, a great deal of work was underway and the United States, whose laboratories and test facilities had been working full time on the technology, was about to field what was arguably the best equipment of the war.

"After we logged about 125 hours in the B-25 for twin-engine training, we were sent to the night fighter school at Orlando, Florida," Anderson recounted. "There we underwent transition training into the A-20."

The Douglas A-20 Havoc was a twin-engine medium bomber that had already seen widespread service overseas. More than a hundred A-20s were modified with radar and other equipment to convert them into night fighters. The modified aircraft were designated P-70s. Judged a barely nominal success, the P-70 was the only American night fighter available before the Northrop P-61 Black Widow became operational during 1944. It was with the P-70 that Anderson and his fellow pilots were trained.

"Also in Orlando," Anderson remembered, "we were paired up with our R/O's—our Radar Observers. We were matched up psychologically. This is where I was teamed up with Smitty." Smitty was John Granville Smith who served as Anderson's airborne teammate through his entire combat career.

"We were sent to Kissimmee, Florida, during December 1943 and that's where we actually started flying the real P-70s. These were converted A-20s but there was quite a bit of difference between the two airplanes, particularly in the weight and balance—you could go about twenty miles an hour and pull back on the controls and the nose would lift up off of the ground!"

Night intercepts demanded precise flying, teamwork, and radar operations. The training was as demanding and thorough as any of the day. Once airborne, the fighter was directed by the Ground Control Intercept (GCI) radar station to take up an orbit at a particular point. When an enemy aircraft was detected the fighter was vectored to a point from where its own short-range radar could make contact. From that point the fighter finished the intercept. Anderson remembered that, "Smitty and I trained to bring an airplane to a point where it would be 500 feet in front of us, 500 feet to the side, and 500 feet above us. That way I knew exactly where to look when he called 'Punch.'"

Advanced night training at Fresno, California, followed duty at Orlando. It was there that Anderson first saw the Northrop P-61 Black Widow. Designed in response to an Army order in December 1941 for an aircraft that could carry the SCR-720 Air Interception radar, the resulting aircraft, technically a fighter, was nearly as large as the medium bombers of the day. With an unusual twin-boom layout—a characteristic it shared with Lockheed's P-38—the P-61 was a complex design that consequently suffered teething problems that dogged the aircraft through its entire service life. The type first flew on May 26, 1942, and deliveries to operational units began during the spring of 1944.

Teething problems aside, the aircraft delivered all that was promised. The radar installation was a success, and although the dorsal barbette with four 20mm cannon was discontinued for a time because of aerodynamic problems, the remaining armament of four, forward-firing 20mm cannon was more than adequate. Additionally, the type was a marvel to fly—in fact, it was more maneuverable than many single-engine fighters.

"I had never seen one before," Anderson remembered. "The first time I encountered it was at Fresno when I almost ran into one. I was parking a P-70 when I lost my brakes. To be honest, at the time I really didn't know anything about it."

He found out soon enough. "I was sent overseas and got off the ship in Liverpool, England, on July 4, 1944. They sent me over to Scorton where I was assigned to the 425th Night Fighter Squadron, part of the Ninth Air Force. They were operating P-61s which of course I had never flown. These aircraft didn't have a gunner or the turret on top. I got two or three hours of cockpit time and then a check ride. That was about it; 'Okay buddy, you're a P-61 pilot now.'"

It was August 18, 1944, when the 425th crossed the English Channel to France to begin combat operations in earnest. Anderson, because he was a junior pilot, was assigned to bring the ground element into France. From a troop transport he landed with the unit's ground echelon at Utah Beach in Normandy. "It was a hell of a thing," he remembered. Heavily burdened and sweltering under the hot August sun, the poorly-provisioned ground crews ran out of water. Anderson eventually got them to a rest area that had been cleared of mines and cordoned off. "We came across a captain who had an entire Lister Bag of water that he would not share. The men started grumbling—and I mean seriously. I told him that I couldn't guarantee that I could control them if they didn't get some water. Well, he finally gave in, but not before it started to get serious. Anyway, we eventually arrived at our airfield [A-33] near Vannes at 0300 in the morning."

Soon after, Anderson began to fly combat missions. "I had only a grand total of 20 hours in the P-61 before my first combat mission. It was a wonderful airplane though—very forgiving and very stable. I had liked the B-25 for the same reasons but the B-25 was very loud whereas the P-61 wasn't. Our first combat sorties were patrols; that's all we did," he remembered. It was ironic that the Americans finally had a fighter in the night skies over Europe that was the equal of any in the world. But the war had turned in favor of the Allies and there was little trade for the P-61s in terms of enemy aircraft. "I probably chased fifty different airplanes over there that turned out to be friendly," Anderson said.

"To the best of my knowledge I only chased one German aircraft. I was sure that it was a Focke-Wulf 200 Condor, but not so sure that I was going to take a chance and shoot it down. He made me look like a school boy because he sure could fly instruments—but so could I. Because we were in the clouds I just never could get another good visual ID on him. We were at 22,000 feet and the heater wasn't working. I was frozen stiff and was shivering so hard that I could barely see the instruments. I followed that boy until GCI called me off when I started to get beyond their radar range. I was so cold I was almost happy."

Anderson's experiences were the norm for most of the Black Widow pilots in Europe. Like the daytime skies, the night was filled with aircraft of all types from many nationalities. The British routinely ran thousand-aircraft raids into Germany, and the Americans also flew at night; many black-painted aircraft performed clandestine sorties in support of various missions and objectives. Of course the Germans, desperate to stem the Allied onslaught, were also airborne although in much smaller numbers. Sorting through this myriad of aircraft to find and destroy the increasingly rare enemy aircraft was a difficult task and opportunities to score came only very seldom.

The night intercept mission was not only demanding but it was also dangerous. Anderson recalled one sortie that turned out poorly for a squadron mate. "He was running an intercept and just at the last minute he decided that it was not an enemy aircraft. In fact it was a B-17. Well, the rules of the road up there at night were that if you had your guns pointed at someone, then you were fair game—they could shoot you down and no one would say a thing. The tail gunner opened up and really let them have it," Anderson remembered. "He was a good shot. My squadron mate's aircraft caught fire and he was hit in the shoulder. Still he was able to fly it back and he managed to belly it in. It was a pretty rough landing and he got banged up good. His R/O dragged him out just before the airplane blew up."

Sadly, the same crew was shot down and killed by friendly antiaircraft fire only a short time later while erroneously attempting a night landing at a nearby airfield.

"Most of the ground commanders didn't give a hoot about night fighters at first," Anderson recalled. "But after we got there they realized that we were all right because we were keeping Bed Check Charlie away from them." Bed Check Charlie was the nickname given by American soldiers to German aircraft, usually operating as singles, which droned overhead Allied positions to drop bombs and otherwise harass the troops. The intent was to keep the Allies from getting enough rest; any incidental damage was icing on the cake. After the arrival of the P-61s, the activities of the German harassers were significantly curtailed.

It wasn't long before the P-61s were put to another good use. The German Wehrmacht, unable to move during the day because of the umbrella of Allied aircraft, began to move most of its troops and equipment under the cover of darkness. Borrowing tactics from RAF Mosquito units, individual P-61s turned their efforts to ground interdiction missions after being relieved of their night intercept duties. The big black fighters descended to low altitude and prowled enemy-held roads and railroad marshalling yards looking for convoys and rolling stock.

The Black Widows had a telling effect. Soon the Germans found that movement at night was not failsafe protection from aerial attack. Using only their unaided eyes, the P-61 crews flew over enemy lines looking for signs of the enemy. Glimmers of light, shadows along the roads, and flashes of gunfire were telltale clues of the enemy's presence. Once they spotted their quarry the pilots dived out of the dark and opened fire with their four 20mm cannon. Although the P-61 was still unable to carry bombs at that point, the concentrated fire of the aircraft's cannons was deadly enough to destroy any sort of equipment the enemy could field, excepting only the heaviest armor.

The mission was a dangerous one. "We lost three aircraft fairly early on," Anderson remembered. "Although we weren't positive, we guessed that the pilots lost their depth perception while they were staring through the gunsight and that they flew right into the ground."

Anderson nearly succumbed to the same deadly mistake. During late November 1944 he was on patrol near the front lines when he spotted some ground activity near the city of Kaiserslautern, Germany. "I called it out to GCI and they cleared me to descend to attack it," Anderson remembered. "I was up at about 13,000 feet, and I split-S'd down to set up for an attack. Well I forgot that poor Smitty had a cold and I nearly blew his sinuses out in the dive. That poor guy was screaming.

"I leveled off at pretty low level across Kaiserslautern. I hadn't even touched the throttles and was still moving at about 200 miles per hour." Anderson's target turned out to be a railroad marshalling yard. "I set myself up and picked off four locomotives on that single run.

"I slowed it down to about 150 miles per hour by pulling up into a chandelle, turning 180 degrees and putting down one-quarter flaps. There still wasn't anyone shooting at me. I set up for another attack, but was still trimmed for about 250 miles per hour. I was pretty excited and was over-correcting like hell as I tried to put some shots into another locomotive. Well, thank God that Smitty had moved up into the front with me by then. He started to shout a few choice things at me—'Pull up! Pull up! Pull up!' I finally pulled up and I don't think we missed that locomotive by twenty feet. We flew right through the steam from the blown boiler and that gave us quite a lift." Anderson only barely escaped the same deadly fate that had already claimed three crews from his squadron.

He recalled a similar incident when he made an attack against a plant of some sort: "I went into a shallow dive and put the power back on and started firing at the edge of the factory and worked my way back toward the center. All of a sudden I saw a huge smokestack. I just laid the airplane over—the wings were vertical with the ground. And oh, we only barely missed it! Just as I leveled the wings back out, something in the factory exploded and that old airplane was lifted straight up, just like we were riding an elevator."

Accidents outside of combat also took their toll on the 425th. Recovering back at the airfield in the dark, often in poor weather, caused more than one mishap. "One night at Coulommiers all the sorties except mine had been scrubbed because of the weather. I lost my radio as soon as I got airborne and ended up a hundred miles into Germany. When I eventually got back, I had to make two or three attempts to land. Finally, when I broke out underneath the weather, about half of the runway lights were out so I mistakenly set down about 2,000 feet from the end of the runway. I had to brake very heavily and blew a tire and slid off the pavement. I thought I had it made but then the right wheel sank all the way into a bomb-hole that had not yet been filled in."

But others weren't as fortunate as Anderson. "One night there was a column of our tanks getting ready to go into combat," he remembered. "They were only about a mile from the airfield and were lined up on the same heading as our runway. These tanks had vent holes in their tops which were open. It was concluded that the lights from the inside of the tanks looked just like the runway lights because one of our crews tried to land right on top of them. It killed them and burned up three tanks and several tank crews."

December 16, 1944, marked the beginning of the last great German offensive in the West. What was to become famous as the Battle of the Bulge came very near to achieving the German goal of collapsing the Western Front. From their base, A-82, in Etain, France, the men of the 425th were close to the action and ultimately flew a great number of sorties to help blunt the enemy thrust.

Anderson remembered the start of the clash. During the day of December 17, he and Smith took the squadron "hack" aircraft, a Stinson L-5 Sentinel, to reconnoiter near the front for a sortie they had scheduled for that same evening. "Smitty and I took the L-5 and flew across the Moselle River. Once we got across we spotted a bunch of German tanks coming down from the hills. We were pretty low and we could see their faces as they looked up at us. Smitty shouted 'Let's get the hell out of here!' So we hightailed it back to the field and reported it to the intelligence officer."

That same night Anderson and Smith were airborne in a P-61 when they spotted a signal light flashing just beyond friendly lines. "I went down and popped it and it caught fire. Then I spotted another one further down and popped it too. There was another one even further down the line, but

GCI called me back—we were getting out of their range. That's when I saw a bunch of searchlights illuminating the clouds. GCI turned me loose to go get them but when I got close they really let loose with the flak. I couldn't get anywhere near them.

"When I came back I was debriefing with the intelligence officer and one of my squadron mates was standing there and he started giving me a hard time. 'My God, Anderson, are you chicken? Couldn't you even get a searchlight? I'll show you how to do it.' Well, he took off and I just hung around waiting for him to come back. He came back about 45 minutes later with his right engine and his radio shot out. So I asked him if he got a searchlight. 'Hell,' he said, 'I couldn't even get close to them.' I found out later that the searchlights were American. They were being used to illuminate and silhouette German troops."

Anderson's combat career came to an abrupt end less than a week later on December 23, 1944. At the time, the 425th was still operating out of A-82 at Etain, France. "There was an unidentified airplane coming our way and the squadron sent a jeep out to town to get us where we were staying in a bombed-out hotel. It was about 2330 on the evening of 23 December. We piled in and drove out to the airfield and heard two bombs go off. Well it was a gorgeous night, absolutely brilliant, and we could see the aircraft. It was either a Ju-88 or Ju-188. He was low as hell and I was sure that he could see the jeep and would strafe us. I would have if I was him.

"Well the roads were covered with glare ice, and we had a hard time getting the jeep stopped," Anderson remembered. "I was sitting in the back and I jumped out and slipped on the ice then hit some frozen mud and broke my leg. I had a compound fracture of the tibia, and the fibula was just all shattered. The tibia was broken just like it was cut with a knife and the bones came right out through my boot."

The next two weeks were an exercise in patience and pain for the injured Anderson. "They put a Thompson splint on my leg and took me up to a hospital on the front lines about 18 miles away. The next night we got bombed and a nurse and a patient were killed. So then they brought me back to the evacuation hospital at my own airfield." While Anderson waited to be flown out of France, the airfield came under air attack several times. "There was a priest in the cot next to me. He was the nicest guy but he had gangrene in both feet. He had gotten frostbite after walking out of

Bastogne. Well, the field came under attack and they dropped a bomb on us. We both ended up hiding on the ground under our cots. Then we looked at each other and started laughing as we realized that those canvas cots weren't going to do us any good if we got hit by a bomb!"

Anderson's movement to England for more advanced treatment was further delayed until early January by poor weather. "They had some C-47s there to get us out but the weather was too bad. Every morning they'd go out and run the engines, then shut them down. Finally, they loaded us up one day. The weather was pretty fair and we took off. We were supposed to go in somewhere around Portsmouth, England, but the field there was socked in. After that I knew that there was something going on," Anderson recounted. "From my stretcher up against the bulkhead I could see the flight nurse going in and out of the flight deck. I asked her what was going on—were we short on fuel? And she said no, that everything was fine. But she was nervous. She'd tend the patients and then go back up to the flight deck.

"Anyway we finally started to let down," Anderson said. "The pilot brought it down through the weather and touched down on the runway. On landing roll-out the right engine quit—we had run out of gas. After we cleared the runway, I saw the pilot. He was slumped over the controls with relief. There were two other C-47s in that flight and each one had one or both engines quit on the runway. It was that close. Later the pilot came by to see us in the hospital. I told him what a good job he had done—he was really only just a kid."

———

Following an extensive recuperation period, Alvin Anderson went on terminal leave from active duty in January 1946. Exercising his considerable charm, he married the girl next door, who in fact had been warned off of the rogue night fighter by his own mother! He eventually reentered the oil industry and retired from the Atlantic-Richfield Oil Company in 1975 after 27 years of service.

CHAPTER 18

THE SHARECROPPER'S SON
BOMBS HITLER

The immense armadas of American heavy bombers that came to characterize the daytime air war over Europe had humble beginnings. The USAAF flew its first heavy bomber attack against the Nazis on August 17, 1942. It was a short-range raid by a dozen B-17s on the rail yard at Rouen, France. Nevertheless, the United States methodically equipped and manned the England-based Eighth Air Force until it was the most powerful air force ever fielded. Together with the Italy-based Fifteenth Air Force and the RAF's Bomber Command, the Eighth pounded Germany into rubble. By December 24, 1944, the Eighth, by itself, was able to sortie more than 2,000 heavy bombers on the greatest air raid ever launched.

Still, early on, it wasn't obvious that the American heavy bombers would survive. Casualty rates were catastrophic. The odds of surviving a 25-mission combat tour, even as late as the end of 1943, were only about half. But with the introduction of the long-range P-51, and of range-extending modifications, equipment and tactics for the P-47 and P-38, the survival rate improved.

The bomber crews obviously appreciated their increased odds. Nevertheless, the skies remained dangerous until the end of the war. Inside each of the bombers, unseen, was a volunteer crew of nine or more men. Each of them had been someone's baby boy— someone's loved one. Many of them were husbands and fathers. And each of them hoped and prayed to finish their combat tour.

George M. Kesselring

GEORGE M. KESSELRING WAS BORN AT HOME IN GUTHRIE COUNTY, Iowa, on December 11, 1923. "My father was a sharecropper. He farmed rented land and paid the owners half of what he made from it. I was one of four brothers—the youngest—and we pitched in as soon as we were old enough to do so. My father worked hard. And with four boys to raise and a household to run my mother did too. Aside from crops we kept ten or twelve milk cows that had to be milked twice a day; they took up one entire side of the barn. And we also had a chicken coop with laying hens. We sold the milk and eggs in town—Guthrie Center—and that brought in about seven dollars a week. It was an important part of our income."

Food production was a critical element of the American war effort and Kesselring was doing his part on a spring day in 1942. "I was headed out to one of the fields on a tractor—we were putting in corn—when there was a roar that drowned out the noise of the engine. It was a P-51 and it flew right over me. I decided right then that I wanted to fly one.

"My father didn't like that idea one bit," Kesselring recalled. "We were farming three hundred acres at the time and one brother had already left home, another had died of diabetes and the third was drafted. My father wanted me to stay home. He was particularly against the idea of me signing up voluntarily because I wasn't in danger of getting drafted. I was the only son left at home and we were working in a vital war industry. I could have easily gotten a deferment from military service."

Counter to his father's wishes, Kesselring prepared himself to pass the battery of tests required to qualify as an aviation cadet. "I took a night school class at Perry, Iowa, that was administered by the Elks Club. I drove 35 miles two nights each week after working all day in the fields. And I did pretty well; they told me that my scores were more typical of someone who had completed at least a couple years of college. So, I enlisted as an aviation cadet on September 5, 1942, in Des Moines."

Kesselring left home for the first time in his life during February 1943 at age 19. His training kept him in the south central United States. After screening and indoctrination at the San Antonio Aviation Cadet Center, he completed primary training in Corsicana, Texas, basic training in Greenville, Texas, and advanced training in Frederick, Oklahoma.

He remembered how the aviation cadets were used to police their own ranks. "At each phase of cadet training you were an underclassman for about a month and then an upperclassman for about a month. Following that, you were typically sent to a new phase of training and would do the same thing again. Well, upperclassmen were used to discipline underclassmen. At San Antonio, one universally despised upperclassman put me into a chair brace. I had to sit with my back to the wall with my knees bent like a chair and then hold an actual chair while he piled shoes on it. He crawled under the chair and snarled at me and dared me to drop it on him. I didn't. When he was washed out and sent to the infantry a short time later, my satisfaction knew no bounds!

"Later, during advanced training at Frederick, a cadet by the name of J. O. Jeffers was flying without an instructor one day and came in for a landing. He forgot to lower his landing gear and was on final approach while the control tower shouted at him to go around. I don't know why he didn't respond but he landed with his wheels up and damaged his airplane. He didn't get washed out, but from that day until graduation he had to wear a big sign across his chest that read, GUMP. GUMP stood for Gas, Undercarriage, Mixture and Prop. Those were the four items that were supposed to be checked before every landing."

Kesselring's advancement through the various schools and phases was relatively uneventful. After he graduated in February 1944 as part of Class 44B he was sent to Liberal, Kansas, for training on the B-24. "The weather had been terrible for a while in Kansas," Kesselring said. "They were about three classes behind because of it. After sitting around for a few weeks they sent me to Goodfellow Army Airfield in San Angelo, Texas, to be a pilot instructor in the Basic Phase. I spent several months instructing on the Vultee BT-13. I didn't mind it too much."

Following instructor duty Kesselring was reassigned to fly B-17s rather than B-24s and joined a crew headed by John Flynn at Lincoln, Nebraska. Kesselring, Flynn and the rest of the crew were subsequently ordered to Pyote Army Air Field—nicknamed Rattlesnake Field—in west Texas. "It was hot and the temperature sometimes reached 130 degrees on the flight line. We were wet with sweat before we took off and then we froze when we got to altitude. After landing, we were again soaked with perspiration before we even got back into the operations building."

At that point in the war, late summer of 1944, the USAAF was at its zenith and numbered almost 2.5 million men. Less than five years earlier it had counted only about 25,000 men in uniform. What this meant in practical terms was that just one man out of every hundred had been on the job for more than five years. Essentially, although the force was very large and capable, it was also very green.

And it showed. "Things were often disorganized," Kesselring recollected. "For instance, after our crew finished training at Rattlesnake Field, we were sent to Kearney, Nebraska, to pick up a new B-17 so that we could fly it overseas. However, after we arrived at Kearney there were no aircraft available. So they sent us down south to Texas and then east to Langley Field, in Virginia. There we spent a short time flying navigators around for training. Finally, in November 1944, they put us on a ship and sent us to England." It had been more than two years since he enlisted.

Once Kesselring arrived in England it seemed that the USAAF was anxious to make up for lost time. He was assigned to the 323rd Bombardment Squadron of the 91st Bombardment Group (H) based at Bassingbourn, England. He was sent into combat a short time later. "I flew my first mission on November 26, 1944. It was the policy at that time for newly-arrived crews to fly a few missions with experienced airmen so that they could understand how things were done. So, on that day several of us flew with William Koff in *Outhouse Mouse*."

The 91st was part of a group of 118 bombers sent to hit the railway viaduct at Altenbeken, Germany. Much of the coal that fed Germany's synthetic oil industry traveled over the structure. On that day the German fighters defended against the bombers in force just as the group passed east of the Dortmund canal. A large, ill-formed, mixed mob of FW-190s and Me-109s passed below the bomber formation headed in the opposite direction. The enemy fighters then climbed and struck from the rear.

"We were attacked by four FW-190s," Kesselring remembered. "Their cannon fire detonated near our wings and fuselage but didn't cause a great deal of damage. Our tail gunner, Richard Pridemore, was hit by a few pieces of shrapnel and his right side looked like he had been stuck a few times with a pin. After we landed we kidded him about his 'wounds' and tried to get him to go to the hospital so that he could get the Purple Heart." However, not everyone from the 91st was joking. The group lost four ships that day.

Kesselring flew an uneventful mission the next day against the rail yards at Offenburg, Germany, and then again, three days later on November 30, 1944. "Our target was the synthetic oil plant at Zietz, Germany. About five minutes before we reached the target our number three [right inboard] engine started smoking. We tried to feather the propeller but it failed to respond. The engine caught fire and flames reached back across the wings where the fuel tanks were located.

"Not only was the engine on fire," Kesselring recalled, "but it was vibrating so badly that it shook the entire aircraft. There was a good chance that it was going to blow up and we considered bailing out." Kesselring and the rest of the crew prepared to leave the damaged ship. "I learned that day that it was possible to fly the B-17 while wearing a chest pack parachute. It wasn't easy to reach the controls but if that plane exploded and blew us out, I wanted to be sure that I was ready."

As it developed, the crew stayed with their stricken aircraft. "The propeller finally wore itself out and stopped," Kesselring remembered. "Earlier we had cut off the fuel to the engine and the fire was extinguished. We had trouble keeping up with the rest of the formation so we salvoed [dumped] our bombs. Even though we were lighter we still couldn't stay with the rest of the group so we turned back west toward England. It wasn't long before we picked up an escort of P-51s. Words can't describe how good it felt to be protected like that.

"I used to joke about bailing out," said Kesselring. "I shared my last name with a famous German general, Albert Kesselring. He was in charge of all the German forces in Italy. I always said that if I was ever shot down and captured that I would demand to see my Uncle Albert."

Kesselring and the rest of the crew were reunited with John Flynn after their third mission. From that point they started flying missions together as they had trained. "Technically, I was the copilot," said Kesselring. "But I never liked that term. Many people think that the copilot just sat there and watched the pilot and helped him out occasionally. That wasn't the case at all. I flew that bomber as much as John did—we worked very closely together and were a real team. Later, when people asked whether I was a pilot or a copilot, I'd truthfully tell them 'both.'

"For instance, flying close formation was very tiring work. If it wasn't done right there was a good chance that you'd run into someone or that the formation would get too loose. But after a time, concentrating so hard, a person could get fixated and lose awareness about what was happening. So, John and I worked out a system where one of us flew for fifteen minutes while the other rested. Then we switched. Believe it or not, I'd turn my oxygen to the 'pure' setting and take catnaps when I wasn't flying. It was amazing how much rest I could get in such a short amount of time."

On December 5, Kesselring was scheduled with the rest of the group to fly a mission to Berlin, but engine problems forced them to return to Bassingbourn before they reached the Dutch coast. After only five sorties, Kesselring had already experienced several close calls. "I wasn't really superstitious but I started to develop rituals that I kept up through my combat tour. For instance, I wouldn't leave my room before a mission without stopping to look into the mirror and reassuring myself that I was there, that I was fine and that I was going to be okay."

The crew was assigned their own aircraft during this time. They flew their first mission in *Sweet 17,* on December 5, 1944. It was an aluminum-finished B-17G that arrived in England the previous March. It subsequently provided yeoman-like service for several crews and by the time Kesselring first handled its controls it had already completed nearly seventy missions. "I liked that airplane," Kesselring said. "We flew it quite a bit during the first part of our combat tour and it took good care of us."

If the B-17—first flown nearly ten years earlier in 1935—was the iconic bomber of the air war over Europe, the B-17G was the defining exemplification of the type. Produced in more numbers than any other variant, the B-17G was visually distinguished by a defiant-looking chin turret that jutted from under the aircraft's nose and housed two .50-caliber machine guns. German fighter pilots had earlier discovered a weakness in the B-17's forward quarter defenses. They exploited that weakness with terrifying, massed, head-on attacks. The new chin turret—operated by the bombardier—was intended to discourage such assaults. With the addition of the turret, which actually appeared in late production blocks of the B-17F, the B-17G's defensive armament totaled 13 guns. It was indeed a Flying Fortress.

As it was for all the units that flew from England, the weather was nearly as dangerous as the enemy. Kesselring recalled the mission of December 24, 1944, which was the largest bombing effort in history: "It was, on the whole, an awful mission. The weather had been terrible and this mission was the first we flew for several days even though the weather still hadn't gotten any better." The group was part of a large force of bombers sent against Merzhausen, a German airfield near Frankfort. "We had to take off on instruments and we had weather almost to the target. However, the target itself was clear and we completely destroyed it."

Although the mission was a success, it cost the Eighth Air Force one of its early stalwarts. The B-17 of Brigadier General Frederick Castle was hit by fighters. Castle had been called up as a reservist lieutenant during January 1942, was made a captain, and traveled to England as part of the original group of six men who established the Eighth Air Force in England. Competent and hard working, he rose quickly to command the 94th Bomb Group and subsequently the 4th Bombardment Wing.

The Germans didn't care. His ship—at the head of more than two thousand bombers—was shredded by German fighters. He maintained control of the staggering B-17 while seven of his nine crewmen jumped from the doomed ship. He perished when the aircraft's right wing separated and what was left of it plummeted to earth in flames.

Kesselring didn't know any of this on that day. "Our biggest problem once we returned to England was that our airfield at Bassingbourn was completely socked in as were many others. We finally landed at Bury St. Edmunds and it looked like every other bomber in the Eighth Air Force did too."

The foul weather had forced all the Eighth's bombers to recover at just a handful of bases. "There wasn't enough food or beds for everyone that landed at Bury St. Edmunds," said Kesselring. "I wandered around for a long time and finally stumbled across a room they used for drying flight suits. I wasn't supposed to be in there, but I threw a bunch of suits onto the concrete floor and curled up and got some decent rest. Most of the crews froze out in their aircraft and weren't able to sleep at all.

"That next morning was Christmas and we were supposed to fly another mission but ice kept forming on our aircraft. Our crews spent hours scraping the wings but it just formed all over again. By the time they finished one wing, the other was iced up. Finally, the mission was scrubbed and we were all sent back to Bassingbourn in trucks. We arrived in the afternoon and were fed a hearty Christmas dinner. We didn't fly another mission for three more days."

Kesselring had a very practical perspective of what he was doing during those final months of the war. "I sort of likened myself to a delivery truck driver. I had packages that needed to be delivered, but my customer just didn't want them and, quite frankly, did whatever was possible to keep me from getting them where they needed to be."

There were times when Kesselring and his comrades didn't get their goods to the correct address. "There was one mission when we learned during debriefing that we missed the target by eight miles. Eight miles. That was a joke in our crew; we figured that if we could bomb out their Brussels sprouts that we might just starve them into quitting." Still, he understood the seriousness of what he was doing. "Aside from destroying our targets I knew that the bombs we dropped killed people. But it was a war. And of course we couldn't see what our bombs were doing. It didn't really bother me and I don't think it bothered most people."

Moreover, Kesselring was in more danger than the civilians below him. Although he flew on several milk runs they were the exception rather than the rule. On January 1, 1945, a B-17 from the 91st blew up on takeoff. During the subsequent nine-hour mission, *Sweet 17* was hit by flak and the left inboard engine was knocked out, a hole was blown out of the fuselage near the ball turret gunner and another chunk was torn out of the wing. Too, a large piece of flak passed by Kesselring's seat and grazed Flynn's hand. "I thought that was no good way to start the New Year," Kesselring recalled.

On the January 3 mission to Koln, the aircraft's Plexiglas nose was blown away. "And the Plexiglas window over me and Flynn was blown out by flak—it sounded like a shotgun blast." When the crew returned to Koln on January 12, one of their wingmen was shot down. "Bill Meyer's ship caught a shell that exploded right in the plane and only one parachute was seen. He was a really nice young man and had a little daughter. We also got several holes in our plane: two in the left wing, four in the cockpit, a chunk out of a propeller, a hole by one of the waist gun positions and another big one by the top turret gunner."

Antiaircraft fire is perhaps what terrified the bomber crews the most. It was too random. They could battle against fighters—to some extent their skill and training made a difference in whether they survived or not against the German pilots. But skill had virtually no bearing whatever on whether or not an aircraft was caught by enemy flak guns. The bomber crews could do little against them but pray.

Kesselring and the rest of the crew had many close calls with antiaircraft fire. He recalled one incident that underscored the capriciousness of fate during the war over Europe. "There was a flak emplacement near where we typically crossed the coast into Europe. We called it Two-Gun Charlie because it always fired two salvos of four bursts." But rather than two guns, the enemy unit was actually two batteries of four 88mm antiaircraft guns each.

"On one particular day," Kesselring said, "Two-Gun Charlie tracked us. The first salvo detonated just in front of *Sweet 17* and the four bursts trailed off to the right and just barely missed us. Had we been just a little bit right of course, that would have been the end of our tour. And then the same thing happened in reverse. The second salvo exploded just in front of us again and then trailed off to the left. It couldn't have been any closer."

Things got especially ugly on February 14, 1945. It was Kesselring's eighteenth mission. "The weather was horrible," he remembered, "and I thought it would be scrubbed. As takeoff time approached they pushed it back an hour and we just sat and waited. Finally we took off."

There was smoke and high clouds en route and the formation weaved across Europe as it rumbled eastward. "Our target was Dresden. We were supposed to hit the rail yards there." Unknown to the men in the bombers, they were caught up in the jet stream which was a phenomenon that was not readily understood at the time. "We ended up getting blown way off course. Instead of hitting Dresden, we bombed Prague!" Indeed, Prague was 75 miles southeast of Dresden.

"We turned for home and after a while the lead ship in the formation descended to 11,000 feet. Of course, we thought we were over friendly territory and spread our formation so that we could relax. Consequently, we had plenty of room to maneuver when the Germans opened up with their 88mm antiaircraft guns."

The 91st was somewhere near Münster, Germany, rather than over friendly lines. "John and I maneuvered aggressively, but it wasn't enough. We were hit hard and a piece of flak punched through the bottom of the aircraft, passed under my seat and hit John Flynn in the right leg. The middle of his thigh looked as if someone had used their finger to rip out a big chunk of his muscle. I called the navigator, Robert Hodgkins, and he came up and got John down into the nose where he administered first aid. I put the flight engineer, Harley Russell, in John's seat to help me. There was blood all over."

The mission had been a long one and the crew had been lost with the rest of the formation for much of it. *Sweet 17* was very low on fuel. "I leaned out the fuel mixture to the engines as much as I could and decided to land at the first airfield we came across. We got a steer over the radio from a nearby field and got the aircraft on the ground without too many problems. I thought that we were somewhere in Belgium but it turned out that I had put the airplane down at Saint-Pierre-du-Mont Airfield, A-1, near St. Lo, France.

"An ambulance met us and took John away," remembered Kesselring. "Harley Russell wanted to count the holes in *Sweet 17*. I told him not to count anything he couldn't stick his finger through. The final number was 178. I also found out that we had less than eight gallons of fuel remaining. We left the aircraft there and were flown back to Bassingbourn. I only saw John once more after he got out of the hospital before he went back to the States."

Kesselring continued to fly his required missions. "Most of us wanted to fly them as quickly as possible so that we could go home," he remembered. Although the required mission count had been 25 from 1942 until January 1944, the number had been increased to 35 by the time Kesselring was flying combat. This was due to two primary factors. First, the odds of actually reaching 35 missions at that time in the war were realistic—most crews made it. Second, the USAAF's leadership needed as many crews and aircraft as possible to hasten the end of the war.

Although German fighters were much fewer than they had been a year or more earlier, they were more advanced during the last few months of the war. Kesselring saw the jet-powered Me-262 on several different missions, but never so close as on April 10, 1945. On that day, the 91st hit an ordnance depot at Oranienburg. "It was odd that we saw no flak over the target, but it didn't take us long to figure out why: They didn't want to hit their own fighters. Me-262s were all over the place. One swept down in front of us and knocked down a B-17 from another group. It was having trouble and had left the formation to fly east toward the Soviet lines and safety when it was attacked.

"Another Me-262, trying to evade our P-51s, flew right into the middle of our formation. He knew that we wouldn't fire at him for fear of hitting one of our own but he probably had fifty, .50 caliber machine guns trained on him. He was so close I could see his face—it was amazing. He finally climbed out and I watched a P-51 shoot him down and saw his plane spiral out of the sky." Indeed, April 10, 1945, marked a black day for Germany's Me-262 pilots. Of more than sixty jets sent airborne, at least half were shot down. Although the Me-262 was fast and heavily armed, it simply couldn't cope with the huge numbers of American fighters that dominated the sky over Europe during the final part of the air war.

Kesselring flew his last mission on Friday, April 13, 1945. "As I started out I ran into the operations officer and asked him if he was really going to make me go on my last mission on Friday the thirteenth. He said that he wouldn't make me go if I didn't want to—he could find a replacement. I went anyway and it was a rather short and uneventful mission. We bombed the rail yards at Neumünster and were back by mid-afternoon." Ironically, *Sweet 17*, patched up and returned from France, flew its last mission on the same day.

"Of our original crew, almost all of us made it home safe," Kesselring recalled. "Of course, John Flynn didn't get to finish his missions as he was sent home early because of his wound. Our ball turret gunner, Donald Pubentz, was a nice kid from Chicago. He didn't finish his missions with the rest of us because he got a pass to visit his brother who was a P-51 pilot with one of the fighter groups. A few days later on April 17, 1945, after the rest of us finished our tours, Pubentz was flying on a mission to Dresden and his aircraft was attacked by an Me-109. The ball turret was shot away and he dangled from the airplane in the cold for about thirty seconds before he fell to earth. He is buried at Ardennes American Cemetery, Plot: A, Row: 36, Grave: 15."

———

The Eighth Air Force lost nearly 6,000 aircraft while suffering 47,000 casualties including 26,000 dead. Indeed, the Eighth suffered more killed during World War II than did the entire United States Marine Corps. The 91st Bomb

Group's share of those losses—while flying 340 missions—included 1,010 combat crewmen and 197 aircraft.

Following the war, George Kesselring stayed in the USAAF—and later the USAF. He became a personnel and administrative professional and served in a variety of capacities both overseas and in the United States before retiring as a major in 1963. Following his retirement he taught high school in Muskogee, Oklahoma, and later worked for the Oklahoma Department of Corrections. He subsequently worked as a real estate broker before retiring altogether.

CHAPTER 19

COLD AND DEADLY SEA

The North Sea, especially the English Channel, had protected England from invading armies for nearly nine centuries. But to the Allied fliers in World War II it was a cold and deadly barrier—the final obstacle on the return trip from the mortal air combats over occupied Europe. Many damaged and fuel-starved aircraft fell into the icy water far short of their airfields on the solid and welcoming island that was England.

At the beginning of the war it was the Germans who were the most advanced at finding and plucking their airmen from the sea. From 1939 onwards, German flying boats with the Red Cross emblem covered the waters between the Continent and England. The English followed suit with more advanced procedures together with better radio and radar equipment. And the Americans, after some initial skepticism about the value of such efforts, committed wholeheartedly to Air-Sea Rescue with more equipment, personnel, and aircraft.

Such had the art advanced during the war that toward the end, approximately ninety percent of the fliers who either ditched or bailed out over the waters around England were safely recovered. This contrasted sharply with the situation at the beginning of the conflict when less than a quarter of the crews who went down in the sea were rescued.

Donald Whitright

First Lieutenant Donald Whitright leaned forward and looked down past the nose of his P-47. Only fifty or so feet below him the frigid February waves of the North Sea seemed angry—almost as if they wanted to claw him from the sky. Only two hundred feet above him a cold blanket of clouds spat a mix of sleet and snow. But it wasn't the weather that drove him down so low; he would have performed his search at the same altitude regardless. Experience had taught him and the other pilots of the 5th Emergency Rescue Squadron that they were less likely to spot downed airmen if they flew much higher.

If he flew any lower though, Whitright knew he would spend nearly as much time trying not to fly into the waves as he would spend searching. Also, depending on the sea-state, he would be less likely to spot a downed flier in the troughs of the waves. So then, fifty feet was determined to be the ideal altitude for search operations.

Still, the weather was an enemy. On this day, the sleet and rain and snow cut visibility to less than a half-mile at times. Not only did this make his search more difficult, but his wingman was hard-put to help with the search while maintaining formation with Whitright.

He looked back over his shoulder and checked for his wingman. The pilot of the other P-47, its cowling painted in the red, white and blue bands of the 5th ERS, flew a few hundred feet away, stepped slightly up and back to one side. Whitright turned back around and scanned the waves in front of him one last time, signaled his wingman, then eased his big fighter into a turn. After ninety degrees of heading change he rolled back into straight-and-level flight. His search pattern was a series of ever increasing rectangles. A quick glance back confirmed again that his wingman was still with him.

The weather unsettled him. The sleet came harder and he saw a thin layer of rime ice forming on the leading edge of his aircraft's wings. Experience told him that the propeller blades were also picking up ice. The frozen coating robbed the aircraft of lift and performance. If it got much worse he would have to abort the mission.

Whitright continued to look over the sameness of the water. God help those who were out there in it. It was cold. Cold enough that—combined with the near-freezing temperature of the air above it—a man could not last more than about thirty minutes before drifting into hypothermia and, soon after, a numb and indifferent death.

There! What was that? Whitright banked sharply, his eyes glued to a dark object riding atop the windswept water. He strained to make out some detail that would tell him what it was. He had been fooled before. Floating pieces of wreckage or driftwood—even seals—had made his adrenaline start with the hope that he had found a downed airman.

This time he was not disappointed. He rolled up on one wing as he flashed over the object. Looking down he saw a flier huddled into a one-man inflatable dinghy. The man's upraised face, contrasted against the dark water and framed by the yellow of his Mae West life jacket, was stark white. Cold and wet, he raised an arm in a weak salute to the two fighters roaring overhead.

Whitright twisted around in the cockpit, careful not to lose sight of the downed flier. Getting enough separation so that he could set up for his run, but not so much that he would lose sight, he reefed the aircraft around into a hard turn then leveled out again pointed straight at the man in the raft. Just before he passed overhead he released two smoke flares into the sea. Swiveling in the cockpit again, he checked to make sure that they both ignited before he wagged his wings in farewell and started a climb.

Pausing just under the overcast to let his wingman join in close formation, Whitright keyed his radio and called the Air-Sea Rescue coordination center. Receiving no response, he started a spiraling climb into the thick, gray, clouds. After a short time, higher now, he established radio contact and at the same time broke out of the gray murk into the blinding brightness of sunlight bouncing off the top of the cloud layer and into a clear sky. Whitright blinked against the glare and passed the condition of the downed flier as radio direction finding installations ashore triangulated his location. Marking his position, the coordination center thanked him and said that there were boats nearby which would attempt the rescue. A moment later, the center passed the bearing and range for Whitright's next search sector and wished him continued good luck. Checking his wingman in position, Whitright wheeled the two-ship of fighters on course for a new search.

"I never found out what happened with any of the pilots I found," Whitright remembered. "For some reason, higher headquarters never re-layed that information to us."

Donald R. Whitright was born on April 14, 1921, in the small town of Lodi, Ohio. "I was born in town, but not in a hospital," he said with a certain sense of pride. Growing up he had no special aspirations toward flight. Rather, he lived a typical Midwest, small-town lifestyle. "We went out to my uncle's farm when they had threshing or something like that going on. My mother helped cook for the workers. I still see those scenes in my mind as clear as day."

Nevertheless, Whitright's horizons widened as America prepared for war. While working as an engineering draftsman for Curtiss in Columbus, Ohio, and later for Goodyear Aircraft in Akron, Ohio, he grew an affinity toward aeronautical machines. "I kind of got to where I wanted to get in one of those ships and fly." He signed up with the Army Air Corps College Training Detachment, and was called up for flight training in February 1943. His training was typical for the period and included multiple moves to and from various training bases in the southeast until he received his wings and was commissioned a second lieutenant in April 1944, part of the class of 44D.

Following his commissioning, he was sent to Camp Springs, Washington, D.C., then on to Richmond, Virginia, to fly P-47s. "I had a couple of friends from my hometown who had been in for a couple of years. They were flying P-38s. At the time I would have liked to have flown those, but in the end I was glad I didn't. I really liked that P-47."

He remembered his introduction to the big, jug-shaped fighter. "It was a huge thing! I couldn't get over the size of it. But it was so easy to fly. It would almost fly itself. It was the easiest plane to land that I ever flew. You only had to get somewhere near the ground, chop the power, ease back on the stick and it would settle right in."

During October 1944, Whitright was embarked with thousands of others aboard the Dutch ship *New Amsterdam* as a replacement pilot bound for Great Britain. Following an uneventful voyage, he disembarked in Scotland and was sent to a replacement pilot pool. While there, he and the handful of replacement pilots he traveled with were given a few hours of refresher time before being sent to operational units. One of them was killed in a landing accident. "He didn't keep his speed up on final," Whitright remembered. "He pancaked in and was killed."

Whitright finally received his assignment during November. "I was sent to an Air-Sea Rescue unit. It was Detachment B of the 65th Fighter Wing. It had been operating since May 1944. They renamed it the 5th Emergency Rescue Squadron in January 1945, a couple months after I arrived. The unit was operating war-weary P-47s. These planes had an awful lot of hours on them but they were in good mechanical condition." The war-weary birds Whitright remembered were part of a program through which tired, earlier-model aircraft were replaced on the front-lines by newer models. The older aircraft were then put into good mechanical condition and given to units that weren't fighting on the front line. The aircraft the 5th ERS used were early model P-47D "Razorbacks." "We only had four guns instead of the usual eight. They took them out to lighten us up. We also carried a 150-gallon external fuel tank on the belly."

The mission of the 5th ERS was a vital one. Although at this point the Allies enjoyed absolute air supremacy over Europe, the sheer numbers of aircraft airborne on any given day guaranteed that Allied airmen dropped into the North Sea on virtually a daily basis, either due to enemy action or mechanical failure. The incidence of downed airmen was particularly high on those dates that huge missions, numbering into the thousands of aircraft, were sent over Germany. The importance of having a system in place to recover downed aircrews could not be overrated. It was important in real terms—that is, returning highly trained airmen to service. But it was just as important in terms of morale to those same airmen.

"We had a minimum of training for what we did," Whitright recalled. We had lectures on what they expected of us and that was about it. The squadron put pilots either on ground alert, or airborne to cover the return of particularly large bombing raids. Once we took off, they vectored us to areas where they expected us to find someone. We went out at fairly high altitude; we had to in order to get good radio reception. They told us when we were over the right spot and then we descended to just over the water to start our search.

"I started flying missions during winter," he recalled. "It was really rough. There were many times when we took off in fog that was so bad we could hardly see the runway. We flew completely on instruments until we were told to descend over the North Sea. Usually we'd break out of the clouds only just before we got down to the water.

"When we located someone we had the emergency stations take a fix on us. We also contacted British fishing vessels which were out there on the same frequency. It was sometimes difficult to figure out what they were saying. It was a different sort of English—sometimes we just burst out laughing."

Whitright spent the first part of his tour at the airfield at Boxted, in the eastern part of the country. The unit was collocated with the famous 56th Fighter Group, which also flew P-47s. For obvious reasons the men of the 5th ERS enjoyed good camaraderie with their fellow flyers from the 56th. Later, during January 1945, the unit moved to the airfield at Halesworth, which was only marginally closer to where USAAF aircraft might be expected to fall into the sea. Nevertheless, it gave the pilots a few more precious minutes to conduct their searches.

As the unit became more successful and procedures and techniques became more refined, additional equipment was added. "We carried an inflatable dinghy under each wing," Whitright recalled. "With that we could get a bomber crew out of the water real quick. The dinghies were in a compact case. We dropped it from very low altitude and when it hit the water it inflated." The squadron also operated aircraft types other than the P-47. "They gave us a B-17 [SB-17] with a boat on the bottom. We dropped that with parachutes. And we got a PBY (OA-10) too. When the weather was calm enough they could land that on the water. But they had to be very careful because the waves were so big."

Although poor weather was their primary adversary, the pilots of the 5th ERS still occasionally sighted German aircraft over the frigid water. "When we encountered the Germans, they'd just run. We didn't see many, but when we did they'd just run," he repeated. "They were beaten by that time. They had few airplanes, hardly any fuel, and their remaining pilots—especially the young ones—had very little training."

Amazingly, considering the abysmal weather conditions in which the unit operated, Whitright recalled that the 5th ERS lost very few pilots while flying their rescue missions. He recollected an accident that occurred while two aircraft were showing off over the English countryside—it was a fairly typical practice. "One of our pilots took off with his wingman on a day off—he wasn't even scheduled to fly. They buzzed a farm and circled a small lake or reservoir. Doggone if they didn't turn in too tight. They augured in and were killed. Both of them. Right into the lake. I doubt the farmer was impressed."

―――――――

Cited and decorated for their work, the men of the 5th ERS were aboard the

Queen Mary and en route to the United States within a week after the war ended in Europe. They were to prepare for deployment to the Pacific for the same mission.

While awaiting movement to the Pacific, the Japanese surrender obviated the need for the 5th ERS. Whitright left the service in November of 1945 and returned to Ohio. A successful career in the concrete business led to his retirement in Rancho Bernardo, California.

Although these P-51s are from the 361st Fighter Group, they are the same type
flown by Herman Schonenberg with the 55th Fighter Group, and Robert Macdonald
of the 363rd Fighter Group. —*USAAF*

CHAPTER **20**

ESCORTS OVER EUROPE

No image better symbolizes the American air war over Europe than the one of huge, contrail-streaming, bomber formations steadfastly plunging through clouds of vicious black flak. In that picture, if one looks closely, are the fighter escorts. These "little friends"—P-38s, P-47s, and P-51s—arc around the big bombers as they do their best to shepherd them safely across the target and back home again.

The P-51 Mustang, more than the P-38 Lightning and the P-47 Thunderbolt, is the escort fighter held most dear in America's collective memory. As a bomber escort—with its handsome lines and unmatched performance—the P-51 was unequaled, and seared an image in history that has made it the quintessential American fighter of World War II.

Herman Schonenberg

BORN IN ASTORIA, NEW YORK, ON SEPTEMBER 12, 1919, HERMAN Schonenberg was raised in the town of Baldwin, on Long Island, only a few blocks from where the famous Grumman Corporation had its beginnings. "As a kid, and all during high school I just loved airplanes. My brother and I built every different kind of airplane model you could think of. We also read every aviation article we could get our hands on.

"Shortly after I graduated from high school," Schonenberg recalled, "I went to work for a bank in New York City. I just hated that, so I enrolled with my brother at Roosevelt Aviation School, at Roosevelt Field, on Long Island. We earned our Aircraft and Engine Mechanics Licenses and got jobs for Pan American Airways working on Boeing 314 flying boats. But the pay was so bad and the working conditions so poor that we soon started looking for something else." Eventually, Schonenberg and his brother made their way to Corsicana, Texas where they worked as civilian crew chiefs at one of the Army's primary flight schools.

During 1942, with the United States at war, the Schonenberg brothers grew dissatisfied with working on aircraft; they wanted to fly them. In September 1942, they both took and passed the exam for acceptance as aviation cadets in the Army Air Forces. "They called my brother about three months before they called me. Finally, on March 3, 1943, I was called into the service." Nine short months later, Schonenberg received his wings and was commissioned as a second lieutenant on December 5, 1943. He remembered his excitement when he was selected for duty as a single-engine fighter pilot. "I don't think many pilots wanted anything else. That was the ultimate—and I just never expected that I would make it. Except for getting married, I think that was the greatest thing that ever happened to me."

After commissioning, Schonenberg received follow-on training in P-39s. By this time, the Bell aircraft had been relegated mostly to advance training duties. It was not a very popular airplane with most of its pilots and Schonenberg's recollections mirrored that viewpoint. "It was an experience that I enjoyed very much, but it was a dangerous airplane. You couldn't do a lot in it—aerobatics and things like that. It was aerodynamically dangerous. I never felt very comfortable in it."

After further tactical training in the P-40, during which time he practiced skip-bombing, dive-bombing, and other ground attack techniques, Schonenberg received orders for service in Europe. "I left Boston Harbor on July 1st, 1944, on the SS *Brazil*. We landed at Glasgow on July 15, and from there got sent down to some kind of distribution center where they had P-38s, P-47s, and P-51s. Believe it or not, we drew straws to determine which type of aircraft we'd get assigned to. Fortunately, I got P-51s.

"Now, I hadn't even been near a P-51 before," Schonenberg remembered. "It was really a rather simple checkout procedure though. They showed me where everything was, gave me a blindfold cockpit check and then they let me go. Well, it was really a beautiful airplane; it was so much more improved over the P-40 in terms of flying and handling—it was just so easy. I was amazed at how comfortable I felt in it. And it was so reliable.

The 55th Fighter Group, where I was eventually sent, had P-38s before, and that single engine in the P-51 was more reliable than any two engines they had in the P-38.

"It was only a short time after that when I was sent over to the 55th Fighter Group. When I arrived they sent me to the 338th Fighter Squadron. They flew me around a little bit there, maybe about ten hours. They had us new guys fire the guns and do some formation work and high altitude flying. All the way up to 37,000 feet. We'd never had any high altitude training before.

"We were based in the country at Wormingford, next to Colchester— right in the heart of 'Buzz-Bomb Alley,'" he said. "The V-1s came over the buildings there at about a hundred feet. It was very loud." From the middle of June 1944 the Germans launched more than 10,000 V-1 terror weapons at England. They were small, pulse-jet powered flying bombs that made a distinctive rumbling sound as they flew low over the countryside. Although notoriously unreliable, more than seven thousand made it across the channel and killed more than six thousand people. The fastest RAF aircraft carrying mainly cannon, together with the British antiaircraft batteries, were somewhat effective against the small bombs and were credited with bringing down nearly four thousand of them. "We weren't encouraged to attack them in the air because we would have had to get so close with our machine guns," Schonenberg recalled. "They were worried that we'd get blown up when the bomb exploded."

Having arrived in England during July 1944, it was about a month later on August 25 that Schonenberg was put into combat. "I'll never forget the first mission I flew. It was up to Politz, in Poland. We escorted bombers to the harbor at Danzig—they were hitting one of the battleships in the harbor there. We took flak from the Frisian Islands, then again over Heligoland, and Peenemünde too. I had never been in an airplane more than two hours, and that mission was six hours and fifteen minutes—it was the first time I used a relief tube. I haven't walked right since."

Although he encountered no enemy fighters on his first mission, aerial clashes weren't long in coming. On his very next mission, August 27, 1944, his squadron was part of the escort effort for a bombing raid to the German capital, Berlin. Once freed from escort duties, his flight started a descent to strafe targets of opportunity. "We were heading south when we spotted a formation of enemy aircraft, one of which was a Do-217 pulling a glider. The glider was released as we started firing at the Do-217. I flew very close to it as it dove. It was loaded with a lot of troops and they shot at us from inside as we started our firing passes. That was very unnerving," he said, perhaps not noting the irony. "The Do-217 hit the ground and slid for a considerable distance before catching fire. The glider was also destroyed. Both of them must have been heavily loaded with fuel because they burned pretty fiercely when hit. It's not likely that anyone survived."

Schonenberg flew his next mission, number three, on September 3, 1944. "I got my first victory on my third mission," he said. "It was a bombing mission to Ludwigshafen that had been aborted, and I was flying the number-two position in Red Flight. After the mission was aborted we dropped down to a sensible altitude, and between Brussels and Antwerp we spotted a flight of three FW-190s."

Still new to the game, Schonenberg clung tight to his leader as the Mustangs dove down from 10,000 feet, through a cloud layer at 3,000 feet, and finally pounced on the German fighters. "My flight leader expended all of his ammunition behind one of them," he recalled. Schonenberg took his turn and slipped into position behind the enemy fighter. "Being so new, I sort of crept up on him. He was down on the deck and I was right down there with him in the trees. I fired about four bursts of one-and-a-half seconds each, and got hits along the fuselage and wings. I saw the canopy and other parts come off. I pulled up to the right to avoid the canopy and saw the enemy aircraft pull up, snap-roll to the right, then turn erratically to the left. I came back in for a deflection shot then passed right over the top of him. As I did so, I checked, but didn't see the pilot in the cockpit. The last I saw of the enemy aircraft, it was in a steep turn, with the nose down, at about one hundred feet, with smoke pouring from the fuselage. I did not specifically see that aircraft crash. I did see an aircraft crash— burst into flames and all that sort of thing—but I can't tell you that it was the one I was shooting at. Things happened so fast in combat.

"It was kind of an unnerving experience for me," he continued, "because while I was down there banging away at this guy, my flight leader left me. He just took off. I got finished and there wasn't anybody around!" Alone and afraid, still over enemy-held territory, Schonenberg made his way home to England and put in his claim for the aerial victory. "Several days later it came back confirmed which kind of made me feel like I was doing something in the war."

Years later, Schonenberg learned the final outcome of that fight. The accomplished aviation author Donald L. Caldwell was doing research for his book *JG 26, Top Guns of the Luftwaffe*, and contacted Schonenberg for an eyewitness account of the duel. It turned out that the enemy aircraft his flight encountered were from JG 26: the famed "Abbeville Kids." JG 26 was one of the most successful, and perhaps the most widely regarded German fighter unit of the war; its pilots reputed to be among the very best. "Evidently," Schonenberg explained, "this flight of FW-190s was leaving to go back to Germany and we caught them soon after they took off."

When the official German and American records—and first-hand recollections—were brought together by Caldwell, he discovered that of the three FW-190s attacked, two were shot down. Schonenberg's squadron mate, Lieutenant Darrell Cramer was credited with a victory over Hauptmann Emil Lang. Lang, who was killed, was a highly decorated pilot with 173 kills to his credit. The second downed aircraft was piloted by Leutnant Alfred Gross, who bailed out and survived. The third aircraft was piloted by Unteroffizier Hans-Joachim Borreck, who actually survived the encounter and landed back at a Belgian airfield, despite the fact that his aircraft had been badly damaged. His aircraft was subsequently abandoned in the face of the Allied ground advance and he returned to Germany scrunched inside the baggage compartment of another FW-190.

The vast majority of Schonenberg's missions were spent escorting the heavy strategic bombers—B-17s and B-24s—of the Eighth Air Force. In formations numbering more than a thousand, seemingly endless columns of aircraft crossed the North Sea from Great Britain to hit targets throughout the continent. The Luftwaffe, increasingly outnumbered, was less and less able to effectively counter these tremendous raids. As 1944 drew to a close and 1945 unfolded, the American bombers, although still terrorized by deadly and accurate flak, were often left unmolested by German fighters. Schonenberg's memory reflects this: "A lot of times these long bombing missions were very boring. They were just a pain in the rear—literally."

However, the flying wasn't without drama. "With the Mustang," Schonenberg continued, "you had so much fuel, that after you left the bombers you had the option of creating your own excitement. So, after we got the bombers going home and everything was clean, we went down and strafed all hell out of Germany. We were given an area to strafe and were careful not to get tangled up in the front lines." He remembered that with the primary role of bomber escort, his unit wasn't well-trained in the recognition of friendly and enemy ground units.

"But we all knew what a train was. We had a specific setup for attacking trains. The commanding officer would skip-bomb his external fuel tanks against the engine and then the rest of us followed and did the same thing. Then, the newest kid in the outfit got to set it on fire with Armor Piercing Incendiary rounds from his machine guns. We did that several times."

Schonenberg remembered attacking a train in the heart of a station crowded with passengers. It was in Alsace-Lorraine, a border area historically contested by both France and Germany. The time was late in 1944. "We spotted this train that had just pulled into the station. Now, it was common practice to send the youngsters—the green guys—down over a target to check for flak before the whole flight went down to attack. Well, I went down and didn't run into anything particularly, so I rejoined my group and we strafed that train," he explained. "There were a lot of people on the platform. And mixed in with all these people were German uniforms. I didn't want to strafe the train with all those people around it, so I strafed the front of it—the engine. I still have the gun camera film, and I point that fact out to my children.

"Another time," he remembered, "over northern Germany, the low country area, we followed a set of railroad tracks to a junction that split off and went right inside a factory. Well, we dropped our fuel tanks right inside the factory and set the place on fire."

Nevertheless, the strafing was dangerous. Many more fighters were lost to ground fire than to enemy aircraft. Schonenberg remembered that his group leader, Colonel Elwyn Righetti—an aerial ace who was also known as a very aggressive strafer, was shot down. "He bellied in on an autobahn, and the German farmers killed him with pitchforks. It was important not to crash land where you were strafing. American flyers were hated in Germany."

As the war progressed and the Luftwaffe lost more and more veteran pilots, the quality of the replacements, hurried through ever more abbreviated training, suffered. Schonenberg remembered a fight in the autumn of 1944 where the greenness of the German fighters was very apparent. "One day we saw an enormous gaggle—it must have been a couple of hundred enemy fighters. Some estimates put it as high as four hundred. It looked like a giant swarm of bees and we went barreling right into them. There were airplanes everywhere, a lot of people bailing out, parachutes all over the place. I think it was just a bunch of German kids that were bailing out as soon as someone fired at them. This was early on for me too, and I didn't shoot anybody down. I think I was just glad to get out on the other side of all that mess."

Despite the evident deterioration of the Luftwaffe, the stresses of combat still took a toll on the Americans. Many were the pilots and aircrews who suffered from the fatigue and strain brought on by long missions over enemy territory—Schonenberg's missions averaged more than five hours. However, the numerical supremacy of the Americans was such that they could afford to release flyers for rest and treatment at special rest homes. Schonenberg recalled his own experience at the turn of the new year in 1945 with remarkable forthrightness: "Sometime during the middle of my tour I flaked out a little bit. I did dumb things like taking off and forgetting to pick up my landing gear. I'd call my lead and tell him to slow down, that there was something wrong because I couldn't catch up. He'd look back and—in a very harsh way—tell me to raise my landing gear. Or I'd leave my takeoff flaps down and so on.

"When you get to that point you realize something's wrong. I went to the flight doc and told him that I thought that I should quit. He checked me out," Schonenberg said, "and told me that I was like a lot of other guys and just needed a rest. So they sent me to a flak home in southern England. I spent a week or two there, and then I came back and instructed at Clobber College for about a month." Clobber College was a type of finishing school that many of the Eighth Air Force's fighter groups formed as a way of teaching the fine points of air combat to new arrivals. It was taught by seasoned airmen who had been in combat with the unit for awhile and it eased the transition of the new fliers into actual operations while increasing their chances of surviving.

Schonenberg recalled two innovations introduced during his combat tour which made significant contributions to the combat effectiveness of the P-51: The anti-G suit, and the K-14 gunsight. "I loved the G-suit," he remembered. "It made a tremendous difference." Tailored to fit closely around the torso and legs, the G-suit was connected by a hose to the aircraft's vacuum pump exit, and filled with air whenever the aircraft was put into a G-inducing turn. The air-filled suit squeezed the pilot's lower body so that oxygenated blood stayed in the pilot's brain, rather than draining down into his lower body under the force of the increased gravity of the turn. A conscious, alert, pilot was obviously more successful in battle than a groggy, grayed-out pilot. "It was great," Schonenberg said again, "but you had to be careful when you had a full bladder!"

The other innovation, the K-14 gunsight, was a gyroscopically stabilized device that helped the pilot determine the appropriate amount of lead while maneuvering to fire on another aircraft. Rather than having to rely on "Kentucky Windage," the K-14—a derivative of a British model—took a lot of the guesswork out of the firing equation and was critical to the success of several aces. "On one of my first flights," Schonenberg recalled, "I tried to shoot an Me-109 with a fixed sight. It didn't work very well. As a new pilot I was like most guys—excited and more likely to screw up until getting more experience. The K-14 gunsight helped make up for some of that."

Schonenberg's second and last confirmed aerial victory occurred on March 18, 1945, after escorting a bombing raid to Berlin. "We were north of Frankfort and caught sight of a gaggle of Me-109s and FW-190Ds at about 12,000 feet. I was flying as top-cover as the fight got going but it wasn't long until one of the FW-190s climbed up and attacked us. While we were fighting I saw another FW-190D—on fire—dive down and smash into a barn. The pilot of the FW-190D that I was fighting was very good, but I was able to get into a firing position at a point when I was almost completely inverted.

"I hit his plane in the wing roots and he bailed out. I could see he was a big man, and as I flew past him I saw that he was shooting his pistol at me! German records indicate that he was found dead in his chute. The last time I saw him he was very much alive. I imagine he was shot on the way down. This happened on both sides during the war."

―――――

Schonenberg finished his combat tour during April 1945, just before the war ended in Europe. He had flown sixty-three missions during which he logged more than 300 combat hours. He was awarded credit for two aerial victories. His combat decorations included the Distinguished Flying Cross, and the Air Medal with eight Oak Leaf Clusters.

After the war, Herman Schonenberg taught in a civilian aviation mechanics school and eventually went to work for the Grumman Aircraft Engineering Company for the next forty years.

Newly commissioned Second Lieutenant Emilius Ciampa.
—*Emilius Ciampa Collection*

CHAPTER 21

A CAN OF PEACHES

The strategy in the Pacific was far from solidified even in the final months of 1944. One faction of strategists argued that the Philippines should be bypassed in favor of an invasion of Formosa. General MacArthur argued that the Philippines were more important, and that the United States was under a moral obligation to free the Filipino people as soon as possible. In October of 1944, Roosevelt gave MacArthur approval for a campaign in the Philippines.

Ultimately, the effort was a costly one. Like all American campaigns, the operation was extensively supported from the air. A godsend to the forces on the ground were pilots assigned to units as forward air controllers. The pilots, with their understanding of the employment and capabilities of attack aircraft, were directly responsible for the dramatic increase in the effectiveness, safety, and coordination of air support.

Emilius Roger Ciampa

THE SON OF ITALIAN IMMIGRANT EMILIUS CIAMPA—A SCULPTOR of some note—and of a mother of Swedish descent, Emilius Roger Ciampa was born on December 23, 1920, in Cambridge, Massachusetts. He remembered Lindbergh's 1927 flight across the Atlantic and the excitement it created in his family as they listened to the news on their crystal radio set. "Here I was, only six years old, and I decided right then and there that I was going to be a pilot. Not just any pilot, but a Marine pilot. I had an uncle who spent most of his life disappointed because he had volunteered to be a Marine in World War I but they wouldn't take him. So he joined the Navy. I can remember," Ciampa continued, "he would tell me that a good Marine could do anything that a good soldier could do, plus everything a good sailor could do."

Like most veterans of World War II, Ciampa was a child of difficult times. His father, as a sculptor, took the family wherever there was work. During 1926 a hurricane struck Coral Gables, Florida, and destroyed much of the town, including the elder Ciampa's business. "It ruined everything my father had," Ciampa said. "He went bankrupt and we limped back to Massachusetts where our relatives and friends helped us get back on our feet. He no sooner bought a house and got going good again when the Depression hit. So, my habits of cleaning up everything on my plate, and not throwing away shoestrings and such, all stem from that part of my life."

Always with an eye on a career as a Marine pilot, Ciampa completed a high school curriculum weighted heavily with technical courses. He was in his third year at Rhode Island State College studying aeronautical engineering when Pearl Harbor was hit. "What a shock!" Ciampa remembered. "I felt that maybe I owed the country something so I left school as many of my classmates did. It wasn't anything brave—most of my friends did the same thing."

Ciampa enlisted as a Naval Aviation Cadet during April 1942. By that time he had earned his pilot's license through the Civilian Pilot Training Program and had completed a couple of years of infantry training in the school's ROTC program. He easily cleared elimination training at Squantum, Massachusetts, during July 1942. "We flew biplanes at elimination training," he recalled. "They were Navy N3Ns. It was easy, especially if you already had a pilot's license."

Once finished with elimination training, Ciampa was assigned to class 10B at Naval Air Station Pensacola, in September 1942. Again, although the training was thorough, it posed him no great difficulties. "The happiest day of my life," he remembered, "was when I looked at the bulletin board and saw that I had been selected for the Marine Corps, and on another list, that I was going to fly fighters."

Soon after, Ciampa was commissioned as a Marine second lieutenant and sent to Opa-Locka, Florida for follow-on fighter training. "Along with the Navy ensigns, we graduated and put on our bars. We had to ask some enlisted Marines on the base how to wear the uniform because we actually knew very little about the Marine Corps. So, some of the enlisted men who we had gone through training with, corporals and sergeants, they became our mentors. They told us how to act and although they had to salute us they knew a lot more than we did. We learned from them and depended on them."

At this time, early in 1943, the Navy was still short of aircraft, and most of the fighter training was done in the derelict Brewster Buffalo, and the SNJ, the Navy's advanced trainer. Ciampa described the makeshift manner in which his SNJ had been modified for carrier operations on the training aircraft carrier *Wolverine,* which operated on the safe waters of Lake Michigan: "The arresting hook for the SNJ was added almost after an afterthought. To get it down there was a piece of clothesline rope tied to the end of the hook. The rope came into the cockpit and it had a loop on the end of it. You kept that loop over a folded armrest and when it was time to land on the carrier you let the rope go and it would just string out behind, and gravity would pull the hook down."

Ciampa eventually completed his training and was sent to the Marine Corps airfield at Mojave, California, where he joined VMF-225, a fighter squadron flying F4F Wildcats. As part of a large group of new pilots attached to the squadron, Ciampa and his peers worked furiously to catch up to the original cadre, which had been flying the Wildcat for some time. Ciampa remembered his first flight. "For takeoff we were told to get to the end of the runway, set the trim tabs for takeoff, hold the brakes, and put the throttle to full power and tighten it down. Then, we were supposed to let go of the throttle, grab the stick with the left hand, release the brakes, counter the torque with rudder, and get airborne. Once airborne, we had to crank up the wheels with our right hand. It was a little bicycle chain arrangement and it took about twenty-six cranks to get the wheels up. You could always tell when a new pilot was taking off because the plane would bob up and down as he cranked.

"On my first flight I guess I didn't tighten the throttle down tight enough because I heard the engine start to wind down as I was cranking up the gear. We were told never to let go of the crank, because no matter what, it would come around and break your wrist before you could get it out of the way. Now, I had a choice between hanging on to the crank and crash landing, or letting go, adding power and getting a broken wrist. Sure enough, I let go and got a broken wrist. I learned that you can fly that airplane with a broken wrist. Hurts like hell, but it can be done."

During this period, a decision was made to transition the squadron to Vought F4U Corsairs. None other than Charles Lindbergh, Ciampa's boyhood hero, accompanied two Vought pilots to Mojave to brief the squadron on the care and feeding of the new aircraft. Ciampa remembered this time with some frustration: "Finally, after the indoctrination, the squadron received Corsairs. But at the same time the squadron was split in half. The half that had been in the squadron a while and was well-trained stayed with the unit and went overseas. We new guys were sent to fly SBD dive bombers. We were told that we would still be fighter pilots, and that the assignment was only temporary while they trained new rear seat gunners. It was fine for a while, but nearly a year went by and we hadn't been sent back to fighter squadrons as we had been promised. We all were scrambling to get out of there. We interviewed with colonels, and wrote letters and such, and finally eight of us were sent to the Marine Corps station at El Toro in California."

There awaited more frustration. "When we got to El Toro we thought that we were going to be assigned to one of the fighter squadrons. But they looked at our logbooks and saw that we had nearly a year's worth of time flying those SBDs and decided to make us dive-bomber pilots." After getting over his initial disappointment and going through a formal training syllabus, Ciampa was assigned to VMSB-144 flying SBDs.

"We all got through the formal syllabus and were finally ready to go overseas, when they took our SBDs away and gave us the SB2C Helldiver," Ciampa recalled. "It was made by Curtiss, and was a piece of junk." Intended as a faster and more modern dive bomber, the SB2C carried a larger load farther than the SBD but it was plagued with all manner of mechanical and electrical problems. Nicknamed "The Beast," it was a much larger and more difficult aircraft to fly than the SBD and was the most hated aircraft in the Navy inventory. Ciampa experienced several emergencies in it. He remembered a propeller malfunction that forced him to land right next to a practice target that his flight had been strafing. "That night while my gunner and I sat there," Ciampa recalled, "a lady and her young daughter drove up on a dirt road and asked if they could take some photographs of the airplane. We put a helmet on the little girl and put her up in the cockpit. Years later my wife was pregnant with our first daughter and we were looking at those same pictures. She thought that 'Darrolyn,' which was the little girl's name, was nice, and so that's what we decided to call our own daughter."

Finally, in October 1944, the squadron was finished training on the new aircraft and was ready for service overseas. "But it didn't happen. They took those SB2Cs away from us and said that they were going to give us TBF torpedo bombers and send us through a new syllabus."

Ciampa had had enough. "I went to my commanding officer and demanded to be sent overseas. Each month he was tasked with sending a certain number of pilots overseas as replacements and he always sent the worse ones. I told him I wanted to go with the next batch. He refused. He said that we were a team and that we would train together on the TBF and be unbeatable. I told him that he was wrong and that the war would be over before we got overseas. Well, he lost his temper and finally let me go. In fact, he let six of us go. As it turned out, after the war ended and we were shipping back home, we met his squadron as they were leaving the States."

It wasn't until November 1944 that Ciampa arrived in Guadalcanal—by then it was a major transit point for troop movements throughout the South Pacific. Except for three or four days test-flying newly repaired SBDs, Ciampa remembered that he did little during the thirty days he spent on the once hotly contested island. "We finally got orders to Emirau where I was assigned to VMSB-243, the Flying Goldbricks," he recalled. The newly joined pilots were assigned as part of the squadron's ground contingent for the upcoming invasion of Luzon at Lingayen Gulf in the Philippines. They were to build an airfield and prepare for the arrival of the squadron's aircraft once a beachhead had been established.

"While we were loading the invasion convoy I developed a bad feeling for labor unions," Ciampa remembered. "The Merchant Marine union people only worked their assigned hours. When their time was up, they stopped work. So, we Marines took over in order to make sure our gear was loaded aboard the ship in time. Due to our inexperience, we smashed up a lot of equipment with those big cranes. Those Merchant Marine union people just watched and laughed."

The invasion of Luzon began on January 9, 1945. The largest island of the Philippines, it was the key to controlling the entire archipelago. On it were garrisoned 262,000 Japanese troops of the 14th Army under the command of General Tomoyuki Yamashita. Yamashita, who had already lost more than 80,000 troops on Leyte, realized that he could not eject the numerically superior American forces and decided on a campaign of attrition. Rather than fighting on the central plain of Luzon, he withdrew his men into the mountains and forced the Americans to fight for every inch of territory.

Ciampa remembered going ashore on D+1, January 10th, 1945. "They dumped us into a rice paddy that we decided would make a good airfield. Well, we needed bulldozers and other heavy equipment to level the paddies into a workable landing field. But the Army was more interested in unloading their artillery and tanks. They couldn't have cared less about Marine aviation equipment. It was ironic that we were there to support them.

"When we went to them for help they told us that Marines always stole everything anyway and that we'd have to shift for ourselves. Our group commander, Colonel Clayton Jerome, called all the officers together and told us that he didn't want to know how we were going to do it, but he wanted trucks and bulldozers and he wanted that airfield ready in time. So, we forged some orders and signatures and went aboard the Navy ships that were carrying what we needed and took it. The Army and Navy made thieves out of all of us. Anyway, we got the airfield built just in time. The aircraft were brought in and we started flying support missions for the Army.

"So here I was on my first combat mission," he remembered. "The target was an oil storage facility on Luzon Island. I saw the black smoke from the flak coming up all around me; there were even a few holes in my wings, but that didn't really bother me. Then the oil tank I was aiming for was hit by another plane, so I had to switch targets quickly. I rolled over—almost upside down—and targeted a building in the complex. I continued my dive and was right on target. So I dropped the bomb and pulled out. But as I did I felt the tail fluttering back and forth. It was obvious that my tail section was hit.

"I made it back to base and landed the aircraft. As I taxied back to my revetment it became apparent to me that the tail wheel had also been hit because the aircraft was shaking so badly. Back at my revetment I finally shut down and started to crawl out. When I did I had a little difficulty and looked down into the cockpit. My legs were shaking wildly—knocking back and forth and kicking the rudders. During the bomb run and all the way back, although I consciously felt no fear, my legs knew the real story!"

Ciampa recalled that his squadron, part of Marine Air Groups 32 and 24, designated MAGs Dagupan, attacked a variety of targets. These included not only Japanese troops in direct contact with American soldiers, but transportation routes, barracks, airfields, and supply depots. Although the Japanese air forces in the Philippines were nearly routed by early 1945, the flying was still dangerous. Ciampa remembered one particularly difficult mission. "The target was a series of Japanese infantry bunkers along a river which was protected by a box canyon. The day was overcast but we could see the target through the clouds and were able to go in," he recalled. Attacking through intense antiaircraft fire, Ciampa pulled the nose of his aircraft into a near-vertical dive and chose a target for his 1000-pound bomb. "I dropped my bomb, and as I pulled out from my dive I was forced to climb at a forty-five degree angle to clear the mountains. What made it particularly frightening was that the Japanese had strung cables from one mountain peak to another to create a sort of spider web. It was unbelievable, but we all made it out of there without running into those cables."

Bridges were also typical targets. But Ciampa recalled when his squadron spent an entire day trying to protect one rather than destroy it. "We flew from Lingayen Gulf all the way down to Manila. The Army's 1st Cavalry was going as fast as it could in jeeps and trucks to rescue the internees being held in the Santa Tomas prison camp. Whenever they ran into Japanese opposition they called us to bomb and break it up. They were moving so fast that their artillery couldn't keep up, so they used us instead.

"Finally, they reached a bridge that the Japanese were trying to blow. Naturally, they wanted to save it so they asked us what we could do. We kept three SBDs overhead the bridge continuously and every time the Japanese engineers came up with their munitions to blow it, we strafed them.

"We came back with holes in our airplanes after almost every sortie," Ciampa recalled. "They were most often from 20mm and 37mm guns—sometimes even bigger. During the last part of the war when we were flying at Davao, the Japanese started using smokeless powder. We wouldn't see any puffs of smoke at all. I came back from a mission one day and complained to my mechanic that the engine was running rough. At the intelligence debriefing I was telling them that I hadn't seen any enemy fire at all when I got tapped on the shoulder. I turned around and there was my mechanic holding an unexploded 20mm cannon shell that had been lodged in one of the engine cylinders!"

The Marine SBDs were one of the most highly sought ground support aircraft of the entire Philippines campaign. Although they were slow and nearly obsolete, the aging bombers were deadly accurate. "One day we were tasked with hitting a large barracks complex up in Baguio," Ciampa recalled. "Three wings of it were being used as supply warehouses and barracks but the fourth wing was being used as a hospital. They told us to destroy it all except for the hospital wing. We did just that. We went in there and leveled everything but the hospital.

"One of the reasons we were so accurate," Ciampa said, "was that we didn't release our bombs until we were very low. The lower we were, the better our accuracy. Of course that meant that we kept coming back with holes in our aircraft from our own shrapnel. Our mechanics, who were usually older than us—almost fatherly—often gave us lectures against that sort of flying."

Ciampa adopted a cat while he was in the Philippines. "We Marines were pretty tenderhearted and took in a litter of cats that had been abandoned. I named mine Zambo, because he had been born on Zamboanga Island. He was part Siamese, but all black and with a little kink in his tail. I kept him in a little box and fed him milk and bits of fish that I got from the Filipinos.

"But there was a monkey—also a pet—that wouldn't leave Zambo alone. I'd come back from a mission and hear Zambo wailing because that monkey was pulling his whiskers and tail. I'd chase him off but he'd come back just as soon as I left.

"Zambo got bigger. One day that monkey started toward his box and Zambo attacked him and chased him up the tent pole and out the top. I heard them both slide down the outside of the tent and that monkey went up a palm tree and Zambo was right after him. They disappeared in the top of that palm and all I could hear was screeching and caterwauling. Finally, Zambo came out and jumped right into my arms. That monkey didn't mess with Zambo anymore."

Assigned to support Army ground troops during most of their time in the Philippines, the Marine flyers of Ciampa's air group were frustrated by the inefficiency of the system that was in place. "A ground officer—not a pilot—would get on the radio and try to coordinate our attacks by describing his position and the position of the target. If there was any doubt, the flight leader made dummy attacks on what he thought was the target. This was dangerous as it gave away our intentions and made us easy targets.

"Sometimes the men on the ground would get frustrated. They might ask us to do something like 'attack the building with the red roof to our left.' How were we supposed to know which way was their left? And which building out of the fifty that had red roofs was the one they were talking about?"

Another problem the Marines worked against was the degree of distrust the Army ground commanders held toward air support. "At first they didn't even trust us," Ciampa recalled. "They'd had some bad experiences—the Army's aircraft had bombed their own troops."

The solution was to put a Marine aviator on the ground with the advancing army troops. Ciampa was one of the first to do a stint with the Army ground troops in the Philippines as a Forward Air Controller, or FAC. "I followed a Marine communications officer around for a while. Captain John A. Titcomb was his name and he had experienced a lot of success up to that point. When he was killed, I took over full time. I developed a plan that, because it was simple and based on common sense, was effective. It was similar to what other Forward Air Controllers developed.

"When planes checked in on the radio I gave them coordinates, and described the target in detail. If I could, I got artillery or mortar rounds to mark the target. Using cardinal headings, I coordinated the attacks from a position where I could see both the attacking aircraft and the target. Then, as the aircraft attacked one at a time, I called hits and misses and corrections for the following aircraft."

This system dramatically increased the effectiveness of the Marine aircraft and the Army units they supported. A large number of Marine pilots were rotated through duty as forward air controllers. Ciampa served two separate stints, himself. During his first tour he controlled airstrikes during the bloody battle for Manila. His second tour was spent in the southern Philippines.

The Marine Corps flyers continued to develop their close air support procedures during the campaign. At times their lessons were written in blood. Ciampa recalled hitting a target near another target that was already being bombarded by friendly artillery. "As we flew through the area, one of the SBDs simply disappeared in flight—it just blew up. We figured that we hadn't been high enough and that the artillery shell struck the SBD's bomb and that everything—the shell, the bomb and the airplane and its crew—exploded in one blast. After that mission we always coordinated with the artillery units so that we understood where they were shooting and what the trajectory of their shells would be. It was the beginning of what developed to be very comprehensive fire support coordination procedures."

Between the periods he spent as a Forward Air Controller, Ciampa flew two sorties each day to ensure his mission count stayed even with the rest of his squadron. "After proving my worth for three weeks as a forward air controller on Luzon," he remembered, "the air group was moved south to Zamboanga, on the island of Mindanao, during March 1945. We flew in as an entire group, but along the way I lost a friend. I had met him while we were at sea as part of the invasion convoy for Lingayen Gulf. He was an avid bridge player and couldn't stand the thought of being at sea for so long without playing. So he took four of us, and by the time we made the landing, had turned us into fairly good bridge partners.

"Well, on the way to Zamboanga he had engine problems and decided to land at an airfield that was supposedly under the control of Filipino guerrillas. As he rolled to a stop, he radioed that he was being overrun by Japanese troops. We found out later from the Filipinos that my friend and his gunner were captured and tortured for the entire day. At sunset the Japanese cut off their genitals, shoved them down their throats and beheaded them.

"I think about that now whenever I play bridge."

The Marine aviators continued to support the Army operations both in the air and on the ground. Ciampa told a story on himself: "One of the targets I was assigned to hit was a bridge that crossed a river. I hit it right in the abutment and blew it to bits. I was very proud of myself. But only a short time later I was controlling from the ground again and cursed myself. I had to find a way to ford that same river because the only way across had been the bridge that I blew up!"

Support to the Army continued to be the primary focus of the Marine aviators through the entire campaign. As the fight matured, coordination, techniques, and procedures were refined and results continued to improve. Ciampa recalled how this teamwork came together during the period from April 17 to April 22, 1945, while he was serving his second three-week tour as a forward air controller with the 1st Battalion, of the 163rd Regiment of the Army's 41st Infantry Division.

The Army had conducted a surprise landing on the island of Jolo, south of Mindanao, on April 9. By April 17, the Japanese were driven back into their entrenched and bunkered stronghold on Mount Daho, an extinct volcano. While much of the world's attention was focused on the imminent defeat of Germany, and on the vicious battle on the Japanese island of Okinawa, some of the war's most savage fighting was taking place on Mount Daho. "The Japanese had an elaborate system of trenches, caves, and firing positions," Ciampa said. "I arranged for nine SBDs to come over every hour, on the hour, for an entire day. Each aircraft carried one 1,000-pound bomb under the fuselage, and two 250-pound fragmentation bombs under each wing. We were still working targets when the battalion commander said that we had done enough and that he was going to attack. Well, they were only in the attack for five minutes before they retreated under heavy rifle, mortar, machine-gun, and artillery fire. They suffered thirty-eight casualties.

"While the attack was underway I had my aerial photo map out. Every time I saw a Japanese gun flash, I took a compass bearing and marked its position. The next morning at daybreak I again had nine SBDs lined up every hour, on the hour. We hit those positions for five days. On the afternoon of the last day, April 22, we brought in PBJs—the Marine Corps variant of the B-25—and Corsairs, and strafed the whole area while our infantry started a new attack.

"The infantry took that position without firing a shot. The Japanese dead that we were able to find in those positions totaled more than 235. The rest were crushed below ground in their tunnels and bunkers. After the battle, while I was counting bodies, an infantryman approached me. He was about forty years old and gaunt. He said, 'Son, sit down. I have a can of peaches that I've been carrying around since this war began, waiting for something to celebrate. When they told me to attack this morning I thought we were all going to get killed, because I saw what happened the last time. Well, we didn't even have to fire a shot.'

"So right there," Ciampa remembered, "I sat down with this old soldier in the middle of all those bodies—that wretched, stinking mess—and ate half a can of peaches."

Although combat missions claimed about ten percent of the pilots in Ciampa's squadron, combat with the infantry as a Forward Air Controller was a dangerous business as well. "It was a little different," Ciampa remembered. "I could see people—infantrymen—on either side of me getting hit. One time I volunteered to go out on a patrol so that I could find a hill from where I could run an airstrike. We were ambushed and the guys behind me got up and ran back to the rear. At that moment it seemed very unprofessional. They were supposed to crawl so that they wouldn't be a very big target. Then the men in front of me got up and started running back. It turned out that I was the only one left out there, still crawling! There was a stump of a palm tree about a foot high behind me and the bullets hitting that stump sounded just like bees. The ones going over my head made a snapping noise as they broke the sound barrier. I got all the way through the Lord's Prayer before I had enough courage to get up and run back like the others!"

By the late spring of 1945, the remaining organized Japanese forces in the southern Philippines were reduced to isolated, ill supplied pockets scattered among mountain strongholds or on the smaller islands. Still, they were considered a threat and were engaged where they could be found and made to fight. Ciampa recalled a curious action near Davao, on the island of Mindanao, which caused him some amount of sadness. "Every once in a while I landed at a dirt field at Davao and worked with the infantry. They would ask me to look for targets in certain areas. I'd take off and locate those targets, then coordinate with the air group for a strike. When the other planes arrived overhead I took off and led them to the target.

"I remember pulling off of one target in particular," he said, the picture still clear in his mind, "and seeing a beautiful band of wild horses prancing around and running through a field. Well, it turned out that the Japanese who had been hiding out up there were staying alive by killing and eating horses from that herd.

"As you can imagine, we were told to kill the horses. We were told that doing so would save a lot of American lives. So we did," he remembered sadly. "We went in there and bombed and strafed those beautiful horses."

━━━━━━━━

When the war ended, Ciampa had sixty combat missions under his belt and orders to do what he had always dreamed of—fly fighters. "I was going to fly Corsairs on fighter sweeps during the invasion of Japan," he recalled. Instead, the atomic bombs ended the war and he returned to the States and married.

During Korea, he flew another sixty combat missions, this time in Corsairs. During one particularly hair-raising flight he survived an encounter with six MiG-15 jet fighters.

Following his retirement from the Marine Corps in 1964 as a lieutenant colonel, Ciampa taught junior high school for seventeen years before retiring a second time. His personal decorations include three Distinguished Flying Crosses, eleven Air Medals, and two Navy Commendation Medals with devices for valor.

Acknowledgments

Eric Hammel—the accomplished military writer, editor and publisher—put his confidence in me and this concept many years ago. He helped me organize and edit it, and additionally helped me learn a great deal about writing along the way. Nevertheless, other projects and the realities of business got in the way of its publication. It wasn't until I had written several other successful books that I finally finished this work. Regardless, it never would have happened without Eric and I thank him for it.

I am also grateful to the fine people at Casemate for recognizing the goodness of this effort. Thanks also go to my agent, E.J. McCarthy, who took care of all the contract bits.

My wife deserves no small amount of gratitude for not setting the whole project afire after years of stumbling over, and cleaning around, the various files. She was also genuinely gracious and interested when "my old guys" called to chat and I was not home for one reason or another.

Finally, I must acknowledge the wonderful civility, affability and generosity of the veterans themselves. They gave to a degree that, I'm sure, sometimes tried their patience. They additionally shared my enthusiasm for the project and gave encouragement during those rare occasions when my energy flagged.

And to be quite frank, some of them are less unsung than they had been. For instance, Hamilton McWhorter and I wrote a full-length book together that described his wartime experiences. Likewise, Willard Caddell wrote his own memoir and a relative of John Campbell wrote a book about his service. Moreover, I've used recollections of several of the men in other work. Nevertheless, regardless of their levels of anonymity, I owe them all great thanks as well as an apology for taking so long to get this work into print. I hope that the families of those veterans that have passed will find this work a fitting honor to the legacies of their loved ones.

INDEX